The Broker Boys

Michael K. Kenney

CAUSE

CHAPTER ONE

Is it essential?

Peter turned the light on and went straight to the window. He gazed on the outside world – something that, strangely, we all do when viewing a property for the first time. Why do we go inside in order to look out?

"Bloody hell, Mike, it looks like we've a sex shop opposite!" he exclaimed.

Indeed we had. We hadn't noticed the blue door nestled in the ordinary-looking parade of shops, but it took Peter just seconds to spot the single flight leading up to a first-floor shop.

We were above a Jackson's supermarket, one of those chains where presumably the proprietor recognised that the writing was on the wall for local shopkeepers, thanks to the inexorable rise of the superstore, and decided to upgrade.

"You want a supermarket? Then that's what we are, however small." For all the solution was pragmatic, we thought it was somewhat of an illusion; the one below still looked like a small grocer's shop to us.

The sex shop was an establishment that needed to be sought out. You'd never have noticed it unless, like Peter, you were at eye level. The knowledge added a new element of excitement to our newfound base, the material embodiment of hope, ambition and entrepreneurial vigour. Our company. Our venture. Our new life.

That, and the certainty that we wouldn't have the old guard telling us what to do any more.

The insurance industry was full of them. Nobody ever directly went into insurance as a chosen career in those days. It was always a stopgap, if you needed one. These were the times before call centres and direct line operators and, as a result, young people in the business were in a kind of career denial.

Think of the actor who fills in between jobs as a waiter, just until he gets his big break. So many insurance clerks were waiting for a safe position in the civil service or banking industry – just filling time, counting the days.

For some reason I'd hung on and was eventually appointed as a director – someone who would mix it up a little, a Young Turk (whatever that meant) – with a national organisation. I decided to ride it out and see what happened – after all, you were halfway there just by turning up.

Events overtook me when the chairman of that business finally ran out of patience. I took the piss out of him once too often on a miserable Tuesday morning in Preston.

Wanting to earn my keep on appointment to the Board of Directors I was anxious to make an impact, but the welcoming slap on the back came with a warning:

"Obviously you're welcome, Mike, and as you represent the sales staff we need your presence. But right now you're going to be bloody useless, as much use as the boardroom carpet. So keep it shut for at least the first four meetings, that's my advice - just wait your turn."

We held board meetings once every three months, so it wasn't quite the challenging, exciting start I'd anticipated. I thought I'd arrived, being in my late twenties and having worked my way up from a lowly salesman; they thought I'd only just started. Our two points of view would never be reconciled.

I took my director's responsibilities seriously; I was an officer of the company and would have my say. It was democratic in law, I reasoned, with a naïve schoolboy trust.

When I did get to open my mouth it couldn't have been that impressive. Along with the groans of collective impatience at this little upstart, Neville the company chairman peered over his half-moon spectacles and, looking and sounding like a provincial magistrate, said: "Well, Mike, apart from learning how to fit the word 'perceive' into as many sentences as you possibly can, I don't believe anyone around this table has the slightest idea of what you're trying to say."

Was it me or was it them? He had scored a direct hit on a sensitive point – he'd seen me in my Emperor's New Clothes and it was a blow.

As a secondary modern kid, I loved esoteric words like 'perceive'. It gave me confidence and a heightened sense of being a deep, intelligent thinker, with a sophistication older than my years. If I was talking rubbish – which, alarmingly, I often found myself doing – I could bang 'perceive' into the discussion and lean back with a knowing look and a half-smile, encouraging the most intelligent of those around me to search for the hidden wisdom behind my well-structured ideas. Only the best and most intelligent visionary would ever 'get it'; those who did were in my team, and those who didn't were thick.

But it wasn't working here and I'd been caught out. I sank into my chair as the rest of the board laughed, making the most out of my obvious discomfort before contemptuously moving on.

Well, it was only the second meeting I'd attended – I was the upstart and the elder statesmen weren't having it. Having just served my apprenticeship on the road, running a sales team, I'd spoken before the requisite four meetings and was duly slapped down.

I walked out, eyes downcast, trying not to catch anyone's glance. The carpet was threadbare and needed replacing, full of swirling patterns that were popular at one time among my relatives. Yep, the chairman was right again – it was useless.

So, three months later, I arrived at the Preston office with a mixture of determination and nervous apprehension. I'd had ninety days to plan my contribution and revenge in my mind, and this was my chance to settle old scores.

I'd noticed that at the conclusion of any meaningful comment, Chairman Neville would reiterate it with:

>"It is *essential* that xyz happens..."
>"It is *essential* so-and-so is contacted..."
>"It is *essential* we see this through..."

The phrase was often reinforced with a bang on the table for dramatic effect. I'd seen my moment, my way back, and I'd rehearsed it.

The meeting kicked off as usual. The directors had carved up the agenda the previous evening, as was customary. One would tell another not to ask him about a particular topic "for Christ's sake", and in return he wouldn't press another sticky subject.

It all droned on until my moment arrived. Once a conclusion had been reached, I interrupted with a broad smile; I banged the table and snatched the words from the chairman's mouth: "Neville, is it really ESSENTIAL that we document that?"

The room went quiet. I continued to smile, frozen with fear. Neville knew he was being set up. He looked over his glasses, eyes narrowing as he fixed me in his stare, exchanging more in that glance than could ever be communicated via the fastest broadband width.

"Yes, Mike, it's *essential*," he said quietly. "It's *essential*," he repeated through gritted teeth. No one laughed.

"I just wondered, Neville, that was all," I said, by way of apology. It hadn't gone well, my little joke.

Nonetheless, on retelling the story to the sales team, I became more confident and brazen. I was their champion; I'd sworn to represent them. We were all fed up with parochial attitudes and the Preston mafia.

One director had a habit of saying "fair dinkum" – a sort of Lancashire slang for okay. One of the London directors carried around the idea that he'd receive some sort of dividend at that end of the year when the 'third income' came in. You couldn't make it up, and this lot wanted me to be quiet.

I had a smile on my face and had earned the respect of my sales team on relating the story. "Check!" I thought as I strode confidently out of the office and headed home, satisfied with my day's work.

Three days later I received a letter telling me I was redundant. Neville said it was "essential" these financial cuts were made, but we both knew what that meant. Checkmate....

And now here we were. Peter stirred me from my musing.

"We'll have a great time clocking who's going in and out of the sex shop, Mike. We have prime position," he said excitedly.

"We're going to work bloody hard, put everything on the line, and have a great ride along the way," I said. "Let's go, Pete."

We turned the light off as we left. The next time we set foot inside an office it would be for ourselves, fuelled by hope, ambition and a whole load of barely containable fear. The Ward Evans Group was born.

Big Jim

Big Jim Evans was not a guy you could miss. He was the third of our corporate Holy Trinity and responsible for opening our London office on the same day Peter and I looked out at the sex shop.

Jim was nineteen stones of muscle and laughter, a sort of albino Shrek with, thanks to rugby, the ears to match. He had a heart and sense of justice fashioned from years of boxing with the Boys' Brigade and two years' studying in a Catholic seminary.

He was the keeper of the king's conscience. I might have most of the company shares, but if Big Jim said no to something, it was because it was right to do so – and he'd carry the day.

Big Jim had two brothers. John, a bachelor, carved out a lucrative career as a shipbroker in Geneva and Joe was an ordained priest in the *opus dei* religion. It said something about his unique family.

His father was a Catholic policeman from Liverpool in the days when a good old fashioned 'bobby' could give wrong-doers a clip around the ear and take them home to their parents, or give an older guy a nudge in the right direction by saying he was keeping an eye on him. His mum was a Jewish lady that proved a unique mix in that part of Liverpool – strong-minded, wilful and among the first women to fly on a commercial flight. No shrinking violet, she.

"She managed after the early death of her husband to almost single-handedly bring state education to Nigeria when she arrived there on her travels around the world, completely unfazed as one of the first white women travelling independently in that region," Jim explained in his usual honest, but simplistic, way.

"Bleeding hell, Mike, it wasn't hard. What was obvious to her should have been obvious to anyone. What good was it to those poor little buggers reading about Billy fucking Bunter when they were starving? Didn't exactly relate to their life, did it?"

So, spotting this oversight that was apparent to everyone other than the colonial powers, Mrs Evans began re-writing stories within context and meaning that engaged and educated at the same time. She was quite a woman, and it rubbed off on Jim and his brothers.

The Nigerian connection followed Jim wherever he went. Various tribal kings would be feted at City bars and clubs surrounding the office at Tower Bridge, each bringing a unique flavour and colour to the startled locals - particularly when Jim wore the flowing kaftans they graciously brought as gifts.

He was close to his brother, John, and they made a formidable pair. Everyone knew them on the rugby tours as "those Evans boys".

Sometimes they'd go on their own forays; others as part of their local rugby team. It could get serious, then, with many guys checking themselves into hospital with alcoholic poisoning. It became particularly difficult when the fashion turned to bar diving after a few beers; Jim couldn't be persuaded to give it a miss, with predictable results.

The boys held notorious parties where no man could turn up who weighed less than seventeen stones. Fortunately, women got special dispensation. Brother Joe would try and talk the boys round from their wild ways, but John and Jim would start on about their latest sexual conquests and, within minutes, Joe would bless them and be off, shaking his head and promising to pray for them that little bit harder.

On one occasion, the brothers found themselves stuck on a Greek island with nothing other than a fancy wine bar as company, where they were surrounded by a bunch of backpackers from around Europe and – delightfully for them – the usual sprinkling of athletic-looking Germans.

As soon as they realised there were no pubs, nor many Londoners, the boys put dignity to one side and reluctantly frequented the cocktail bar with their new European friends. Their extensive experience of real ale couldn't help them here.

"'Ello, matey," said Jim, in Pearly King dialect straight from his upbringing. "I haven't got a clue what I should be drinking in this place. Tell you what, give me two of them green fuckers, please."

Jim downed his in one. "Well, it ain't London Pride but it's got a bit of a sting to it, I admit to that," he acknowledged, ordering another. So every night after the beach, they were back to the cocktail bar.

"'Ello, matey. Give me two of them green fuckers, please." And so it went on. Eventually, the bar had to order in more bottles as all the boys' new European friends were treated to the green devils. And they themselves, not wanting to seem ill-mannered, asked the bar staff: "Could we possibly have a round of green fuckers like those Evans boys, please?"

Other than developing a taste for crème de menthe, the boys soon got bored. The days were filled with walking along the beach front and strategically placing an empty Coke can twenty feet from another one carefully filled with sand. Jim and John would wait for a gaggle of Germans to stroll barefoot along the beach and then shout, gleefully: "Hey, Germans!" before proceeding to boot the empty can as far as possible while shouting: *"Beckenbauer scores for Germany!"*

Inevitably a poor German would feel obliged to respond and, with a lot of cheery encouragement from his friends, would shout back: "Hey you, Englishmen!" and then with great enthusiasm shout "Bobby Charlton!" as he took a swing at the sand-filled Coke can in his bare feet. The otherwise tranquil setting would be disturbed by the resulting agonising scream......

Staff at the local hospital couldn't understand the sudden increase in foot injuries on the island, but eventually all Coke cans would be given a very wide berth until a new batch of unsuspecting Germans climbed off the ferry and the cycle began again.

One night, sitting on the sea wall and looking out to the horizon, Jim noticed the number of backpackers camping on the beach overnight.

With an idle mind and ever-competitive nature, he turned to John and said: "I bet I can move more backpackers than you."

"You're on," said John, wondering what his brother had in mind.

Jim went off and returned wearing a white, flowing Nigerian kaftan. A convincing-looking Greek with a wild excitable manner, he shouted "OK!" to the backpackers striding out onto the beach before drawing a line in the sand from the sea to the wall. He turned to the baffled onlookers, who were by now stirring and trying to avoid eye contact with the mad Greek with a slightly suspicious Cockney accent.

"Not here," he pointed at the people. "But here!" Pointing to one side of the line and gesticulating with both hands, he repeated again and again "Not here - but here! You understand, no? Not here, but here!"

Jim counted twenty three people who moved, which made him happy and content with his work.

The local police who did the nightly rounds every few hours stared in confusion when they turned up. Why had all these people suddenly started playing a strange form of sardines, cramped on one side of a line that had long disappeared, while a whole section of beach opposite was left empty?

The boys liked this. It broke their boredom. The next night it was Brother John's turn, and double or quits.

He did the same thing and got thirty six people to move, which encouraged Jim to have another go. On the third night, not wanting to be beaten, he stroke out in his flowing kaftan, waving his arms wildly, shouting confidently and pointing.

He was roundly told to fuck off by most of the now wise and tired backpackers. As crestfallen as his brother was delighted, the two retired to the cocktail bar for Jim to consider his next move. He needed a solution, and finding one occupied another day in keeping boredom at bay. After a few more drinks Jim settled on a cunning plan, but he needed Brother John's help.

John had to dress as a backpacker, mingle, and eventually settle with the crowd as they again prepared to spend the night on the beach. He was told things would soon fall into place and no further explanation was necessary or given. For want of anything to break the boredom, John agreed with the plan.

At the appointed time, Jim came along like a demented Greek and drew the line again to collective sighs. This was clearly going to be a difficult audience. Jim needed something special.

He said as loud as he could, "Not here… But here!" pointing to one side of the line again.

"Fuck off!" came the collective response, at least from some of the old travellers who had seen this carry on night after night. A few moved, nonetheless.

Jim shouted again: "Not here - but here!" and started to swing his arms about wildly. A few more moved. Jim burst in outraged mock anger and, his Shrek-like ears turning red, ran like a madman at his brother. To say John was astonished was an understatement.

Jim pretended in this sandstorm to kick and slap a truly startled John, who was just as alarmed as the onlookers, before picking him up like a sack of spuds and throwing him in the sea. He then turned and strode confidently back, still rambling like a mad man.

"Okay," he said, "now you all move!"

On the way back to the wall, Jim counted a top score of over sixty quickly moving to one side of the imaginary line.

This continued for the rest of the holiday. More than a hundred people slept sardine-style, shoulder to shoulder, contrasting with the wide-open space on the other side of the imaginary line.

Word got round about the mad Greeks with the dodgy accents. The police never got to the bottom of it and used to stand in astonishment shaking their heads as people automatically took their place on the right-hand side of the beach, a few of them nursing broken toes.

Satisfied with his work, a grinning Jim strode off to the cocktail bar.

"Better have two more of those green fuckers, matey," he said. "My brother will be here in a minute!"

Pete

Peter stood at just over six foot and had an affable charm that secured his position as the reasonable face of Ward Evans. The one that was calm, collected, thoughtful, and wouldn't – unless very necessary – knowingly upset anyone. He was instantly likeable with youthful looks and an easy manner.

I had interviewed him in the previous company run by Neville. While not an obviously pushy salesman he was always well liked, and patiently took care of administration around new business. He handled final and delicate negotiations with insurers. If we ever needed a certain deftness of touch, Peter would be called in.

It certainly wouldn't be left to Jim or I, who had what might be described as a more direct approach to problem-solving. Because insurers liked him, he got deals that were difficult for others to achieve. It was this hail-fellow-well-met air that allowed him to forge relationships with our insurer panel and act as our go-between; this was extremely important to the success of our venture in terms of insurer relations.

His charm didn't go unnoticed by the opposite sex, either, but while he might not have been oblivious he was much too careful to take advantage of it. He had a beautiful wife and it always seemed to me that this relationship was based on equal beauty. If he stepped out of line, she was equally up to responding in good measure - a sort of nuclear deterrent based on mutual destruction should either of them misbehave.

A single mistake in that direction would mean an instant de-balling and subsequent divorce. The consequences were restated every so often; Peter knew where he stood and that was good for him.

He was an accomplished musician and played in a rock band, copying his hero – French guitarist Jean Paul of The Stranglers. He adopted the same non-committal persona on stage and, while on anyone else it would have looked silly, Peter pulled it off.

His frequent appearance on stage at a shady pub rock venue often raised the kudos of a particular gig. He'd turn up in a brand new black Porsche 911 Turbo with an assortment of other flash cars outside from supporting directors of the group to challenge the general entourage of U2.

People would see the cars and think some chart-topping band was playing a secret venue to sharpen up before a world tour. They'd often stop him to exclaim: "Fucking hell, mate, how many discs have you cut to pay for this lot?"

Everyone thought he was someone, and indeed he was – just not quite the 'someone' they thought.

Peter's looks were complimented by his sense of style. If you or I tried to copy it, the same clothes wouldn't look anything like as good as they did on him. But he was never big headed about it; he was just our nice, good news guy. He wasn't into conflict or pushy business – that was left to Big Jim or me.

We sat opposite each other at work and socialised at the weekend. Peter became like a younger brother to me, and it was a rewarding and enjoyable partnership. We often pitched for business together up and down the country, leaving the office unattended with only an answer phone and a taped recording to say all our lines were busy and we'd get back to you.

To do this, given we didn't have mobile phones then, meant travelling thirty miles or so and stopping at a phone box to collect our messages from bemused clients. Sometimes we'd sneak into London to pitch for a potential client, just to take the piss out of Jim and boast about it. It was hard work, but equally it was all good fun. It worked well, with each personality complementing the other in presentations. We all brought something different, and it allowed us to equally share the failures. I'm sure the company couldn't have even considered success without the partnership that helped us both to get over disappointments as well as celebrate good news.

It would have been a lonely existence without him alongside; a simple case of the sum of the parts together being greater than that of the individuals.

The office opens

We wanted to keep the launch of our little venture as quiet as possible. If word got out, our old employers might take defensive action and lean on insurers to not even discuss doing business with us. So it was a bit of a shock to see one of our old colleagues walking down the road towards us as Peter closed the door of our new York office after we first viewed it.

Paul dealt with administration for our existing employers. Always ready with a sardonic smile and a slightly cynical perspective on life, he was one of life's nice guys. Notwithstanding this, the prospect of coming face-to-face with him in these circumstances was too much for Peter.

"Bloody hell," he hissed, darting back only to find his escape plan foiled by a locked door. He hit the wall in a Spiderman pose straight out of an amateur mime school, hoping he was invisible to Paul's smiling, quizzical gaze.

It was too late for that. Paul, looking both surprised and delighted to see us, strolled up.

"Hi Mike. What are you doing here?"

There was no getting out of it.

"I've just signed the lease on this place, Paul. I'm starting business next week on my own."

"Good for you, pal! Keep in touch and let me know how you get on – I might want a job!"

"Will do, Paul, take care."

Paul glanced at Peter, who in his mind was still making himself as invisible as possible. Paul, looking bemused and slightly concerned, nodded towards him and looked at me expectantly.

"Don't worry, Paul," I said. "Peter's a bit nervous at the moment."

"I see," said Paul, carefully, and walked on without another word. The silence was broken by Peter peeling himself off the wall.

"Did he see me?" he asked.

I wondered what to say, and heard myself answer: "No, I don't think so. You really blended in." He was wound up enough without worrying about anything else.

A few months later Paul became our first employee, and Peter was never allowed to forget his invisible man act.

Life in the office was quietly routine as we settled into our scary, new environment and tried to feel relaxed and purposeful. I tried to hide it the ever-present knot of nervous tension in my stomach – after all, who would deal with us?

We'd taken the precaution of printing corporate brochures to hand out to potential clients. In truth they were nothing more than an emotional crutch to hold onto in terrified anticipation of being told to clear off from every door we knocked on and telephone call that we made. But at least we could offer something concrete, no matter how abusive the contact, and that was how we spent most of our days – apologising for our calls and sending brochure after brochure out to companies that hadn't asked for them.

We only had one computer, which Peter treasured with such passion that he dismantled it in the evening and took it home in the boot of his car for the first few months, until he grew tired of it. He was also adept at keeping an eye on the comings and goings at the sex shop opposite, and dutifully reported back any activity to break up the monotony. We got quite imaginative, guessing what people might have bought. The sex shop window was shielded with blinds. Unnervingly, these moved occasionally and a thin, angular man could be seen peering out with dark, sad eyes. It was a disturbing sight that would cause Peter to produce a gasp of horror, often in mid-sentence to a potential client. It was as if this creature wasn't allowed out of his little den and was gazing out of the gates of Hell to momentarily glimpse the world on the other side.

"Crikey Mike, look – he's at it again. The bloody devil himself!"

We never saw all of him, just a hollow, deathly white, angular face. We never spotted him going in or out of the premises or doing anything remotely 'normal' like going for lunch. He just stared out at us with cold steely eyes, as if trapped in a place of everlasting misery.

It certainly helped us get our heads down, lest we caught his gaze and he cursed us. We needed all the luck we could get. Fortunately, within a year, we'd won enough clients to move to another office with more potential growth and a better – if less interesting – view.

We could fit about thirty people into two converted houses just off a main road out of York. Much to our delight we could put up a big sign truly announcing our arrival that would be seen by the main traffic flow between York and Hull. We hoped beyond hope that important people in our industry would notice our great neon sign as they flew by. Quite why they would find themselves on that road was politely overlooked as we lavished great pride and much polishing on our new HQ. Ward Evans was loud and proud, as it to compensate how we really felt – just plain scared.

The business

Having opened the new offices, we were anxious to fill them full of clients. Jim, Pete and I got together one afternoon to chew over how we would actually make the business work.

It was rather alarming as we hadn't really had that discussion before; if we had, we might have seen too many overwhelming problems.

Jim got the beers and I kicked off the conversation: "You know, there are people out there who think insurance is even more boring than we do, and however excited we are about setting this company up we have to face the fact that nobody gives a bugger and the world doesn't need another broker!

"I mean, it's great driving past the new sign but we'd better get our corporate arses into gear otherwise we won't be able to afford to turn the lights on."

Jim sat and contemplated the sad fact that too many brokers were chasing too few clients, and lots of insurers just didn't want to know us.

Root and branch changes were just starting to show themselves in the industry. The banking and building society sector had already seen sweeping changes with redundancies, consolidations, and business practices that were more in keeping with a modern, technology-driven and customer-focused marketplace.

This wasn't yet the case in insurance, but previous market agreements to share information on claims and pricing in the insurance industry had just been binned, encouragingly, as they would have been deemed illegal under anti-cartel arrangements had they remained. So, however reluctant to contemplate change, the industry had to – or lose out to foreign competition.

The solutions we needed to fill our empty offices with clients were fundamental. We needed to take steps, and it wasn't enough to answer "bloody big ones" when asked what those steps might be. We needed proper ideas.

Jim spoke as Peter and I stared sullenly into our drinks.

"Everyone is trying to protect their own business for as long as they can but it's got to change. There are more foreign insurers out there that want a slice of the action and they're not going to get it by sitting on their backsides waiting! And all this clap-trap as to how we have to follow certain procedures to get new business isn't going to last. We're not going to do any meaningful business sitting on our backsides either. We have to do something."

You might think we'd have given this some consideration before we set up the offices, but sometimes there is a distinct advantage in not seeing all the problems in front of you. We thought it best to deal with them one at a time, as and when they appeared. A sort of "by the inch, it's a cinch" attitude.

Problems should be easy to categorise. There are generally three types:
- Those you can deal with today
- Those you can deal with tomorrow
- Those that can never be dealt with

Ours wasn't a small problem and we hoped as we sat in that bar that it didn't fall into the last category. Industry protocol in trying to secure new business was Draconian and, however well-meaning, conspired to minimise red-blooded competition.

You were obliged to obtain a letter from the client to present to the existing insurers in an effort to establish the claims experience, even if the client already knew the information. Such a system served only to act as an alarm call for the current insurers, who would naturally do anything in their power to stop it; they'd have been foolish not to.

When the existing broker found their business was under attack, the real fun started.

Corporate tantrums and teddy bears were ceremoniously thrown from prams. There were dark threats as to how the impertinent client might never get cover again if they didn't take a 'longer view' of things. Members of the funny handshake club met in darkened corners.

"It's a right circus, just too much hassle for any new client," Jim concluded. "It's all that bleeding drama that we need to protect them from. I mean, it wouldn't bother me and I'd tell them all to piss off, but for some it just puts them off and they can't be arsed continuing with it."

This was a truth we had to face and, even if we persuaded the unfortunate client to carry on, there was still trouble ahead in the form of a dog-fight among the same list of possible insurers. To get a competitive price in these circumstances was rare indeed, regardless of the risk. But Jim was on a roll, and his inspirational third beer.

"Who wants to bother with that? Even insurers get pissed off. It's a complete waste of time," Peter calmly summed up. "Competition without any chance of winning is no competition at all – we could be screwed here."

It fell to me to remind us all that since we didn't actually have many clients – although we did have two offices, lots of empty desks and a very vain, flashing neon sign – we'd better find a way of getting some. We certainly needed to do things differently as it was obvious that following the old rules and playing the game wouldn't get us anywhere. Business wasn't moving simply because there was no financial incentive to persuade the client to do so.

Our only hope was the beating march of globalisation that had started to emerge. The French, German, Australian and Italian insurers - no respecters of tradition - weren't going to play along with this smoke-and-mirrors game either. They wanted a slice of the UK market. They too sat in big expensive offices with what appeared to us as very little to do. They too knew that if they played the game it would take years to build a market presence. Their needs and our needs coincided. The enemy of our enemy was miraculously positioned as our new friend.

"It's amazing what you can achieve with a bit of relaxed thinking," Jim reassured us all, whilst lining us all up with another pint of it. He drew a map of the city and marked out our target companies.

"It's simple. These new foreign boys want what we want, and all we have to do is go tell them the good news!"

We drew up a plan of attack. Jim suddenly went quiet – it was like an eclipse, and you couldn't fail to notice it. "Do you think any of these underwriters have ever been to any Greek Islands?" he asked.

"I don't know Jim. What sort of question is that? God, the way your mind works sometimes... Why do you ask?"

"Forget it Mike, I'll find out soon enough. But I'll duck out of the German meeting if that's okay?"

We were right. Our overseas friends were more than receptive and excited at the prospect of a new approach that would gain them market share.

Our *modus operandi* was simple. We'd quote on businesses that were the most profitable for them, businesses any idiot could underwrite and make money on. The risks were straightforward so we were able to persuade them that we didn't need to go to existing insurers and alert them to our activities.

We loved it. We'd discovered a new angle and laughed as we considered that the first time they knew they were under fire would be when they learned they'd lost the business.

"Imagine their faces..." We revelled in our new found confidence.

"We're not going to get marks for popularity," remarked Peter. This was an understatement, but clients loved us as we delivered great prices. And so did our new-found European contacts, who enjoyed piling on the business and making money.

As Jim said: "I'm proud to be British, but the future is in Europe, matey."

I never thought I'd hear Jim sound so presidential, but for our own selfish reasons we had all suddenly become Europeans.

"Bugger the Pound, give me the Euro," Jim would say to all who knew him. "That's the real currency!"

A united Europe sprang to life in the corners of those empty offices – or, more precisely, the Dog and Duck. Ever committed, Jim had his first taste of lager but after a few pints of what he dubbed 'Euro fizz', he nearly exploded with a gigantic belch. After that he decided some traditions should remain for the common good – and we were all pleased about that.

Small beginnings

We had just one client when we opened both offices - a company   where I knew the proprietor of a sizeable hotel and building business – and that didn't pay very well.

But we knew Malcolm and his custom were at least guaranteed, as he'd put ten grand into the business in exchange for shares.

Malcolm was a non-executive director. A chartered accountant and ex-Oxford man, he gave us the extra dimension we needed to appear credible before we really were.

"Imagine, Mum," I told her. "Who'd have thought there'd be a director on your son's board that went to Oxford or Cambridge? Me, a comprehensive kid who failed his Eleven Plus!"

"Well, think on, that's all I can say," Mum said, as Dad glowed with pride. But I could see she was impressed; after all she'd seen *Brideshead Revisited.*

"You'd better shut it and bloody listen," she warned me. She knew her son, and I did shut up when I met with Malcolm.

"I've made many mistakes in business Mike." Malcolm talked in a sage fashion that became his age and status. "If I can stop you making the same mistakes, I will. Anyway, I think I'll enjoy the ride."

Little did we all know just what a ride it would be, but for now it was reassuring to have him on board. He was our 'grey-haired man', the one we produced if we were too young, sharp or fast for a client or insurer.

Malcolm had studies philosophy and politics during his time at Oxford and had the unnerving knack of arguing one side of a problem and then, frustratingly, the other side – bringing us back to where we started, just more confused. We often felt as if we were part of some bizarre after-dinner game.

A philosopher was once described as someone who wouldn't take common sense for an answer. We told ourselves that perhaps what Malcolm knew wasn't worth knowing on a practical level, but if any thinking was involved it was him we turned to.

He'd had plenty of practice at debating with the best of them; he dropped in the fact that the Rt Rev Ian Paisley attended the same lectures as a mature student at Oxford. I asked if he ever succeeded in getting a few points over on him.

"No way Mike – God himself couldn't get a word in edgeways with that man," replied Malcolm. You sort of knew what he meant.

The fact that Malcolm was a qualified accountant, together with the personal connection I had with him and his experience as a successful businessman made him an excellent non-executive director. We felt lucky to have him as we all wanted a properly-constituted board.

We might be mad in the marketplace, but in the boardroom we wanted to be the model of sobriety and formality. Every board meeting found us suited and booted in recognition of what we were trying to achieve and the ambitions we had. It might have seemed a little pretentious, but when there were just five or six of us – including the office temp – we still had those formal meetings. It was simply a case of fake it to make it – we acted as a big company because we wanted to *be* a big company. One day, we promised ourselves, we would be.

Jim, Peter and I poured our lives' savings into the venture, with family and friends chipping in. When you have absolutely nothing else to go back to, it's easy to concentrate on the way forward. Failure just wasn't an option; this wasn't a toe in the water exercise. The business was designed for success and we had to work at it.

A non-competition clause in our previous employment contracts meant we were precluded from handling clients from that time. All business going forwards had to be won or lost in the unforgiving cut-and-thrust.

We relied on our own skill sets. Jim and I were happy to take on the main role of acquiring business, having done that many times before. Jim sold on sheer personality and physical presence alone, often shrugging his shoulders and confessing to the potential client that he knew "diddly squat about Bo Diddley".

His job was to kick the technical boys back at base if there was a problem. People loved him and nobody wanted to say no or deliberately abuse his kindness. You never knew how Big Jim might react if he felt double-crossed. Mostly he was very likeable and clients loved dealing with him – his personality in what otherwise would be a boring insurance meeting lifted the dullest of appointments. Often he'd get to the end of an allocated client meeting without a word of business being uttered, and then say: "Bollocks to it! I'll get one of our guys to write to you about your renewal. Any problems, let me know."

Either way policies were renewed, as he'd practised the art of simply talking the client out of time. No one could compete with that. "Bish, bash, bosh – sorted!" as Jim would say.

Having got the insurers on side we needed to ensure we had a system, a design process of selling; something others often had difficulty doing in a natural way. In writing down these guidelines, we made the process transferable and allowed many less experienced executives to do the same amount of business by simply joining the dots. The idea of making skill sets transferable was given to me by my old chairman. He was a cunning old fox, as I'd discovered to my cost, but his idea was brilliant. I was called to his office, prepared for the flattering plaudits I'd come to expect and, rather arrogantly, believed I deserved. Instead, I got a bollocking.

"Mike," the chairman said, peering over his half-moon specs. He always had a habit of slightly unnerving you, even if you felt you were doing reasonably well.

"I don't think you're doing what you can in this business."

I immediately went on the defensive, quoting the top sales figures by a mile.

"Listen, listen," he went on. "You do a hundred grand's worth of renewable new business a year and I'll pay you as a good salesman. But you get others to do a hundred grand like you and your value to me is triple anything a good salesman on his own could achieve. Think about it. I'll pay you as an entrepreneur: the choice is yours. Write it down and make it transferable, let people into the secret and train them to do what you do. Your decision, Mike. Do you want it easy and stay at the same level, or do you want to aspire to bigger and better things?"

I didn't need to think about the answer. It made perfect sense to me and was a changing point in my life.

Terms of reference made what we did transferable. The result was being able to take an average guy and turn him into a better salesman by applying those terms, even if he didn't quite understand why they worked.

Pete was our safe pair of hands on administration, the Mr Nice Guy every company needs. He was the one who could charm insurers into doing deals that allowed our business to flourish.

Together we made a great team and within six months we had our blueprint for success. All we needed to do was stay on track.

Doing the numbers

Much thought and debate took place about the name of the company. It had to be a 'clean' name that didn't conjure up anything old fashioned, nerdy, or too flash.

Jim suggested a democratic combination of all our surnames – Ward, Evans and Kenney. But it didn't take a genius to work out that, when amalgamated, it formed the name Wankee Insurance Brokers. Catchy, memorable, maybe true – but not the image to attract the clients we desperately needed.

We weren't big on egos back then, so we settled on Ward Evans. Jim and Peter could say they had their names on the business, showing extra kudos to potential clients, and I could large it up as managing director if needed. We all had an angle. The name also sounded familiar, so we didn't need to apologise about being in business for only a few months.

The business couldn't pay us our previous salary levels so we all went on subsistence money until it got on its feet. That meant that I had to move my family out of the matrimonial home during the summer and rent it out as a country cottage to pay the mortgage. We stayed with family and friends for about twelve weeks of the year, returning each week to clean up in readiness for the next holidaymakers. It provided much-needed income, and we promised ourselves it would be worth it.

Ahead of us stretched days, weeks and months of mind-numbing phone bashing. We knew any business would have to start with a back-to-basics mentality and we were all prepared to get our hands dirty. Folding envelopes, going to Kwik Print to have our letters typed up and licking stamps were all part of our new duties.

From every twenty one calls we made to potential clients, we could expect one meeting. That didn't seem bad, but sometimes we had to face being told to bugger off 100 times in a row before the next five calls got us five appointments. This was the law of large numbers – just like if you kept betting heads or tails, yes and no evened out at 50/50 eventually.

The work was soul-destroying, but unavoidable. We weren't machines, and often had to retire to the pub for some 'relaxed thinking'.

"How much is it costing us to make these calls?" Peter asked. Jim, ever resourceful, suggested that we should instead ask what it paid us.

He was onto something. We needed to work back the value of the phone calls in order to keep going with a smile on our faces; anything to keep the phones hot.

We worked out our statistical conversion rate from meeting to client appointment as one in four. An average client would pay a fee of around £2,000. Simple arithmetic suggested that every call we made brought us just over twenty quid.

"Holy shit!" Jim said, "It bleeding well doesn't feel like that!"

In his simplistic way, though, he was right. And that was the point. Pick up the phone and be told to piss off around twenty times, and the last one who listened would produce enough money to pay for those who told us in many and varied, clear and wonderful ways to take our brochures and stick them. In the hard and lonely days, the only way to keep going was to smile and say: "There's another twenty quid earned." Looking at it that way, life wasn't too bad. It was a lesson in changing how you look at a problem by taking a step back. This provided an emotional as well as practical platform in using this system to get new business.

We clung to that belief – that if we made the calls, we'd be fine. We lived it like a religion and practised it every day. Phone bashing was our only way to greater riches, every call earning us £20 on average. Who wouldn't do that with a smile on their face? Often when flagging we'd egg each other on: "Hey, how many people earn twenty quid to be told to piss off? Let's do five more calls and make a hundred!"

It didn't take long to have an enviable database. We knew who potential clients were, when they wanted us to call and what they were paying. The database became our life-blood. Our success wasn't left to chance – we designed our company to be super-athletic in the pursuit of new business, and then keeping it on service.

Peter was right about our popularity. Every client we won was taken from another broker – so our gain, their loss. Each one was a reason for other brokers to hate us. We developed a useful counter-strategy when occasionally one of our clients was attacked, encouraging them to seek at least six references from the competition with contact names and rough spend. We persuaded our clients that they needed to be assured the other broker could demonstrate good service.

We'd worked enormously hard to ensure we kept the account and, if successful, it didn't end there – it was payback time, as Jim said. He'd call the referees and explain why they needed to talk to us. The other broker tried to nick one of our clients and lost, because they were too expensive. That suggests you might be paying over the odds as well, Jim would say.

"I mean, competition's good mate, I welcome it. Now we have one happy client who knows we're good because he has just tested us, but when did you test them? I mean, fair's fair wouldn't you say?"

It was a persuasive argument, and many of the referees would allow us to quote on their business, much to the misery and dismay of the incumbent broker. Even if we didn't win, by the time we finished we'd have ripped the remuneration of the broker to pieces and either way, they'd lose money. Most of the market felt we were too much hassle and were best to leave us alone. It was exactly what we wanted.

In insurance broking, particularly if you were active in acquiring new business, prospecting friendships within the market wasn't possible. We had to find that fellowship within, closing the door on the outside world and becoming our own friends and family.

As we piled on business, everyone seemed to hate us. We embraced it and stopped apologising for who we were and what we were doing. Instead, we began to enjoy the notoriety; we were called terrorists, traders, crooks and rogues. Really we were an ambitious family of like-minded people with a common purpose and a shared vision. We were a close-knit team and, consequently, the business gained momentum. Things had taken off. We employed people who needed a special sort of courage just to come for an interview, let alone work for us. We managed to be different and stand out in an old industry.

Competition was essentially confrontational, and if brokers ever did get together it was usually at an annual institute dinner. Fights and jealous hissy fits were prevalent just below the surface – one careless remark and the whole thing could kick off. It was, in our view, remarkable that these dinners went ahead at all, but there was sometimes an underlying desire to poach staff and settle old scores in a more traditional way outside the doors of the Queen's Hotel in Leeds.

Any suggestion in those days that the middle man might go the same way as the milk man was met with derision and grand talk that the noble art of broking had its rightful and permanent place alongside other professions. Bugger any talk of that slightly tacky subject of commerce and business. But when you asked clients what they wanted, it was only for their claims to be paid and to pay a reasonable price for their policies in a fair, free, open market.

These were the days before call centres and direct line operators. The older guys still ruled, wearing their institute medals, which we young bucks fondly took the piss out of.

It all seemed a million miles away from the business we'd just set up. Peter, Jim and I looked around, and the more we saw of the decay, pomposity and disregard for the changing times, and the demands of a new generation of owner-managed clients, the more certain we felt that we had a fighting chance of doing something way beyond our original expectations. We might just be onto something here.

CHAPTER 2

Off to London

Through relentless systemised calling in an effort to gain appointments, selecting each 'good prospect' by applying terms of reference and being ruthless on pricing while offering the same cover, business continued to expand.

Within a few years we had over fifty people working for the organisation, many of whom were solely engaged to go out and win new business. Profits were starting to roll in at last and, after a few years, I no longer had to rent out my home as a holiday cottage and could take things a little easier.

It was wonderful to take my parents to see a West End show in London for the first time as a gesture of thanks for their help, support and the money they had provided. We drove down as far as the last junction of the M1, where Jim had advised we'd be able to park up and get the Tube, commuting straight into central London with minimal hassle.

Mum was fascinated that we were catching a train "on the underground" which patently was above it, as far as she could see. She immediately made a beeline for the driver and the guard, drinking tea from a flask and clearly on a break.

"Do we have two trains, love? One for above ground, then one for below?" she asked. The guys did a double take to ensure that they were not being accosted by the usual type of lunatic that must frequent the Tube at least once a day. They laughed and explained that she didn't need to change but would have to hold her breath when it went underground.

This was met with laughter, as Mum knew this was wrong. So they went on to explain that it ran on electricity and could go as far as the plug allowed, so it was environmentally sound and we were all doing our bit to combat global warming.

Mum stood her ground, oblivious to the piss-take and concluded: "So an underground train is just like an overground train, is it then?" She seemed content with the answer before walking off to see how long the train was.

We made the mistake of settling in our seats as the door closed. Fortunately, the guard was in shouting distance, as we panicked the train was going to leave her behind.

"Bloody hell," said Dad. "We haven't even got into London yet and she's missing!"

The guard made one announcement. No response. Then another. Within seconds, Mum could be seen running back down the platform, shouting: "Wait for me, love! I didn't know how long it was - I ended up right back there!"

She eventually barged her way on and sat down while we thanked the guard for his patience. Mum considered the staring faces and tuts of disapproval and then said in a fluster: "Well, I only heard the second announcement!"

"How did you know there were two, then?" I asked with a smile. Mum gave me one of her looks – it said everything.

"OK, love," she turned to the guard. "Let's get on, then. We've tickets to collect!"

Settling on her seat, she told the guard she'd been looking for the restaurant carriage so she too could have a nice cup of tea. Sharing the joke he confirmed that the dining car, where complimentary lunch would be served just as soon as the train eventually pulled away from the station, would be available shortly.

"Daft bugger!" she said, smiling at the guard. "I know you only serve tea on these types of trains."

I could see her mind was racing. She was excitable, adrenalin flowing, wanted to say something, anything. It got pretty random when Mum was in this mood.

"Anyway, what's this bloody global warning you're talking about in London?"

"It's OK," I said to the guard again. "We're from the north. I'll try to keep her quiet. I put it down to her diet and fizzy drinks, and she hasn't had her afternoon sleep yet." The guard walked away shaking his head. No doubt we confirmed too clearly that it is, in fact, grim up north.

I'd bought the show tickets from Mickey Tickets – there was little to know about him other than he was recommended by friends of Jim and, as it was on his 'manor' he'd ensure it was all 'good' for us.

We were instructed to meet Mickey at Knightsbridge underground station.

"Don't worry, Mike," Jim reassured me. "He'll be there in a white suit with four top tickets for Phantom of the Opera."

These were the hottest tickets in town at that time, with Sarah Brightman and Michael Crawford in the leading roles. We were delighted to have secured them even if they were from a dubious source. It turned out Mickey Tickets was a go-between – a bridge between the actors on stage and the ticket allocation they got for every performance.

We got to Knightsbridge half an hour late, stressed, hot and worried the guy would have done a runner. But there they were – Big Jim and Mickey Tickets, the latter smart in a crumpled white suit, standing together the best man and groom at some bizarre wedding. They smiled at all who passed by, both looking self-conscious in the busy station foyer.

"Crikey, you were pushing it," Mickey started. "I could have sold these ten times over!"

"You wouldn't do that with me stood here, pal. But I'm sure Mike takes your point," interrupted Jim. "He's here now. And how was your trip, beautiful?" Turning to Mum, he planted a big kiss on her cheek. He always made a fuss of her, sensibly. "Welcome to London, honey!"

"Don't get her talking, Jim!" I said. "Thanks so much, Mickey, I really appreciate it." And I handed over an envelope full of cash. We gave our thanks and goodbyes and off we went, looking forward to our evening.

Arriving early at the theatre was exciting in itself. People bustling, the occasional star sweeping in. Mum couldn't believe we were outside the theatre where *Live at Her Majesty's* was broadcast and half-expected to be grabbed by someone saying the tickets were fakes and we'd been conned.

We were somewhat relieved to be shown to our seats and have the curtains go up and lights go down without being tapped on the shoulder and asked to leave. I looked at Mum and wondered what she might make of it, given that the last stage performance she saw was my sister and I dancing around a maypole.

The show didn't disappoint. We had a fantastic, glorious, wonderful night. Michael Crawford swinging from the ceiling provided a fantastic spectacle that mesmerised everyone, especially my parents.

"I didn't think they could do all that on a stage," said Mum, shaking her head afterwards. "Bloody marvellous. I nearly had kittens when I saw him. I said, Tom, didn't I, where the bloody hell will he appear next?"

I said I thought it might be the Bradford Alhambra, but she didn't get the joke. We climbed into the waiting limo outside as Mum went star-spotting – but Dad was carefully tracking her this time.

"Only bloody Shirley Bassey saw the same show, in the same audience," she said gleefully. "Imagine that! Her car's not as big as ours, love," she told the driver.

We took off for a beautiful French restaurant in Soho, where Jonathan Ross was dining with Jane Goldman, his future wife. Mum gave him a dressing down about wearing white socks with black shoes, and he was kind and courteous as she explained where she'd been.

"I won't spoil it for you, love," she said, "But he doesn't get the girl in the end. I'm not surprised though, He's got an awful face, that Michael Crawford," she concluded. She sat down at last, saying to us in conspiratorial tones: "Nice bloke, but you'd have thought he could afford better socks, wouldn't you?"

The night came to an end and I bade them goodnight in the hotel foyer. Next morning, they both looked a little worse for wear when we met for breakfast.

"Your dad and me had a late one, love," smiled Mum. "Well, we thought since you went to the trouble of stocking up the fridge with all those little drinks, we didn't like leaving them. It was lovely of you, so Tom and I had a few."

"What fridge? Do you mean the minibar? You didn't drink all of them?" I asked incredulously, as I quickly tried to estimate the cost.

"Don't be bloody silly!" Mum said.

I breathed a sigh of relief. "Thank God for that," I thought.

"We're not bloody daft," Mum continued, with a wicked look in her eye and a cunning smile. "Those we didn't drink your dad and me brought with us – can't you hear the bottles in my bag?"

Mum, (Doreen) and Grandma Clara

My mother, Doreen, was in her seventies and weighed six stone nothing in wet clothes. She had a fighting spirit that shocked and astonished those around her for a woman of her size. She was always on the lookout for anyone trying to pull the wool over her eyes, but who that might be and why was often unclear – until one night we got something of an explanation.

"They have to get up early to beat me, old love," she'd say, completely out of the blue.

"Who the hell has to, and why?" we'd ask.

"Anyone!" came the hissed reply.

"What the hell is she on about?" I asked my sister one day. "Something must have happened in her life that's resulted in her casting a suspicious eye over everyone she comes into contact with, other than the immediate family."

We tried to trace it back, but the only thing we could come up with happened a long time ago and we howled with laughter when we considered just what an effect it had. Mum had gone into hospital for a minor operation and bought some new, bright pink slippers from Marks and Spencer. She loved them and wore them whenever she could as she tripped around the ward, stopping occasionally to appreciate her new footwear.

"They're like walking on air," she said, smiling down proudly at her fluffy pink feet. When the time came for her to be taken down for the anaesthetic they were still stuck on the end of her white little legs, but when she came round later the first thing she did was look down and notice they were gone.

Who knew those slippers would cause such a sense of outrage and fury? Mum demanded no bed was left unturned until they were found. The realisation someone had nicked them while she was under anaesthetic was a turning point.

"In a bloody hospital!" she'd say, shaking her head. "In a bloody hospital. You wouldn't credit it, would you? They had to bloody knock me out before they could get one over on me, but they'll only do it once, they won't do it again."

She meant it. From then on she'd keep a watchful eye out, and God help anyone if they had a similar pair.

Mum had a shock of ginger hair and a pale complexion – not, it has to be said, a good look with pink slippers anyway. She took to wearing her favourite cream trouser suit that made her look like a matchstick from a pack of Swan Lights. An incessant smoker, she went about her business with a cigarette hanging from her mouth and a blue haze permanently above her head, a look not dissimilar to that of albino Cuban tobacco workers in old films about Castro and Havana.

Her eyes shone bright blue, loving towards her immediate family but with steeliness in them to anyone else. They belied the great hardship she endured in her youth.

Mum's parents were both born deaf and dumb. In those days, such an affliction was treated more like a mental illness than a physical disability.

They couldn't hear air raid sirens during the war and her father refused to get out of bed. Mum, with her sister and brother, would sit in total fear until the all-clear sounded.

Her father, not unnaturally, given his disability and treatment by others, was a man who didn't mess around if he felt he was being talked about or ridiculed. He'd thump anyone who glanced at him the wrong way in many a public house, never giving the benefit of the doubt.

I often wondered how many were the consequence of an innocent look, perhaps a comment about his flash suits or the fresh flower in his striped jacket. But either way, Granddad wasn't going to take any chances. It didn't matter if there were one, two or three guys.

Cartoon-like bar brawls ensued, not unlike those in the saloon scenes of old westerns. Then everyone would disappear except for Granddad, who hadn't heard the police siren or instructions to drop to the floor.

Inevitably he was arrested and didn't have the vocabulary to offer a defence. They thought he was 'mental' and locked him up.

Grandma Clara was dressed permanently in her Victorian get-up, all lace and fineness; she was a very handsome, strong woman. She always had a dog that acted both as a companion and help for her hearing. A very strong bond developed between her and Queenie, the family pet. Queenie was a faithful mongrel that constantly smelt of the carbolic soap that Grandma used to keep her nice and clean.

A problem arose that wasn't dissimilar to Granddad's, but with different consequences. If the poor dog looked at her for more than a few seconds – as happened often – Grandma would convince herself that the dog was trying to communicate with her, trying to tell her something or ask for something.

Most people might reasonably assume the dog was hungry or needed a walk, but my grandmother concluded that Queenie had a headache. So she plied her with a good few aspirin and other medication mixed with milk.

We tried to explain it wasn't a good idea, but Grandma was having none of it. It was a miracle the poor dog wasn't overdosed, but I think towards the end Queenie got the gist of what was going on. At any rate, she steadfastly refused to look at anyone – it was a new take on Pavlov's conditioning.

Queenie would run towards you with a sideways gait, not wanting to look you in the eye and risk another druggable offence. She'd rather pass with her head down and an apologetic tail tucked away, thank you very much. Clever dog.

Although born profoundly deaf – and therefore dumb – Grandma tried her best to learn to speak. As the years went by her immediate family could understand her, but no one else had the least idea what she was on about.

One of my earliest memories is of sitting on Grandma Clara's knee listening to her sing *My Girl's a Yorkshire Girl,* although it was only many years later I recognised the song.

She had an endearing habit (at least, for us children at the time) of nicking a few odd items in Woolworth's for us, and always buying Easter eggs in Thornton's in County Arcade, Leeds. The added value was that the shop would ice the name of the recipient child on their egg. I can only wonder at the scene when she told them my name was 'Maggle', which appeared as clear as anything.

Grandma was undeterred, and every Easter my sister and I would look forward to the eggs and try to guess what names might appear, and whether we could successfully identify which was which.

She used to look forward to her annual holiday in later years with the deaf and dumb club that was her social life. The anticipation was at least half of her enjoyment, preparation being everything.

The holiday would be pre-empted by a two-week stay in the local hospital, timed to perfection so she could save a few quid, have a rest, and be on top form for her trip. This was before the days of super-bugs and the like – on reflection it shows what a sorry state we are in, that some hospitals are now a more dangerous place to be than at home.

In those days, though, Grandma got first class treatment and proper nursing. We marvelled at how she could time her comings and goings, convincing doctors that her 'funny do' meant a brief stay was the ideal precursor to a trip to Skegness.

As we now consider holidays begin at the airport, so did Grandma Clara's start in hospital.

Her bags were packed months in advance. A small 'just in case' hospital bag rested alongside the holiday suitcase, giving the game away about the sudden illness that would befall her in the run-up.

Goodness knows what would have happened if the doctors had insisted on her staying in and spoiling the actual holiday.

On the day she left, the strong smell of lavender would stun you and take almost a month to disappear. You could actually taste it all the way down the street to Victoria Coach Station, as she and her deaf and dumb crowd bullied the driver into loading the suitcases. It's reasonable to assume that such a disability heightens other senses, so we as a family often speculated on what the other poor unfortunates on the coach made of my Grandmas pungent wildflower smell. It was probably enough to give everyone a high chance of hayfever.

I hated school dinners as a child and would go to Grandma's for lunch every day. They were idiosyncratic and amazing – I'd have a lamb chop, bacon, a fried egg and peas all on the same plate with a Yorkshire pudding. I remember that exotic mix with relish today, no matter which fancy restaurants I've frequented in later years. A plateful of goodness-knows-what was always tasty, if surprising.

Grandma always visited us for Christmas and sometimes babysat in the evening. They were joyous times, apart from when she indulged in her obsession of fiddling with all the clocks – she'd wind them up, and walk around oblivious to the many alarms that she set off at the same time.

My grandparents' disability didn't make for an easy childhood, but it did hardwire a special strength and resilience into Mum's character that meant she could take whatever the world threw at her and ensured she kept her cautious eyes wide open. "Shit to them!" she'd say, quite alarmingly as it came out of the blue from a flame-haired, five-foot-nothing fireball.

"They have to get up early to beat me, old love," she'd reassure herself and anyone else in earshot.

When we moved our offices to larger premises, I had the habit of working on Saturday mornings. Mum and Dad would come across to meet me at the office as they stayed most Saturday evenings.

Mum was prone to taking up a duster, tutting and moving bins, and I paid her a small amount of money for a few weeks whilst she blasted around.

"No one can bottom a place like me, love," she'd say, with justifiable pride. "Would you look at those bloody cups in that sink? The dirty buggers. Don't your staff know how to wash a pot?"

Eventually, unknown to me, she started leaving notes on people's desks if they were particularly untidy.

"Who's bloody Doreen then, the cheeky cow?" they'd say on Monday morning, until they realised it was the boss's mother. They took notice, then, and the yellow sticky notes from the Dreaded Doreen were the first thing they'd deal with when they got in. I often contemplated letting her loose on the slackers from the sales side.

Mum was always uneasy with modern technology. Not just computers and the obvious stuff, but what most people would be quite familiar with, such as an answer-machine.

We had one at the matrimonial home and if Mum called and it picked up she'd treat it with suspicion and aggression, as though she'd interrupted a burglar.

We'd come home to messages such as: "Oh bloody hell, not you again. I wanted our Michael. Ask him to call me, would you, love? I'm not saying any more to you."

When we challenged her, she'd say: "Well, I haven't a bloody clue who it is I'm speaking to, have I? So I'm not saying anything to them. Could be bloody anybody." It wasn't worth the explanation.

Once, I'd deliberately asked an employee to come in for a disciplinary on a Saturday morning, reasoning it would be easier and less stressful for us both to do it with a heart-to-heart outside business hours.

When the formidable Doreen turned up she wanted to get into my office to collect coffee cups but was stopped at the door by my PA and told we couldn't be disturbed.

"Bugger that," she said, interrupting our meeting by bursting through the door. "He said that, did he? The little shit!" Ignoring me, she turned to the other guy and said, "I've just come in for the cups, love."

"Mum!" I said with exasperation, "I'm here to talk to Roger." (The unfortunate sitting opposite me.)

The reply was instant.

"Well, if I know you, he'll be here a bloody long time listening to the shit you come out with!" she sniped, clearly ready for the fight. "And if you think I'm waiting outside that door you've got another think coming! Who the bloody hell do you think you are?"

Turning to Roger, she added: "Don't let him have a go at you, love. You should be home with your family on a Saturday not listening to his crap. Tell him to bugger off. I would!"

With that, she left and banged the door shut. Roger didn't feel comfortable or reassured, thinking it had been going all right until she got involved.

"You're sacked!" I shouted. Roger went pale. "Not you," I said to him, "that daft bugger outside!"

"Shit to you!" she shouted from outside.

She was back the next week, dusting and cleaning. She didn't say a word, but cast me the occasional glance as if daring me to say something.

Persistence and resilience were qualities she possessed in abundance. In her case, they were necessary to get through everyday life. I hoped she'd passed some of them on to me in small measure at least – they'd be needed in the days ahead.

Doing the business

Business continued apace. The sheer relentlessness of calling potential clients, gleaning information and logging them onto our dedicated new system meant competing brokers thought we were everywhere.

The truth was, we were. Peter, Jim and I continued to hit the phones with our account executives, making between five hundred calls every month, six thousand a year, speaking to three thousand new companies per year. It built into a database of around a hundred thousand companies, telling us when their insurances were due for renewal, when they might like a confidential review, how to attack the account and in many cases where the business was placed and what they were paying

If an insurance company did the dirty by alerting the existing broker when the client had specifically asked this wasn't done, we'd gently remind the insurer that we had all this data and, at the flick of a switch, could attack all the accounts held by them.

It was no guarantee we'd get the business, but it concentrated the insurer's mind when faced with having to compete against us on a large load of cases. They could lose premiums amounting to millions just because we selected potential clients insured by them. They'd have to aggressively compete with the lowest premium in the market. Clearly this was to be avoided so we had to decide how and in what circumstances we'd threaten to push the nuclear button. Once done there would be no going back, so only Peter had the authority. I don't think he ever used it, as he skilfully persuaded insurers to keep to client instructions. At the end of the day, we were all there to do our clients' bidding.

Many brokers wondered at our success and asked how we could do all this new business, but they never really stopped to think that the way in which we systemised everything meant the chances of failing were minimal. There was no real secret; we were simply designed to go out there and find business. We did, however, foster relationships with a few brokers where we had an informal 'non-competitive' agreement.

One came to look at our systems and data, and went away saying that while he now knew how we did it, it was impossible for him to replicate it. The culture was so different he'd need to almost cease trading, sack the existing staff and start again. That was the benefit of starting when we did. We had a clean sheet of paper and could design the company for success without any problems associated with previous cultures or practises.

The only cloud on our corporate horizon was that the more successful we became, the more competitors blackened our name. We weren't totally immune to this; egos, pride and feelings were hurt. But however we looked at solving it, the problem remained. How could we be liked when we were always pitching in a competitive situation – and winning? Nobody would thank us for taking business from the existing broker. There were other brokers who were expanding, a few at the same pace as us, but they

22

were buying the businesses from the proprietors so all they got was a slap on the back. All we received was a metaphorical smack on the head and bad press.

I remembered again Chairman Neville stating the three types of problem:

- Those you can deal with today
- Those you can deal with tomorrow
- Those that can never be dealt with

And half the solution is putting them into the right category.

I put our problem in one of the latter two. All we could do was acknowledge it and, as Churchill said, *KBO* - Keep Buggering On!

Our reputation of being off-the-wall, different and exciting was beginning to attract characters that wanted to be part of this crazy army of well-paid executives.

There came a time when interviews for new candidates took place almost every week. We'd developed a certain reputation, and that alone brought momentum.

We employed a full time personnel consultancy which, in turn, had various external consultants including industrial physiologists and interpreters of character and work ethic.

This tended to give us more information about a potential employee than we knew what to do with. Jim cut to the chase when he commented: "All we need to know is whether they can at least give the job a good go and whether they'll fit in."

We found an essential quality was a sense of humour under pressure, and Jim quickly devised a series of questions that cut across any deep profiling. Just before the candidate would be offered the position, he'd crash the meeting, stare the person in the eye and say: "One last question mate... Important this..."

The candidate would straighten up and be on max alert.

"You're doing well, but I want to know one thing to settle an argument that rages in this office. What's the wonderful thing about Tigger?"

The candidate would usually check to establish they'd heard correctly. "Tigger?"

"Yes, Tigger, you know! Come on, what's the wonderful thing about Tigger?"

They'd usually reply, with a smile: "That's easy; the wonderful thing about Tigger is that *he's* the only one!"

"Wrong!" Jim would assert. "You've not got a head for detail, have you? You didn't put that down on your CV as a weakness!"

If the candidate came back at Jim this was a good sign; it was someone who'd stand up and say what they believed with a smile on their face. Some just didn't get it, blushed and stayed quiet. Sadly for them, they would never flourish in this environment. Some went away baffled, thinking it had gone well until the lunatic crashed in.

But most got it and a row erupted. There was immediate bonding and it usually ended with Jim telling the now successful candidate the correct 'corporate answer': "The wonderful thing about Tigger, mate, at least so long as I'm in this company, is that he's flouncy flouncy bouncy! It may not be important to you, but it bloody is to Tigger!"

Once employed, the majority went through a shock to the system and then settled in. But the occasional person, who couldn't cut it and didn't want to be there, left – a cause for great celebration by the rest of the industry.

"There you are," they'd say. "We told you so – they're a hire-and-fire organisation. We knew it." Competitors mounted viral campaigns about the leavers who, individually, simply felt it wasn't for them.

We understood that. Our kind of philosophy, ethos and values weren't for everyone. In a strong, close-knit community you're bound to find people who don't share those views or feel threatened by such a strong corporate culture.

But the idea we didn't care for our employees, who were the walking, talking assets and hard-working talent of the business, was offensive and hurt more than we cared to admit.

We commissioned research and learned that, compared to industry average, the number of people leaving us was higher by a couple of percentage points. Bad news, but not surprising as we also had more people going through their first year of training and development.

In short, we were recruiting more people than average too. Where our competitors' employee numbers were pretty static, ours were expanding considerably. Those who joined us and got through that initial year were more likely to stay, so the research underpinned the message we wanted to send. Plainly and simply, we were saying: "If you think you have talent, come to us. If you prove you have talent, stay and enjoy a greater salary and bonuses."

Those who just wanted to hide as a number in a large, organised structure, who felt uncomfortable being accountable, would find no place with us. There could be no hiding with regard to performance or figures. Everyone, including directors, would be exposed in that way.

It all seemed a far cry from the days when Big Jim would lose the keys to the office and we'd be locked out, standing around the front door as he looked for a spare set, praying that the ringing phone wasn't our biggest client saying their factory had burned down.

Both offices were growing, and in London it was so crowded that we had one desk just two feet outside the toilet door. Jim, creative as ever, made good use of its unfortunate position.

He called it the dunce desk. There was a silver ashtray on it that wasn't allowed to be moved, and anyone who went to the toilet was encouraged to put lose change into it. The account executive who'd ballsed up that month would be obliged to sit there and say thank you to people when the coins hit the tray.

Simple, effective, and fun – if a little harsh. No one wanted to be the monthly toilet attendant and it was an imaginative solution to problem performance, if not particularly PC. It was more effective than withdrawing bonuses and was done with the humour that Jim brought to all his business dealings. The money paid for drinks on a Friday.

We had a different solution at our new office in York, where we had a giant aquarium full of piranhas. Nobody quite believed what they were until they saw them feed on raw meat. The tank stood some six feet across and five feet deep, and legends grew about what we did to failing executives. There was talk about someone's head being dipped in there if they didn't wise up – it was only talk, I promise.

In the foyer, adjacent to the tank, were a couple of sofas where nervous job candidates would sit and wonder what we idiots were doing with these fish, only to jump out of their skin when the large cuckoo clock behind them would strike on the hour. The silence was interrupted by loud chimes and the banging heads of two goats – we loved being different.

Peter and I used to visit London each week and looked forward to feeling the clearly identifiable pulse of the City. We'd walk from our little office on Jamaica Road and stare like Dickensian tramps into the plate-glass kitchen windows of Pont de la Tour as the chefs prepped for lunchtime service.

It was a different world, but one that was starting to open up for us. My first visit there was one autumnal afternoon. We arrived at around 2pm; service would continue until 3pm. Jim couldn't understand why I was rushing, but I thought the place would empty and that the ambience would disappear with the people, as in some provincial town eatery. I loved the idea that the place was still heaving at three and four in the afternoon, meals and deals being done everywhere. All having fun, when we should be behaving ourselves in the office.

I had a childlike wonder for the whole culture, made more exciting because it just felt so naughty to be there when surely we should be at work – I couldn't believe we wouldn't be in trouble for being out.

And there was the joy in knowing that I really didn't have to report to anyone, save the clients, and they were happy enough. It felt like true freedom.

I sat looking at the famous Tower Bridge, beautifully illuminated against the city skyline and the yellow and blue lights of Lloyd's of London. I drank in the effortless efficiency of the waiters, the chatter of moneyed business folk, the practised welcome of the maître d' that made me feel like he'd shagged my girlfriend and owed me one. It was a circus of beauty. It was a world I felt a desperate need to belong to.

I wanted to be there among my friends and work colleagues. It wasn't the food or the alcohol, which of course was served in abundance. It was the sense of occasion, the indulgence – I mean, it was 4.30pm, they were still serving and it was still full!

We sat there, a happy team, knowing our fantastic group of happy people was working hard back at base – a bit like Andy Warhol's Factory with a lot of production, some flair and a lot of joining the dots.

I was moved to say: "Please, if the Good Lord can hear us, let no one take this away." I never wanted to be poor again. We'd seen how the other half lived. Better than that, we'd become the other half. They'd let us in, we were part of the secret. The one that everyone holds back, the knowledge that while most people are working their balls off, there's a huge party going on out there. But behind closed doors – you can only join if you have an invitation. And now we did – access all areas. Somehow, we'd become members of this privileged group.

We had also just found a gorgeous, two-bedroom flat just upstairs from the Pont, overlooking London Bridge and the Thames, at Butler's Wharf. We'd worked out that the cost of people going up and down the line and staying in hotels could be more than covered by renting this pad – it was a no-brainer.

Within a week we were toasting our new domestic base on the balcony overlooking the river.

"I tell you what," said Peter, "it's a bloody long way from the sex shop and the devil himself!"

It was; but with what the City had to offer, I wasn't sure the devil was too far away. I swear I could still see that face peering out, calling us in to who knew what.

Lloyd's of London

Lloyd's of London still dominated the world's insurance market and was a heck of a difficult place to get into to do business. You had to be a member of Lloyd's simply to place a risk with a syndicate in the building.

It was an extremely important market, particularly when the insurance industry was hardening. That meant capacity to take risk was reducing, and as a consequence, premiums would rise or you might not get cover at all.

We weren't big enough to apply to be a Lloyd's broker, so we had to use a middleman to get to those underwriters; effectively, a middleman going to a middleman before the risk got to an underwriter. And the poor end user, the client, had to pay for these middlemen along the way.

Occasionally we were invited into the building as guests, and were instantly mesmerised by the dramatic escalators and lifts. As Jim said: "It's like a bloke with his guts on the outside, don't you think?"

His view of architecture was more traditional than mine. I loved its elegant frame – it generated excitement and a feeling of untold opportunity. I reminded myself as I walked through the swing doors that I was entering history, a place with the famous Lutine Bell and the little desks that were called boxes.

We heard stories that, given our experience of the general marketplace, we felt were true. Underwriters would seek to ensure their box was as near the ground as possible as brokers simply couldn't be bothered to ride the elevators to go higher up the building. Rather like a Marks & Spencer high street location, a close box had greater value. Location was everything.

Another rumour related to one of the first women to walk the floor of Lloyd's. Inventive – and sexist – as ever, it was alleged that some syndicates started laying odds as to which member of a broking team would have his way with her first. Dignity and reputation was at stake, although not that of the unfortunate and unknowing lady. The story went that the Lloyd's committee got wind of the plan and put a quiet stop to it, fearing press comment.

Inside and out, the place was full of 'Ruperts', as we called them. They looked the same - Sloane types fresh from the same senior public schools across the land, each with the floppy fringe favoured by Hugh Grant in most of his films, with accents to match. Little pads in the City for the week, and off to the country pile at weekends. Many spent years just queuing to see underwriters on the first three or four floors of the building. In those days appointments were rare and you had to stand there, papers and submissions in hand, waiting. Often a Rupert, having stood there for a few hours would get to the front of the queue, take a deep breath, and the underwriter would stand up, put his pen down and bugger off to lunch without a word.

"I'd fucking follow them," Jim said, when he heard why the Rupert couldn't get an answer. Jim had a quote to get and would be more persistent than most. He'd turn up in the bars and general watering holes, insisting the Lloyd's broker went with him, and 'accidentally' bump into the underwriter. Some of the most interesting business was done during Jim's accidental meetings with a Lloyd's underwriter, port or brandy in hand.

"'Ow's it going, mate?" he would ask perfect strangers, having the personality to get away with it. "I've got this risk, money for nothing, sweet as a nut. Show it to him, Rupert," he'd continue.

Most work was completed in the Mitre Club, a basement wine bar in easy walking distance of Lloyd's and temporary office to many of the best underwriters. It was one of those places where you needed to know where to go, down some stairs that opened onto a large bar, throbbing with suits and a blaze of vertical lines and spilt drinks. Further along was the restaurant, but it seemed nobody really bothered with that – they preferred to eat at the bar, chewing the fat with fellow underwriters. A few of the brokers in the know were there, hovering around, ingratiating themselves, with the occasional Lloyd's slip-paper containing the minimum information necessary to the underwriter.

Word was that one evening, when the IRA detonated a large bomb at the nearby Baltic Exchange, the front door of the Mitre was blown in. No damage there then; most of the guys hardly noticed. They were asked to evacuate but, used to risk

26

assessment, decided it was safer to stay put. Underwriters hardly paused as they checked discreetly whether they were 'on for the risk'. Those who weren't got another bottle in as they celebrated their near-miss in more ways than one, while generously commiserating with those who were.

The Ruperts were tremendously arrogant when you bumped into them in the clubs and wine bars – perhaps it was payback for the humbling experience of constant queuing.

"Have I seen you in Lloyd's? I don't recall your name. You're not a member, then?" they'd sniff. It's something we had to put up with – we needed those jerks, they didn't need us. There were more risks chasing too few insurers or syndicates. But it never failed to amaze us that these expensively-educated guys thought so much of themselves when they were really little more than bag carriers.

The senior broker would clear off while a Rupert stood in line for hours. When he got close, he'd page the senior broker who would step in to have the risk 'scratched'. Off the Rupert would go to stand in another queue. Sometimes, if he was lucky, he occasionally got to say something.

The demand to work in Lloyd's was tremendous. I was outside the building – as a non-member, I had to wait for someone to give me a visitor's pass. I became engaged in conversation with a young guy, nervous and sweating as he waited for Lloyd's broker to collect him for an interview.

"Good luck, mate," I said as an older, aristocratic, pinstriped man with greased-back hair swept through the revolving doors and bellowed the poor boy's name.

He immediately stood to attention as the broker spoke only in the deep tones unique to the breeding of that social group.

"Hello there, sorry I'm late; bloody fuck up in the market at the moment. Here's your pass, come with me, stick close, don't get lost..."

With that, the man turned with a flourish and headed for the revolving doors that still spun from his exit. The Rupert didn't say a word; he just blushed and, with military precision, fell tightly in behind the broker as he entered the doors. Unfortunately, possibly out of nerves, he stepped into the same quadrant as his leader.

As the broker was halfway in, the Rupert, eager not to be left behind, had stepped a little too close for comfort. The glass hit the back of his shoes, causing the front panel to slam shut as the Lloyds Broker pushed vigorously. The guy turned around in close confines as Rupert tried to feign transparency. His gaze met the poor Rupert's, who had nowhere to hide. The broker shook his head in disbelief, but the bollocking had to wait. They had a problem to solve – getting out of the revolving doors with as much dignity as possible.

Rupert, poor lad, went puce and surely wanted to die. But to get out meant they had to work together – cooperation and teamwork were needed. Looking at it objectively, it was the perfect interview test – could they work together under stress? They both made a slight side-stepping walk, similar to penguins on ice. Slow but steady progress was made. Rupert tried to apologise but could only talk to the back of the aristocrat's head, whilst trying to make enough space to allow decency rather than looking as though he was trying to back-scuttle his future boss. Mind you, senior public schools and all, that might not have been a bad thing. They eventually managed to get to the other side. Not the most elegant entry into one of the world's leading members only clubs, but one he wouldn't forget.

I sometimes wonder whether he did get that job, or saw the light and decided to go live in the real world.

The big cars arrive

In a mad moment, I'd ordered a brand-new, hand-built Aston Martin straight from Newport Pagnell. It was a big V8 coupé that rocked gently when the engine turned over, it was so big and powerful.

I knew nothing about these cars other than they looked marvellous and you didn't see many around. When it arrived at the office a few of us went outside to look at this monster being unloaded.

It was racing green, a truly British car that looked like it had been built on steroids. When you opened the bonnet you could still see the name of the guy responsible for building it emblazoned on the engine head, a truly remarkable way of instilling pride in the final product and providing a connection from the factory to the final owner. I learnt that over ninety percent of all Aston Martins ever built still run today, their history monitored and traced as befits any thoroughbred.

The car had a sporting handbrake, which meant an idiot like me couldn't move it, and I consequently drove around for half an hour with it on.

"Holy shit, Mike!" cried Peter, our resident petrol-head, "You've still got the bleeding handbrake on!"

"Bloody hell, it was fast enough anyway," I said. "What's it going to be like with it off?"

Peter quickly arranged for me to go on a speed training and safe driving day organised by Aston Martin before I killed myself. Jim had a Jaguar XKR that he treated like an old kitchen – crisp packets here, old sandwiches there. It looked like someone had been squatting in it – within weeks, it was a real mess.

While Jim's gracious nature meant he wouldn't say no or seem ungrateful when it was suggested he get a flash car, he never looked happy in it. He always drove it with a slightly confused and uncomfortable look on his face and, before long, he'd gone into a ditch on his way up to the York office.

"Sorry, guys," he wheezed, "I got distracted by something flying out of the car."

"What the bloody hell was it?" I asked. A silly question – half of Jim's life was in the car and it could have been literally anything from his house deeds to his lunch.

"I don't know, we'll have to wait and see what's missing." I couldn't attack the logic of his argument.

"I can't get used to this," he continued. "Too many dials and the like. All I want to know is how fast I'm going and how much petrol I have in the tank. That's all I need."

We had a heart to heart and asked Jim what he truly wanted, rather than what Pete and I were happy with. It was wrong to impose our preferences on him.

"Well, those great bloody Volvos look the business to me. They may be big buggers for you, but they're just the right size."

We traded in the now bent but still beautiful XKR and got him a top of the range Volvo. It lasted a few days until he forgot it was diesel and filled it up with petrol. We gave up on Jim and cars.

Peter, the car enthusiast, got himself a black Porsche Turbo 911 with what seemed like six extra exhausts and flared black arches. It was what Jim and I would call a boy racer's car, but we knew how great it was – and that Pete was the only one capable of driving it and enjoying it to the limit.

He loved it, even though he couldn't escape us taking the piss by calling it a 'hairdresser-made-good' car. We'd see him in the car park and catcall: "Well, I'll see

if I can fit in on Saturday but I have Mrs Plumb's cut and blow dry darling!"
This was usually answered by swearing from Peter, growls from his exhaust and a
scream of tyres as he let us know what he thought of our comments. It was all done in
good fun.

Meeting Sir Chay

We were invited to the Southampton Boat Show by Sir Chay Blyth as potential clients
of his company, Challenge Business. They arranged motivational days out on a fleet
of large yachts, doing team building exercises and straightforward ocean going races,
which enabled that work to be put into practise.
We'd previously been guests on Sunsail, but what Sir Chay offered was a notch above
that.
We arrived in good time thinking we'd have some fun first. We'd never been to a boat
show and soon found the famous Guinness tent, promptly named base camp, where
refreshment was had by all.
Suitably fortified we finally tore ourselves away and visited the various stands, a
bunch of wide-eyed boys. It must have been a logistical nightmare getting everything
together for this event and I was full of admiration for the teamwork required to get it
up and running.
The Sunseeker stand was for VIP s only, so we stood behind the ropes and gazed at
the beautiful vessels, wondering if we'd ever climb the dizzy heights and actually own
one. We certainly had the desire and the ambition.
A few more years, we promised. We all needed objectives, a reason for expanding
and going forward, and the beautiful Sunseeker was now one of them. Sunseeker sold
dreams, and everything was designed to enhance that image. Nothing was left to
chance. Whether dreams could be turned to reality was another issue.
 We eventually got to meet Chay, which we were all looking forward to. He was, after
all, a living legend, a real character.
Distinguished by his blaze of silver hair and ruddy, cheeky face, an intelligent twinkle
in his eye, he was every bit straight from the yacht club in his smart navy blazer and
slacks – just with a harder edge and a Boy's Own reputation. He had a habit of saying:
"Ha, lads, well, you know, it's only money," with an engaging smile that stayed
firmly on his face, whatever the circumstances.
We got on famously and I think he thought he might be able to pass on a few wise
words for the benefit of our corporate adventure. He obviously thought we needed it.
But then again, he'd seen it all, met them all and done it all.
"You know, Mike," he'd say, "any fool can make money. It's keeping it that's the
problem."
He and John Ridgway were the first people to row across the Atlantic. They did this
purely for queen and country – they were the last of that breed. They'd heard an
American team was preparing to try for the Atlantic record and Chay wasn't happy
about that, so he and Ridgway got leave from the Army to compete.
The two Americans set off first, with Chay and Ridgway in hot pursuit. The American
pair drowned, under-pinning just how treacherous the trip was, and Blyth and
Ridgway became the first guys to row unassisted across the Atlantic, having nearly
drowned themselves on many occasions.
Single-handed, without any safety boats, they completed a near impossible task. Even
to this day, when one hears of adventurers crossing the Atlantic in rowing boats, it's

rarely the same stretch of water from America to Ireland that Chay and Ridgway completed. Their bravery and courage was beyond doubt, and was central to Chay's character.

Chay had never rowed before other than on the park lake and for general fitness – he did no specific training. There was no time, and he thought excessive rowing would wreck his hands – an inevitable occurrence he might as well suffer on the trip, rather than tear them up beforehand. Such a pragmatic approach was typical of him, his life and attitude to it.

Rather than being upset by the British taking the world record, the Americans loved their success and invited Chay to Hollywood for screen tests. He was very happy with the prospect until he eventually heard the part he was testing for.

"I turned down a lot of money," Chay said, shaking his head. This was indeed serious for a man like him. With a raised eyebrow and an air of astonishment, he shook his head and continued: "They wanted me in the Robin Hood film. A big blockbuster, lots of money, lots of famous stars. They wanted me you know. I was offered a part."

It sounded good so far, and I didn't understand the problem.

"Well..." he hesitated, as if traumatised with the memory of it. "Well....I eventually heard they were thinking about offering me the part of Friar Tuck!"

We laughed so much we nearly fell over. What we would have given to see those original screen tests! When we composed ourselves, I said: "You made the right decision. I could never see you being part of anything where you gave money away – it would be totally unbelievable!"

I always found talking to Chay in quiet moments fascinating and inspirational. His life was full of adventure and mishap.

He'd casually mention events like the time he spent twenty one hours in an upturned boat in the Southern Ocean, completely alone and in danger. I asked what he could possibly be thinking about while down there.

"You get interested in everything that might float by," he explained helpfully. "For example, I spent some time trying to keep a can of beans from floating away – you never know when you might need them."

Peter thought for a moment, wondering why anyone would be interested in a can of beans in that position, before piping up: "Maybe that's just because you're Scottish, Chay?"

Sir Chay went on to break so many records and run the very successful Challenge Business events which, at the time of meeting, included the premier round-the-world yacht race, the BT Global Challenge.

His straightforward attitude to business and life was: 'They say NO but we say YES'. It seemed a perfect mantra for our company.

He offered to do some team-building on races in the Solent on his fleet of ocean-going yachts. We were invited on an away-day and loved it. We developed the idea of a yacht race the week before Cowes – with nine yachts carrying twelve people each, it wouldn't exactly be a small event.

We agreed to meet at the Pont de le Tour the following Thursday and I went home to tell everyone. My father was so excited I invited him to stay at the Butlers Wharf flat with me so he could meet Chay.

I knew it would be a special evening, one I'd never forget. It turned out even better than I could imagine.

CHAPTER 3

James

I met James for the first time when he came for interview with my previous employers. He was young, even by our then-tender years, but came across as a smart and charming man, one to watch out for in the future.

He'd just won top prize in an insurance debating competition and was clearly well-educated and intelligent with a massive ambitious streak.

He was also well-connected in some distant way to a top Yorkshire family so he had some useful contacts. With sharp manners and a tie that never seemed to loosen around his neck, he struck a military bearing. He was polite, quick-witted and showed steely determination – visibly a man in a hurry to make a real name for himself.

He was a good fifteen years younger than the rest of us, but when he talked he did so with maturity and authority; people listened.

On hearing about his debating success, Jim commented: "There's only one thing to debate in this business - why do the buggers always look for a way to turn a bloody claim down when I need to rely on the policy for the first time in years?"

He had a point – that's how many people thought about insurance. It was last on the list of things to buy, and always a distress sale.

James replied that the question was rhetorical, that you couldn't debate that for more than a minute as we all knew why, and we moved on. James seemed to have an answer for everything.

I advised him to spend another year gaining a little more experience before coming back, which he duly did. We'd left to set up our own business by then, but this unexpected talent walking into the office was too good to be true for Chairman Neville and they snapped him up.

I'm sure it was also seen as a tiny victory over our expanding venture too. We saw James as our seed-corn, and we wanted him back.

A few years later I heard great reports about James and thought we were now big enough to accommodate his fierce ambitions, which if not sated could make him a dangerous player in a smaller, slower-moving company. He really was on fire in terms of his unflinching discipline in applying terms of reference and – importantly – getting others to do the same. He was also heading a team of people that, as far as we could see, was the only other group doing anything like large amounts of new commercial business across the UK.

I bumped into him at the Institute dinner – where else? As well as experience and success he'd acquired a little arrogance, which I'm sure was closely associated with the results he was achieving and the plaudits that went with them.

We invited him to talk to us. He said he was busy but would fit in time to have a chat. "Clever shit!" we all thought, but in this case it was wise to bite our collective corporate lips, as we knew he could be special and people rarely come in perfect square boxes without fault. He was good and he knew it, and so did we. The ones that cause more problems are the ones who think they're good but aren't. They bring over-inflated expectations and under deliver. James always delivered, and then some.

We were due to meet the following Wednesday at 11am, and I asked Big Jim to make a special effort to be there to attend the interview with Peter and I. It was a big request as Jim, we all knew, was dangerous on roads north of Watford Gap – he said they were too green and boring.

"It all looks the same and I sort of become hypnotised," he explained helpfully.
I knew that if we secured James it would have a big impact on the business, so I wanted all key players present.
He didn't show at 11am. At around 11.50am I got a call from reception to say he was on the phone, and immediately knew he was ringing to say either that he was late or had decided not to come.
Either way I was pissed off, as it had taken Jim time and trouble to be here and I was genuinely excited at the prospect of him becoming part of our team.
I asked for the call to go through to my PA.
"If he's late tell him he can join us for lunch, or we'll be available after lunch," I said.
The PA came back and said he wasn't late but very busy – he had to visit a very important client and would have to rearrange. He'd advise us of another date.
Now that *really* annoyed me – *he'd* advise *us*?
I replied that he couldn't and that we'd gone to considerable trouble to get everyone here to see him. We were happy to see him later in the day.
This was duly communicated, and the message came back saying he was unable to meet that day.
It was fast becoming an angry stand-off. I said in that case, he needn't come back at all. Quick as a flash, via my PA, he said that was my prerogative.
Wanting the last word, I replied: "Tell him thank you for reminding me of my prerogative and, as he's done so, I've exercised it. Tell him goodbye."
The line went dead, I was told. It was another year before we inevitably bumped into each other, again at the Institute dinner. It was a case of pistols at dawn or kiss and make up...... We made up over a glass of champagne and agreed to meet the following Monday.
"Be on time," I warned.
He was.

Dinner with Sir Chay

A deal was quickly done with James. He joined us and was immediately identified as one of the smartest, most intelligent and well-mannered executives we had. His talent at pulling new corporate accounts was massive, even by our high-volume standards, and his military and formal style of leadership was much needed and respected in a company that had grown through informality with like-minded people. We had to change and employ people not necessarily in our own image. We needed more depth. James was more of an organiser than any of us. We had a lot of staff and needed parameters for a certain level of formality, no matter how reluctant we felt about it. There were simply too many people to have no systems or order.
James's employment marked the start of an inevitable change. The company was taking on a size and momentum of its own, and we needed to shape and manage it into tight little units that were easier to handle.
We tried to ensure we had all the qualities of a larger, established business, with corresponding structures, while still breaking each aspect down to bite-sized pieces that we hoped would maintain entrepreneurial flair, and not lose the characteristics that had made us such a success in the past. It wasn't an easy call and James got more and more involved.
He soon made his way up to becoming a member of the main holding board. Having

also shown a talent to micro-manage he was very much our detail man, and it was important he was with us when we met Chay as agreed at Pont de le Tour.

James was delighted to be involved and play an important part in the discussions. He had in mind a *Blackadder*-style cunning plan, so it was with big smiles and lots of laughter that we assembled at a beautiful table in the middle of the restaurant. My PA had told them we'd have a celebrity with us – which we did, albeit a minor one by their standards – and insisted we should have a good table.

I stood proudly at the bar next to my father as we gazed out at Tower Bridge against the City night sky – a sight one never tired of. It was fascinating to watch the different people being led through to the restaurant – all shapes and sizes, dressed in their finest. What stories would their lives tell? What brought them here? Where were they from? This place truly felt like the centre of the universe, and my smile could not have been larger or brighter. I felt privileged to be there, surrounded by my director friends with my father at my side. What could be better?

Even Big Jim looked smart, a gigantic effort for him. His shirt was tucked firmly into his trousers, rather than gaping at the stomach; his tie went all the way down his shirt instead of ending halfway up his barrel chest; he wore a new, blue, well-fitted suit. We'd poked fun at him, as you can only do to a man of Jim's size if that person really knows you really respect and love them.

"Don't turn up in a shiny suit, Jim, for God's sake," I said

"What shiny suit?" he complained with mock outrage. "I don't have any shiny suits."

"You don't see your arse, Jim!"

"To me that's an advantage, Mike. It's a bit like the wife – I know it follows me around, but I don't see it too often. Anyway fair point. I'll sort it."

And here he was, all scrubbed up with rosy cheeks and a broad smile, looking as if he was about to take his first Holy Communion rather than embark on a night of excess.

I spoke to the maître d' and inspected the table. It was perfectly positioned with sparkling wine glasses – one for red, one for white – and an assortment of water glasses all neatly laid out. We'd already ordered white wine for the starters and the bottles sat chilling in silver buckets.

"Crikey," I thought, 'I hope Big Jim isn't as clumsy as usual." I could imagine the state of the table at the end of the night, when we'd had a few drinks. It made me smile rather than being nervous. Tonight was our night, we were family, and we were going to do the deal of our lives.

Chay turned up, and after being introduced to my father was led into the restaurant. Once we were seated, he looked around nervously.

"Anything the matter, Chay?" I asked.

"Who's paying for this lot then?" he said with a twinkle and a smile.

"That depends on the deal we may or may not strike tonight," Peter replied, calmly.

"Any money deal I do I'd better build in a contingency for this lot. It's not going to be cheap," Chay responded. I didn't think he was joking.

We got down to enjoying ourselves. Jim, as ever on big occasions, was on top form. He had the craic with everyone, including my father and our guest.

"Now, Chay, I've been reading about that Robin Knox-Johnson, from the Clipper organisation, now there *is* a living legend! Bloody great sailor you know. A natural. Went around the world you know, made bloody good time as well," he teased.

Jim was also in charge of the red wine, a responsibility he took seriously and with great ceremony. He'd heard me many times ask for the advice of the sommelier, which he had copied and made his own.

"'Ello matey, this red wine I'm looking for, it's not too fruity, more vanilla, and not too strong but not too thin, nothing too acidic but not too weak..." and so he'd go on. The sommelier would listen patiently, forget what Jim had said and suggest something different that was always acceptable. He'd bring the wine and pour it after tasting. Then, just as he was leaving the table, Jim would call him back.

"Excuse me, mate, I don't want any fuss, but I expect that bottle of wine is much more than twenty quid a go, so where's the bleeding basket that goes with it, eh? You must have loads in there, are you selling them or what?"

Jim's other little party trick, which he always conducted in a very well-mannered way, was to catch the eye of an attractive waitress.

"'Ello sweetheart," he'd open. "May I say you're looking very gorgeous tonight?"

"Thank you very much, sir."

The waitress would usually respond coyly as she got on with her duties, not paying much attention. But Jim would stare at her for a while until she knew that she was expected to say something, that the client wanted something. But what? Finally, after an awkward moment, he'd break the silence and say to bursts of laughter: "And ME?"

The evening went beautifully, with Chay enjoying himself on one side of me and Dad loving it on the other. He couldn't get over the level of service attentive but not intrusive.

Thinking we should have wine and the like out of the way before we got down to business, he'd make one last effort to finish his glass, only to have it automatically refilled by the waiter. This became a bit of a competition until I realised and quietly explained Jim had given instructions that everyone's glass should be kept full. Thank God we intervened. Dad wouldn't have wanted to seem ungrateful and waste any. Coffees, brandy and cigars were eventually served as the place quietened and we finally got down to business.

Chay thought it would be a financial walk in the park, as Jim, Peter and I were not particularly known for our heads for detail. But on meeting James for the first time, he was surprised to be cross-examined about the proposal.

"We didn't want one boat for nine times a year; we wanted nine boats for two days a year. The week before Cowes," stated James.

Chay took notes on a napkin.

We'd heard that Chay had some four years previously resurrected a challenge based loosely on his own world record for a team of two-man boats to cross the Atlantic to see if it was viable and a relatively safe thing to do. We picked up on this and demanded to be the main sponsor of the Atlantic Challenge, as well as having the nine boats for three days per year. We wanted to sponsor a fifty two-man boat race on the safer trade winds route of Tenerife to Barbados. That would be 3,000 nautical miles, with no assistance. Each boat would have to carry our new logo; there would be television, promotional videos, newspaper and radio interest. We'd hope to gain maximum publicity to coincide with our massive sales expansion plans in the UK. When our growing team knocked on the door of a potential client, we wanted them to have at least heard of us.

It would help enormously. In insurance, you're essentially selling a promise and if you're not well-known it's harder to convert a prospect into a client – no matter what the financial saving or service commitment you offer.

It would also define us as being different, apart from the crowd. It would give all our employees something to focus on, particularly the new ones. We needed something that could be easily identified with our hopes, aspirations and values – the qualities needed to cross the Atlantic under your own steam – courage, determination and,

34

above all, persistence. It was everything the company stood for; it would act like cohesive glue.

We might be by ourselves within the industry, but we were a growing family. And this would tie us all together.

We wanted that sponsorship very badly.

Calculation after calculation was done and re-done on napkins and then thrown away, only for Chay to get them back so he could follow the track of thinking and shove them in his pocket. With the occasional shake of his head, he'd say: "You lot of young upstarts! Why should I even consider you sponsoring an event like this? This is a Blue Ribbon event and I'm looking for an equally big blue chip company. You can hardly call yourselves that, can you? I've got Richard Branson at Virgin chasing this, why should I give it to you?"

Chay hammered this home and I thought all might be lost. He liked dealing with 'names'.

Whether this was a diversionary tactic, we couldn't be sure. But we did know that Chay had recently been with Richard Branson on the Virgin Blue Ribbon World Record Challenge, when they tried (and failed) to cross the Atlantic in the fastest time in a powered vessel.

"Hold up a minute!" Big Jim protested when this was mentioned. "Just hold up."

The whole restaurant thought he was talking to them and fell silence.

"Didn't that bleeding boat sink?!"

Collapsing with laughter he went on to drive the point home, finger prodding.

"It bloody did. It did! I saw it on the telly. And weren't you the technical director?"

Chay blushed. "We hit something, that's all," he whispered, shaking his head.

The whole table quietened. Jim was onto something.

"Branson can't be your mate at the moment and I bet you're not his! You were only a few miles off success when you had to abandon ship. Right?"

Jim might not be good at detail but he hadn't missed that point and made sure Chay knew. Dad told everyone to calm down as great excitement reverberated. If Chay was going to work with us, he needed to be able to take it. He could certainly dish it out. Peter, who was listening quietly, talked calmly.

"The thing is, Chay," said Peter. "If you take this project to Richard Branson, do you even think you'll even get a mention in publicity? He'll take it over lock, stock and barrel - you won't have a chance. I bet he's done that before, hasn't he? This would be the Ward Evans Atlantic Rowing Challenge, in association with the Challenge Business Group. Go with Branson and you won't even get a mention. In fact, it won't be your race. You'll be reduced to manager. Go with us and we're both winners."

This was our ace card, beautifully timed to perfection. It clinched it.

On the back of a napkin in the Pont, the three-year deal was done. More brandy and bigger cigars were ordered.

"Bollocks to that," said Jim, "I haven't enjoyed myself like this for years!" He rocked with laughter before adding: "Here, get me one of those large green bastards please... Anybody else want one?"

"Just a minute," said Chay. "Who's paying for this dinner?"

We tossed for it. Chay won, of course. We paid.

"Never mind," said James. "We've just got nine yachts for three years, and main sponsorship of the Ward Evans Atlantic Rowing Challenge, *and* we've just *made* money my friends." A great smile spread over his face as he leaned back on his chair.

"How come?" everyone asked at once.

"Well," continued James, "I made a few phone calls and have eight insurers willing to sponsor each boat per day in the Ward Evans yacht challenge. I've already pre-sold the event. I've told them they'll have four Ward Evans employees on board, which they need as they want to get close to us in order to drum up more business for themselves, four of their clients that they want to get close to so they keep their accounts, building up client loyalty, and four of their own employees whose places can be used as a motivational tool. It's a perfect package for everyone and it's not going to cost us a penny because we have all the costs sub-sponsored out via our yacht race!"

"Bloody hell," said Chay, "I've under-estimated you lot. I've sold this lot far too cheap!"

"It's only money, Chay," I said, "It's only money!"

Later, in the early hours of the morning, Dad and I sat on the balcony overlooking the Thames.

"I can't tell you how proud I am of you, son," he said. "That was the best deal with the best dinner I've ever experienced in my life."

"It doesn't get better than this does it?" I asked.

"No, son, it doesn't. Take it in, Michael. These moments don t last for ever."

I went cold. I wanted it to last for ever. I wanted friends round me, I wanted to do deals like the one we'd made that night. I felt sad the evening was over, and I knew what he meant.

I honestly didn't want the morning light to come. But we had plans, sponsorships to arrange, a yacht race to organise and a business to run.

The bar had raised a few notches. We had to get out and spread the word. We needed to make the most of the opportunity we'd been given.

The tattoos

Communicating our plans back at the office sent a frisson of excitement through the organisation. Who would be on the boats at the yacht race? The places would be given to those who were on target, qualitative or quantitative. Equally, from those who gave exceptional performance, we would take a small number to the final event that we were now contracted to on the napkin. The Ward Evans Atlantic Challenge was very much a desirable destination.

Chay's administrative department called and asked if we'd be happy to sign a formal contract. We said we had, and no further elaboration or lawyers were needed or desired. A lot of this was a matter of trust, but we were happy with what had been discussed and the manner in which it had been agreed.

All we required was a copy of the original napkin, and that's exactly what we got.

We needed to get a PR company and event management company to handle the two separate events. One was the annual Ward Evans regatta; the other was to liaise with Challenge Business about the logistics and resultant PR opportunities associated with the Atlantic Challenge. This was an enormous opportunity that might never come again, so after a beauty parade of various media, event management and PR briefs, final proposals to get us through the next three years with maximum positive exposure were presented.

We settled on what we felt was a clear favourite. They showed strong leadership in what they would and wouldn't do for us. They weren't the cheapest, but we felt we got on well with the main characters and they would deliver, napkin or no napkin.

They insisted on a free hand, recognising that frankly we were amateurs at event management and would get in the way, doing more damage than good even with the best intentions.

We agreed, as long as they brought it home within budget, and we in turn wanted to measure the column inches and exposure we'd paid for.

Some wise guy suggested we just might get more than we bargained for and said we should have the bottom of each rowing boat stickered up with the Ward Evans logo and the strapline *"RELAX - WE'RE INSURED WITH WARD EVANS"* which would be visible to all.

But when we saw the bloody things from a rescue helicopter on a live link-up, floating upside down on *News at Ten*, we were all stunned. This had been a great adventure, a laugh up until then. That people could actually die suddenly hit us. "Jesus, that's wasn't funny at all," I said as we eventually realised the serious point identified by the new PR company about the absolute need for careful handling. People could get hurt, could die, and we had a duty of care through Challenge Business to ensure their absolute safety as far as we could.

We needed a crisis management team on standby at every stage, otherwise this event might kick us up the backside. It could cost lives, and be a complete human and financial PR disaster. We needed professional advice, which the PR and events company insisted we take at all times.

Profiles were sent to us of the many people who wanted or intended to take part in the race. They were a mixed and varied group – some from the armed forces, other primary school teachers; some moving and inspirational, recovering from serious illness, others doing it for deeply personal reasons; some looked like they'd struggle to cross the road while others could demolish a building with their bare fists.

But we knew from previous trials that it's not always the fittest-looking or youngest that get through. And of course, many didn't want or expect to get in the top ten. They just wanted to survive the crossing. The Atlantic Challenge represented something more than the crossing of an ocean.

We also had to be careful of the elaborate suicide. It had happened before, apparently. Just fifteen hundred nautical miles out and some guy says goodbye and decides to swim back to the beach. At least he had some style. But we had to watch for that.

We announced our sponsorship, which was received with enthusiasm, excitement and valuable exposure. We were drawn to talking about all the characters we'd meet and what made them different from us, these great adventurers.

We got worked up about this. Inspirational became aspirational. We all agreed this would turn a new corner in our soft, lazy lives. We'd train with the rowers, get fit, desperate not to be seen as a podgy load of sponsors with too much money and time on our hands. (Which, in retrospect, perhaps we were.)

The PR company said Chay and I should partake in some publicity event to introduce the challenge and it was decided we'd row around The Needles. Wherever they were. I don't remember who came out with it as we were kicking this unreal testosterone-driven conversation around, discussing the possibility of throwing hats in the ring and rowing three thousand nautical miles to representing our own company.

But somebody spoke up – and nobody later admitted it was them, for reasons that will become apparent.

"Don't know why we are talking about it. We're all bloody cissies and would pass out at the thought of a tattoo, let alone a sixty-foot wave in the middle of an ocean..."

All hell broke loose and, with collective bruised egos, we set off to the local tattoo parlour. A few of us – me included – secretly hoped the place was closed. But we muttered and talked at each other, how we'd show 'em, keeping our bravado going.

"I'm having one! Are you, Jim?"

"Sure I am, Mike! What about you, Peter?"

"Certainly!"

"Sod it, we're all having them, and that's an order!"

When we arrived, our determination was waning. We were about to forget it when the door opened. Our faces dropped.

"What can I do for you, lads?" asked the Hell's Angel lookalike.

"We'd like a tattoo, please, right arm," said Peter nervously.

"Sure, you look just over legal age," the hairy man said, acknowledging our fresh faced, if uncertain, dispositions. "What would you like?"

James stepped forward, detail being his business. "We'd like that," he said, pointing to our letter head.

"Not the bleeding address," said Jim. "Here, I'll go first. Bang our corporate logo on that." He held out a tree trunk of an arm.

"Jesus Christ, he's doing it!" I said. I couldn't let him down, so I went next. All the main directors had tattoos of the Ward Evans logo on their right arms. James nearly passed out, and I made a mental note of that for later. Not very military after all.

Two of our regional directors heard about it, and before we knew it they'd got their arms tattooed as well.

"Bloody hell," said James again, who'd recovered his colour. "It's upside down and on the wrong arm!"

They looked crest-fallen, but we didn't make them go through it again. I knew we were a great team, and now eight of us had a permanent reminder of our company, the great provider of this lifestyle, family and adventure.

Two weeks later we were listening to our PR and media company go through a set of proposals they insisted on doing if we were to be successful in getting the right profile out there. But their final comments caused uproar and a massive amount of Mickey-taking.

"Sorry, folks," the PR guys concluded. "I don't know how you'll take this, but you did say we'd have a free hand in our engagement letter. And this is extremely important if you're going to get your money back on this major sponsorship."

"Yes," I said, getting tetchy.

"And it's for the best..."

"What is it?" I asked, getting anxious now

"Well... We're going to have to change your logo."

" Fuck me!" A voice rose from behind us followed by suppressed giggles, which seemingly came from the secretary taking the notes.

"You've got to be bloody joking," said Peter.

"No, guys," said the PR rep. "I don't know who designed the other one, but it's an old-fashioned design and, guess what? It belongs to a major haulage company. They'd sue you if they saw it on the television."

"Off the back of a fucking lorry!" Jim burst into laughter. "I knew I'd seen it before! It always looked bloody familiar. We've been done! We got our company logo off the back of a bloody lorry! Would you credit it?"

Somewhat appropriate, I thought.

"What about the bloody tattoos?" asked James, to an alarmed PR team.

"What tattoos?" they asked, looking confused and concerned.

"Just forget it mate," I said. I'd heard enough

"What have you done, guys?" they asked, perhaps learning more about the company in that moment than at any other time. "Just forget it and change the logo."

"Beer, anyone?" said Jim.

Business as usual…

Deep Water Bear

From the moment we agreed to be main sponsor of the Atlantic Challenge we had a close association with the Southampton Boat Show. This would be where we met with the potential rowing contestants – a natural and enjoyable venue to discuss all things nautical.

It was also where Chay did a lot of his new proposals on behalf of Challenge Business and where he could hold technical race meetings for potential contestants in a nearby hotel.

Southampton became a great venue for all Ward Evans staff to take a few days' break and catch up at base camp, aka the Guinness tent.

We talked about what we might call our boat when we were lucky enough to buy a beautiful gleaming white and blue Sunseeker. At the time it was fantasy, but playing the name game brought it closer to reality. Imagining one of these boats as ours gave a meaningful buzz that provided a welcome – if brief – distraction from the cut and thrust of a business going through warp-factor expansion.

I'd seen a Richard Attenborough wildlife film a few evenings before about Alaskan bears. It was the season when the salmon came upstream to spawn. Peter and I discussed how amazing it was that these bears and their families fished for salmon in strict territories.

The film concentrated on two families, the first of which were Deep Water Bears. These are the unfortunate, slightly down-trodden, fur-matted families of adult bears who wait at the banks of the river for salmon to swim upstream. They'd eye up a particular salmon and rather optimistically dive in after it with great gusto and, it has to be said, an enormous belly flop. The bears chase one particular fish but, needless to say, the bear has little or no chance of catching it as it nonchalantly flicks its tail in the deep water and is gone.

But life has its compensations for these unlikely anglers, and as the poor bear sulks back to the bank, an occasional salmon bangs into it. As Jim might say: "Bish, bash, bosh – sorted!" This happened rarely, but often enough to keep the family fed. A simple case of you have to be in it to win it.

These ravenous bears eat every part of the fish; nothing goes to waste. They repeatedly drag themselves out of the water, only to dive back in again. It was bloody hard work. It struck me as not dissimilar to the way we prospected new business – diving in, dragging ourselves around the market, heaving ourselves out. We'd chase one client and then bump accidentally into an occasional win. Every pound increase in turnover was won through the hard hunting procedure and inevitable aggressive spat. We were part of the Deep Water Bear family.

A few hundred yards upstream, the river flows into the Shallows' area. The salmon have a harder time getting through the bottleneck; they're slower and often maroon themselves on the rocky riverbed. In the middle was the fattest family of bears. Life was good here. Lying on their backs, they occasionally held out a paw to grab one of a plentiful supply of salmon, take a bite of the best underbelly of the fish, and throw the rest away.

The unfairness of their position compared to the Deep Water Bears really struck me. If only the deep water bears moved a few hundred yards upstream, there'd be rich pickings for all.

I turned to Peter, who seemed preoccupied with the Sunseeker stand.

"You know Peter, in this business we're like Deep Water Bears, throwing ourselves around the bloody market place. Making a living, but if we just went out and bought businesses like our competitors, rather than fighting over every new client, we'd be fishing in a different pond. We might not be hated as much either. We need to be Shallow Water Bears."

Peter stopped walking and turned to look at me with a quizzical expression.

"Are you doing drugs, Mike?" he laughed, "Or maybe just try keeping off the Guinness for a while."

"I'm serious, Peter," I persisted. "If we ever buy that boat we're going to call it Deep Water Bear, because we've not done this the easy way. And when we make mega-money, then we'll call the second boat Shallow Water Bear."

"Whatever, Mike," Peter said. "I don't care what you call it; just to have it would be good enough for me."

I made a mental note. One day, one of those will be ours. We now had the name, and it became almost real. If you ever want something desperately, you have to visualise it and invite it into your life. I went further. I'd named our boat. Now we just had to earn the money to buy it.

Trouble at Home

Our relentless growth continued and our headcount was over a hundred staff.

It was impossible to avoid press comment, good or bad, which underlined the mantra that PR companies use – we all have PR, whether we like it or not. You just have to decide whether you'll manage it or not.

The national newspapers contacted our office as they somehow heard about the tattooed directors. We thought it was a hoot that we might be mentioned in the likes of the *Sun*, but our PR company went pale and insisted we didn't give any attributable comments.

It was explained to us in blunt terms.

"I don't know about your personal life, but I wouldn't like them looking at mine," we were told. "I'm not sure it could stand up to that sort of scrutiny. Get my drift? It could be a massive set-up."

We thought about all the sins we'd committed in the last few years, public and private, and went pale.

The business was split into three companies, all shares held by a non-trading holding group company. There was Corporate, which did commercial broking; Financial Services, which did what the name suggests; and Ward Evans Direct. The latter handled our small business and we had ambitions for it to operate rather like Direct Line Insurance, where retailers from hairdressers to fish and chip shops would be dealt with on the phone *en masse*.

The company employed a firecracker of a man called Johnny who originated from Manchester. We didn't hold that against him, though, since he was thankfully a Man City fan and not Man Utd – that would have been a different matter for us Leeds

United supporters. He became very popular with his abundance of enthusiasm and can-do attitude. The only problem was that he was based on the floor above me, and you could always tell when Johnny was on the phone as he banged his foot up and down for hours on end with nervous anticipation of a deal or target met.

"Tell you what, why don't I get some music up here, and we need a few plants and the like - leave it to me," he said. "At least the banging will be in time with the music." Managing this group of people would be very much different to dealing with corporate executives. These guys needed bells and whistles, all of which were right up Johnny's street. "We have to make it fun, Mike," he'd say.

The office was our first attempt at telemarketing. A constant supply of motivational enthusiasm was an essential requirement and the ringing of bells and whistles whenever a sale was made was down to Johnny's expertise of this sector.

We called their room Club Tropicana. You never knew what you might see in there. Flowers, drinks, music, noise and general organised chaos with young kids phone bashing and enjoying themselves in a way I'd never seen – and, it has to be said, with great enthusiasm. They consistently met targets.

We ended up being one of the largest brokers for hairdressers, making our jokes about Peter's Porsche a bit too close to home.

Chris was our corporate group accountant, a quiet and considered man who was also a cricket fanatic. He did an excellent job of keeping everything in order and wasn't at all like most of the people around him. He was a private person, engaged to be married, who liked a no-stress life. He always seemed to be with us but not one of us, which ensured a certain respect whenever he spoke. He prided himself in getting the profit results reflected in our management accounts to within a few hundred pounds of the actual audited figures. He was an excellent member of our team and had a good handle on things.

We had the same set of auditors from year two. They knew our systems and seemed to work well with Chris. Their credentials were good, having previously worked in large multi-national accounts before more regional practice. So while we were a large client for them, paying a lot of money, we weren't paying multi-national prices.

All the profits from year one were retained within the business. We never paid dividends, though we later learned this was a mistake. Cash flow could have been saved had we done it the other way around. Instead, we paid ourselves roughly the same as we expected the company to retain in profit. Paying half, saving half. Whichever way you looked at it, what we did seemed prudent enough to us as a private limited company with no outside directors or shareholders.

Life was good, the company was doing well and everything was rosy, other than in my personal life. I had for too long been obsessed about the company, even to the point of opening spreadsheets on Christmas Day.

It's a classic mistake when you put so much effort, energy and enthusiasm into one part of your life and leave little for others. You simply get out of the habit and sleepwalk towards losing that which should be the most important to you, the reason why you're building a business in the first place.

My wife and I decided to separate. It was all too easy, as I was spending a lot of time in London, so it was simply a case of being at Butlers Wharf more often. When I returned north I used a corporate flat in Harrogate, North Yorkshire, so I could see the children easily.

Eventually, and sadly, pretty much the same happened with Jim. Suddenly, the success we enjoyed seemed a little hollow – or at least came at greater expense than money.

Peter took heed and ensured his family stayed together. Success can come at a high price and not getting up in the morning and seeing your children should be too much for any parent.

He stuck closely to his lovely wife. He was, after all, the reasonable face of Ward Evans. Someone had to get it right, and Peter was our best bet.

It was another hard lesson learned.

CHAPTER 4

Moving in certain circles

Chay invited me to a restaurant in St James's, an extremely posh and traditional establishment that many, including me, would never have known existed.
Its reservation book was pretty much closed to all but regulars and aristocrats. I certainly hadn't crashed into it before, and we'd done a pretty comprehensive A-to-Z of the best restaurants in London. Some wag even called us a food laundering business once.
The evening went well. We talked about the sponsorship and Chay's personal take on life and business. He'd lived to the full by anybody's measure and I always found him and his stories fascinating. He had a high regard for royalty, never failing to mention he had a home near to Princess Anne at Gatcombe Park, always accompanied by a wink and a twinkle of the eye.
"Mike, you know Prince Michael of Kent is very interested in rowing?"
"Yes, I've heard that said," I replied tentatively. You always had to be careful when Chay mentioned royalty.
"Well, wouldn't it be a great honour for you – for both our companies – if we offered him the role of patron for the world's toughest boat race?"
"And how much will that cost, Chay?" I asked, knowing I was out of my depth with this one
"That's the trouble with you, Mike. You can't buy class, and I'm trying to direct you here. It's not about money it's about prestige." Chay went on the attack.
"Chay," I said patiently. "How much?"
"Well, flights, possible use of an Equerry. Maybe another assistant. The Princess may come. Hotel for a few days. Not much at all."
"You what? The Bloody Princess might come? Forget it. No way," I said determinedly.
It seemed like an open chequebook. I couldn't have Big Jim going around saying "Don't eat this" or asking "How many bottles have they had?" It wouldn't have been fair to him.
"It's only money, Mike!" Chay encouraged, "If they come, I might be able to effect an introduction for you...." This supposed inducement had a negative effect.
"Bloody hell," I said. "So I'd pay for his expenses and might not even meet him?"
I could see I'd have to keep my wits about me moving in this sort of circle. I went to the toilet and was immediately star-struck when I saw Michael Palin. Trying to be casual, I said: "How are you doing, Michael?"
He turned to me. I knew as soon as the question came out of my mouth that it was stupid, impertinent and irrelevant. I was going to get hammered.
"Well this is the first pee I've had tonight. I'm doing OK as far as peeing goes. Best pee I've had in a while actually," he said with a half-smile as he nailed my inane question. "Anything else you want to ask?"
I shook my head like a naughty schoolboy and remained silent. I was fiddling in my pants, which in retrospect wasn't a good image either. I decided against shaking his hand. He gave me a withering look, which I fully deserved, and left abruptly.
"Fuck, fuck, fuck," I said. "I'm definitely going to have to be careful mixing with this lot."

It was a whole lot different back at home, where people would approach us and say something like: "Hey you flash sods, you've got a million now haven't you?" To which we'd reply: "Good God, no. Wouldn't want to go back to those hard times again!"

Then we'd leave them looking a little bemused until they worked it out.

In London, we got our collective come-uppance.

The East Coast Conference

The mad, bad days in London stood in great contrast to the time I had in Yorkshire. It really was the best of both worlds – London for the pulse, the cut-and-thrust of business, then Yorkshire to a slower pace, where our administration centre was based. Peter's dad had a fishing boat in Whitby, and made a happy and relaxed living from it. Consequently, Peter grew up knowing all the nooks and crannies around that part of the coast. This was how we discovered Ravens Hall, once a very posh Victorian hotel and now one of the many that was comfortable but with a somewhat decaying elegance.

Despite threadbare carpets and rubber pheasants for dinner, its charm and old-fashioned grade were still there to be enjoyed. We loved it, often holding board meetings where we invited about half a dozen senior guys from each company to make a presentation and discuss progress and problems.

Breaking for coffee, we could walk around the gardens and see the vast cove leading to Robin Hood's Bay and beyond, all framed by dramatic landscapes and crashing seas straight from a Brontë novel. It was also the only place where you could get a mobile phone signal – we must have looked like a line of Buddhists giving praise and chanting to the great horizon as we all stood there in a line, facing out to sea.

The days were long, with meetings starting at eight in the morning and often finishing well past seven in the evening. But the mix of being away in such a remote location and taking views from middle managers socially later on in the bar seemed to work, and the feedback was invaluable.

The relaxed environment allowed for free thinking. The discussions were priceless and changed the direction of the company from time to time. Certainly most of the important decisions were made when we were doing a bit of blue-skying.

We knew that at least fifty percent of our fixed overheads related to salaries, so we could increase or decrease the rate of growth to what was available in terms of capacity to write new business.

That in turn depended on the many and regular peaks and troughs of capacity within the market place. These were hard and soft markets where premiums would generally go up when capacity was low, and correspondingly down when every insurer wanted a piece of the action.

The company would be safe so long as we knew where we were, and took whatever decisions necessary to cut our cloth accordingly. Much discussion centred on 'what if' scenarios.

It always amazed business commentators just what a fickle and frankly short-term market this commercial insurance sector was. Not what you'd expect from an insurance market where the premiums of many over a longer period of time would pay for the claims of a few, and therefore a business where a long-term view was essential.

But there never seemed to be any consistency, and trying to size the sales team became guesswork. An insurer, for example, would spend millions in writing another form of insurance for them to throw the business open again a few years later. No-one seemed to lose their job over this at executive management level – it was blamed on 'market conditions' where the great and the good would nod sagely while thousands lost their clerical jobs through redundancies lower down the chain as a direct result. Eventually, as a result of this mis-management, British insurance underwriting was reduced from having a global lead to being a bit-player. You'd be hard-pressed today to find a truly international insurance company that is British-owned, alive and kicking. Lloyd's had its own problems, where accounting rules meant they were literally counting the cost of a disastrous soft market and appalling natural disasters from three years previously, as part of their three-year accounting rules.

Lloyd's name backed by personal family wealth was suicidal, and great changes were made in that area that only now are yielding results.

However, a changing market place was a good one for an attacking broker like us, as no one could really predict a good price anymore. With uncertainty on pricing, potential clients could be persuaded to check out the competition. Our job was to make sure we were the ones they chose when they came to a conclusion. More often than not, they were in our data bank.

The effect of a few days at Raven Hall was that everyday business was left behind and a bigger picture emerged that was hard to see while sitting in an office.

We used to arrive as Group Plc directors, work out what we had to say, and then over the next three or so days, have various middle managers and senior personnel up for a day and a night so we could discuss what we wanted to achieve. In management terms, this was a typical tell-and-sell approach.

It took many meetings over many years to understand we'd got this the wrong way round. What we needed to do was listen to each team and then meet at Group Plc level to discuss the feedback. In other words, listen and learn. Decide on a course of action, then plan implementation.

This was exemplified when I bumped into the chairman of Scottish Widows one Christmas. His daughter was a friend of mine and he was nice enough to invite me to lunch when I was next in London. He knew I was a new boy in town, so this was an act of kindness.

It was quite a big deal for me as I'd never done a City lunch before, and thought it would be good to get in and among the great and the good; people who might be influential in the future.

There was talk about the possibility of floatation on the AIM market and if that were to succeed we'd need contacts. We definitely needed a bit of an image makeover to be more acceptable to the institutions.

Colin was a hell of a nice guy, and I needed all the help and advice I could get. He was also chairman of the unit trust association – you couldn't get much more established.

The lunch was arranged at some grand old office in the Square Mile, and having told everyone remotely interested that I was going, including my mother, it was with some nervous anticipation that Jim dropped me off outside and wished me luck

I was met by a guy dressed in full red military regalia-like costume. I knew immediately I was out of my depth. As I walked along the corridors of power – real, financial power - I could feel the strength in my legs sap and worried I might not reach the dining room

Colin bounced out of a side office and immediately set about making me at ease, but he could see I was a little overwhelmed. I ate and drank very little _ on reflection, no bad thing. I was amazed how intelligent these guys with serious jobs really were. They were in a different class.

Colin asked my views on certain issues of the day relating to the conduct of financial services. Not one of my strong points, even if I was a major shareholder of a business employing over thirty people in that sector.

I was brought through the ranks on the general insurance side, so the well was pretty dry when I called for water. But I wasn't going to let a lack of knowledge stop me. I went for it, filling the silence with unconstructed arguments and disjointed thinking, thinking maybe the size of the content might compensate for the lack of substance.

My lunatic ramblings finally came to a halt and I looked at Colin for a response. He could tell from my expression that I expected him to say something – anything – it was his turn, after all! I leaned back and thought it was just like my bad old days with Chairman Neville all those years ago. But nothing was forthcoming from Colin.

I looked at him quizzically and started to feel nervous again. Colin carefully put his knife and fork down and wiped his mouth slowly with a napkin. He looked straight at me, and said: "You expect me to reply, but I've nothing intelligent to say on the issues you have raised."

"Bloody hell fire!" I said in a release of nervous energy. This was a new concept for me. If we played by these rules back at my office, it would be like a monastery with silent orders!

Colin could see I was clearly in need of a lot of good advice, particularly about the conduct of board and management meetings. He was interested that each board was properly constituted. We had an outside non-executive of some mature years as a trained accountant. He seemed happy with that. Importantly, he explained the need never to queue or allow others simply to queue to speak, when someone else is talking. If you, do you will not be listening properly

"Listen hard," he said. "Listen anaerobically. Are you queuing, or listening?" I tried to remember this advice but, of course, fell short on many occasions.

I walked away from that lunch in true awe. It wasn't just about the building or Colin's position. He didn't just get lucky. I wondered how much listening he must have done in his time to occupy such an important position and be so respected. I couldn't even aspire to his achievements. I liked the sound of my own voice too much.

Jim was outside to collect me. I repeated what Colin had told me.

"Bloody hell, Mike - listening? That's a new concept for us wouldn't you say?" he said with typical wit. "Don't you think it's just a passing management fad? Don't worry, it'll never catch on. Let's get back to the office and do some shouting. You'll feel better for it."

After that, Raven Hall was a place where the board tried, really hard, to listen to what our troops told us. Listening is a two-way street, though, and some of our employees were less than helpful in their individual attempts to reciprocate.

Maybe it's a lesson that meetings shouldn't go on for too long, but we uncovered a game that was sweeping our office and invading our meetings – Bullshit Bingo.

It was an ingenious game designed to keep boredom at bay for those being lectured to. The simple rules were that, before a meeting and unbeknown to management, people would write down the favourite words that they believed would be heard. Common examples included 'target', 'professionalism', 'prospecting', 'power', 'pressure' and 'micro-manage' – buzz words that used to trip off the tongue on a regular basis without us realising it.

The delegates would write the words down, put them into a hat and each randomly pick out three or four. Armed with fresh interest, they'd file into the meeting room with smiles on their faces, eager to listen to every word for all the wrong reasons. The first person to cross all the words off their list would win, but they had to claim the prize there and then – which could be dangerous, as they had to devise ways to shout 'House!' or 'Bingo!' without alerting management.

Various spluttering voices would be raised with a rasping 'house' sound while they pretended to clear their throats, while one cunning individual asked loudly: *"House that go again, please?"* Some held up signs while our backs were turned.

It passed a few hours – until we got wind of it and started to spend the first ten minutes coming out with all the words needed to get it out of the way so we could get down to serious business. But you had to admire the inventive nature of our group. Our challenge was to excite them so that such games weren't necessary.

The East Coast Conference, however, was a place where people really did get on with things, and everyone had the right to be heard. Those days were some of the best, and least expensive, times we had, often gathered around a real fire in the main lounge going through various issues. As unfashionable as it was, it remains a firm favourite in my mind, holding its own against the fancy restaurants of London.

Every evening, having had feedback on each company, we'd grab a fleet of taxis and travel into Robin Hood's Bay. Peter would phone The Laurel pub in advance, where we'd play guitar and have a general get-together.

The Laurel was a small, traditional pub – no jukeboxes or the like, just good beer and a cosy, welcoming atmosphere. It didn't take much to let your imagination run wild and wonder what acts of smuggling and trade took place there in years gone by.

We particularly liked the place on dark, cold evenings. The pub landlord would tell a few locals we were coming and we put bottles of whiskey, brandy and the like on the bar for the local crowd as a thank you for allowing us to crowd out their pub. We gained a reputation for having a good time; they used to ask when the Ward Evans lads were having their next meeting.

There was a certain magic, particularly in the middle of winter, when Peter used to feign an old salty sea-dog accent and talk of fishing yarns and smugglers' tales.

"'Tell us a yarn,' said the captain to the mate, and the mate began:
'It was a dark and stormy night, and the captain said to the mate, 'Tell us a yarn. And the mate began…" he'd say.

After a few drinks, some of the guys got quite confused by that story.

We grew quite friendly with the husband and wife team who ran the taxi company, too, and it was with great sadness that we learned their history one night.

One of them had taken their eleven-year-old daughter in the back of the car on the exact same journey from Ravenscar to Robin Hood's Bay, and she was tragically killed when the passenger door flew open and she fell out. She hadn't been wearing a seatbelt.

A more awful tragedy is hard to imagine, yet this couple outwardly kept cheerful, laughing and joking. We heard that they planned to build a play area in memory of their daughter but were having problems raising enough money to finish the job. And no child could play there until it was finished and the council deemed it safe. They had started well, but needed £3,500 to finish the project. They didn't ask, but one night on the way back to Raven Hall we invited them to come inside and presented them with a cheque for the full amount.

They were overwhelmed and truly grateful; we felt truly humbled. It's the only night I know of where the taxi drivers checked themselves into the same hotel as us and joined us at the late bar for singing and general chat.

The playground remains to this day at the top of the steep incline down to Robin Hood's Bay, and it's still well-used by local children.

All sorts of interesting people passed through used the hotel at Raven Hall. We met Lord Linley there, who seemed as shocked at seeing someone else in the hotel on a dark November evening as we did seeing royalty there..

It was nice to meet with him, and we learned he had a thriving workshop in Whitby. It seemed really cool to us that he was having all this beautiful furniture handmade in Whitby before selling it to the Hooray Henrys in Chelsea.

"Shame Chay wasn't here," Jim reflected, "We would have had to have bought a sideboard or two just to keep the peace," he added unkindly.

Other celebrities came and went after playing on the coast in Scarborough and holing up there before moving on with their tour. One of the best nights we had was when we crashed into Peter Noone of Herman's Hermits, who took all our laughter, jokes inevitable piss-take and bad guitar playing as we belted out *Something Tells Me I'm into Something Good*. This was in contrast to Wayne Fontana, who was there and playing on the same bill. He took one look at us lot and when Peter asked: "Hello aren't you Wayne Fontana and the Arse Bandits?" he promptly went to bed.

Bonding

The evenings away were usually rounded off with Jim making the most of the esprit de corps and finishing with the company song. He'd developed it so we could all join in.

This sort of thing is so embarrassing when done badly, and fantastic when it's done in a natural way. When everyone gets involved it's really motivational, but it's also something that can't be forced. Often visitors to our gatherings would shake their heads and say: "I see it, but I can't copy it."

And you can't. It would be like trying to bottle magic. It had taken years to put together and the environment had to be right to grow and nurture this group. One last thing – you don't get many like Big Jim, either.

He didn't think too much or analyse how it would motivate – he just did it, and everyone engaged.

We were aware it wouldn't be very clever to employ everyone in our own collective likeness if the company was to grow and mature; we needed many and varied types, each bringing their own unique quality. The only requirement was to contribute in their own way and share the same values.

Jim, to great applause, would stand on a chair and start like an opera singer:

> *Climb up on Sunshine Mountain when you're feeling low,*
> *Climb up on Sunshine Mountain faces all a-glow.*
> *Turn, turn your head from sadness, reach up to the sky*
> *Climb up on Sunshine Mountain*
> *YOU and I*

When he sang 'Turn, turn your head from sadness' the idea was that you had to turn on top of the chair, a difficult manoeuvre after a few drinks.

At the end of 'You and I', he'd jump down and encourage whoever he pointed at to get on the chair with him and sing the song again, keeping the line going until the guy got up.

So we had, at this stage, maybe three or four people up on chairs. This would be repeated until everyone was on the chairs singing at the tops of their voices.

This wasn't about one; it was for all. No one was embarrassed or excluded. We were all in a trance-like state afterwards, wondering what the hell we were doing on all the chairs at the end of it. The hotel management wondered, too.

We once burst into the bar lounge of Cameron House Hotel in Loch Lomond and bumped into Ian Botham, and a bunch of cricketing people. They appeared to be a load of high-powered people that might have been talking about the state of English cricket while playing a bit of golf.

We gave them the benefit of our collective view and bought bottle after bottle of whiskey, which inevitably led to the grand finale of *Climb up on Sunshine Mountain*. Ian and the cricket guys joined in as Jim wove his hypnotic magic even on that esteemed company. If only he could have been let loose on the English football team.

Back on the east coast, Jim would keep the tempo going with one of his Cockney songs:

> *All my life I wanted to be a barrow boy*
> *A barrow boy is what I wants to be*
> *I wheels me barrow*
> *I pushes it with pride*
> *I'm a Costa*
> *A Costa*
> *From over the other side*
> *And*
> *I turn me back on all the high society*
> *And go where the green tomatoes go....*
> *I charges them a shilling*
> *it's how I earns me living*
> *I wish I'd been a barrow boy years ago*
> *Get off me barrow!!*
> *I wish I'd a-been a barrow boy years ago...*

The astonishing thing about this was that halfway through the song he'd tuck his thumbs into his waistband and dance a jig. To say he was approaching twenty stone he was tremendously light on his feet - must have been all the rugby training.

It never failed to get us all going. Some time later, we opened a Glasgow office and had a welcome addition.

We initially opened an office in Mid Calder, equidistant between Glasgow and Edinburgh, because we couldn't decide where we needed to be. Glasgow had the manufacturing base, Edinburgh the financial centre.

The dilemma was settled by one of Scotland's most famous sons, Billy Connolly, when we met him in Malmaison up there.

Billy was a true star. Since there was only his party of friends in the bar and ours, he came across to say hello and engage us in conversation and general revelry. He seemed genuinely interested in what we were doing and when we told him where we were and asked his advice, he was pretty clear

"Fucking hell, guys, Mid Calder is an Englishman's answer to a Scottish problem! It's easy really, just go where your clients are!" We did, and promptly moved to Glasgow. The Glasgow staff certainly didn't intend to miss out on a few of their own favourite songs while with us on the east coast. Taking Jim's lead, the Jocks would charge into a couple of Proclaimers' classics. Goaded on by the rest of the team, we refused to call them Scottish and took the piss by calling them Northern Britons.

*"I would walk 500 miles...*and when you go, will you send back a letter from America? How come all the best Scottish songs are about Scottish people who don't live there anymore?"

It ended with the great *Flower of Scotland.* By then, there was no stopping them. I swear if we'd sent those guys off over the border at that moment to march on some poor unsuspecting broker, particularly an English one, it would have been pretty ugly. The scenes would have rivalled those outside the doors of the Institute dinner! There was passion, drama and excitement, wrapped up in a force that bound the company. We were on the inside, and the world at that time was on the out.

Yes, we had minor fallouts, but as Peter once sang at a grand prix ball when he climbed on stage with Sister Sledge playing live, singing and dancing and pointing to our table: *"We are family!"*

City business and romantic interludes

I was spending increasing amounts of time in the City, and enjoying all it had to offer. Peter, Jim and I were often courted by some blue blood sniffing us out with regard to either flogging something or trying to create a deal where we bought or sold the business. We got wise; a lot of them weren't to be trusted, and half of what they said was pure fantasy. Their job was to create interest where none existed and, in doing so, generate a fee out of it. Many corporate marriages started that way.

It would often start with lunch, which always got the three of us there. Gently, in conspiratorial tones, the conversation would be steered towards our future exit strategy. It was obvious they usually had made up our minds for us and just needed our agreement. They would initiate discussion by saying that a broker who couldn't be identified was interested, almost passionate, about buying us or at the very least merging if the circumstances were right, chemistry strong, synergy high and so on. It would be a marriage made in Heaven. We took the view that the divorce rate was high and by the time the corporate lawyers had you up the proverbial aisle, so to speak, it was too late when you looked at the new in-laws!

Any barriers could be overcome by waving an obscene amount of money in front of us. Generally we played the blushing and reluctant bride, reminding them that we weren't for sale but if they were really talking that sort of money then of course nothing was impossible.

The truth was that it was unlikely the passionate suitor existed – or not yet, at least. So interest on the other side needed generating – a kind of kids' courtship, where I will if you will. Information would be put on the corporate wire to another restaurant somewhere, where some equally astonished guy would listen patiently to another blue blood saying why Ward Evans was desperate to be part of their organisation, given the right deal, circumstance and chemistry.

The way they got away with this fabrication always fascinated us. By the process of asking the right questions, I got Jim to agree that given the right circumstance he would shag Vera Duckworth – and indeed, he would. But it was taken out of context – he was actually answering a question that forced him to choose, if his life depended on it, whether it would be Jack or Vera.

And so it was with these financial games, although the questioning would be a little more subtle. But someone, somewhere, would promise another CEO that they'd sat with the Ward Evans boys and they'd said they were up for a sale.

We were enjoying a lunch at the Pont de la Tour and listening to another blue blood about some financial instrument that would make us easy fortunes when I was joined at the toilet by Peter.

"God help us, Mike, I know he's paying for this lunch but what a boring, patronising bleeder! Have you noticed that every time he makes a point he starts stabbing out with his glasses in his hand, and then when we speak he puts his glasses on again quickly and peers over them? What's all that about?"

"I wondered what it was but yes, something about him irritated me. It's bloody unnerving. Do you think he's trying to intimidate us?" I asked.

"I don't know, but let's do it back to him; it will be a bit of a laugh," suggested Pete.

"Right – the rules are that the guy with his glasses off gets to speak. To interrupt you have to take yours off quickly and everyone else has to put theirs back on. Let's see how long we can go without laughing. Do you think he'll realise we're taking the piss?"

We returned to the table with broad smiles and saw the pinstriped blue blood stabbing away at Jim, who wore a glazed and confused expression.

Peter interrupted, his glasses off and ours on. I got back a few words. Peter quickly put his glasses on like lightening, Blue blood on, mine off and pointing. Peter tried to say something - his off - and before he could speak, I interrupted by taking mine off meaning his were on again. So it went on. We loved this – it changed the conversation and brought a certain pace and rhythm to it. This confused and baffled Jim even more. He knew something was going on but couldn't quite understand what. Eventually, he could stand it no more and said: "Hold up, hold up everyone. I don't know what's bloody going on here but I've got a bleeding question for the City. Answer me this: what's the wonderful thing about Tigger?"

Both glasses off, Peter and I burst into laughter, Blue Blood's glasses back on.

"Forget it," we said. "You don't wear glasses, Jim! Lunch over – we're not interested, but thanks anyway."

I often wonder what rumours went round after that lunch and whether the City people pondered why Tigger had suddenly come up in conversation. Obviously matching us with a passionate partner and a marriage made in heaven might take a little more time.

We'd somehow secured part of the top floor of what was then the World Trade Centre for our office. It was a beautiful, six-floor building, all marble atrium, uniformed security and the flags of multi-national corporations and various nations flapping proudly outside.

We had fantastic views on each side – Tower Bridge and the Thames, the Tower of London itself, St Katharine's Dock with boats of all shapes and sizes and a flourishing café society. This was even more remarkable as it was a stone's throw from Lloyd's. The illuminated city in the evening, seen from the front of our building, was like a beacon of light to guide our corporate ship safely home.

We thought we had all angles covered and were justifiably content with our newfound elevated status. It got even better when we discovered a little pub selling real ale and fine wines in the basement of the adjoining building.

Maybe at that time we could be forgiven in thinking the gods were smiling on us. We didn't think that it could equally be the Devil himself, doing deals with a bunch of willing, giddy, just-got-lucky lads.

We worked hard initially, but had long separated ourselves from the push and shove of everyday life by promoting a protective layer of middle managers.

Jim had met a lady and, not to be put out too much, asked her to meet him in the basement. Peter, Johnny and I decided to go along for a beer. Johnny, always one for an opportunity, decided it would be a good idea to persuade the multi-national owners that occupied the largest part of the building that we had a legitimate right to fly our corporate flag outside.

The problem was, we didn't have one.

Jim, having had a traditional Roman Catholic upbringing that included staying in a religious house for a few years, felt that any flag should have a coat of arms written in Latin. Whatever message or design we landed on, if it was written in Latin it would give us more *gravitas*.

"See what I mean? Gravitas...Latin!" he said helpfully.

There was much debate and merriment in the pub while waiting for Jim's girl to turn up and beers flowed freely as various staff came and went, adding their own increasingly outrageous view as to what our corporate mission statement should be.

I don't recall which bright spark came up with it, but just before Jim's date turned up he had written it out and it was ready for discussion.

"Right lads, I can see this flapping over our office if Johnny goes and sells it. We need to be careful of the design but the motto on the coat of arms should be '*Erectum peni nils consiensum*'."

It sounded *gravitas* enough, we agreed, but what did it mean? We all formed a circle, eager to understand and embrace the slogan that would explain in just a few words what we were about, what we stood for, what our values were.

"Well lads," said Jim, milking the silence, "*Erectum peni nils consiensum* stands for... An erect penis knows no conscience! What do you think?"

We burst into laughter and Johnny dropped any ideas for corporate flag flying. Jim's lady walked in and I felt sorry for her. I wouldn't want to be the one walking in to meet us lot.

I didn't really see her, though. I saw her friend, the work colleague she'd brought as she knew Jim was seldom alone.

And there she was – a wild-eyed, hippy-type chick who apparently worked in IT at HSBC headquarters. All flowing, flowery, layered dress, topped by short, dark, spiky hair. She looked like she'd stepped from an early Salvador Dali picture, maybe a trust fund girl fresh from the VIP section of Glastonbury.

But when she spoke, her voice was a contrast. She sounded to me like an actor from EastEnders, a young Dot Cotton maybe - not what you'd immediately think of as attractive, but I found it enormously engaging and addictive.

I found myself listening quietly. That was a first.

It brought to mind scenes from My Fair Lady, but this one wouldn't take elocution lessons from a man. In the words of another strong woman, this lady wasn't for turning. She didn't seek to soften her accent, she was justifiably proud of her roots and heritage. Effortlessly individual in a square mile full of Sloanes that looked the same, she could have stood out on populated land of fifty square miles and beyond. Her style was no easy off-the-peg, credit card designer image. She confidently wore a kaleidoscope of colours each layered in a way where conflicting shades seemed to blend and startle at the same time. Out of place yet absolutely right – on her.

Maybe it was the vintage clothing accessorised by individual pieces of jewellery, the absolute essence of cool. I understood for the first time the meaning of that term – to be cool meant to have your own unique style, not easily copied and certainly not bought. To be cool isn't to care, to follow or lead. It's simply to be.

She had an independent, confident, almost arrogant attitude. She could look straight into your eye and level you with nothing more than a glance. That possibility made me feel very uncomfortable. I felt immediately self-conscious; suddenly, my oh-so-cocky Armani suit became an impostor of style by this measure. It was bought simply and obviously at a reassuringly high price and, always a deciding factor for me, because it fit. She saw right through it, and in that moment I felt fake. I think she saw it. She said nothing, but I felt it.

My senses were in overload. She had cobalt blue eyes framed with heavy arching eyebrows, the longest lashes. There was the wickedest smile that curled at the edges, with the nastiest mouth if anyone tried to take the piss. She certainly looked capable of verbally taking anyone apart just for the sport of it.

And, of course, that's what we did, in turn, out of nervous bravado. And she shot each of us down in flames.

I loved it, but I couldn't get to grips with what I should say or do. I'd never seen anyone quite like her before, and just to top it off she carried a copy of National Geographic.

We asked her opinion of our new corporate motto, and she considered it before turning to face us. No shrinking violet, she.

"You little boys should start to consider thinking ABOVE your trousers, and I'd recommend you start by getting a few female directors on your board."

That told us. And she was right – insightful. I learned she came from Romford and had formed a limiting view about us Yorkie boys.

"Where do you actually come from? I mean the little mill village you soot-ridden, clog-footed, cloth-capped, whippet-racing idiots come from. Is it called *Scuddlythorpe* or something?"

I was drawn to her; better still, I was a little scared of her, and that made it exciting as well as dangerous. I knew this had potential for real passion and conflict. If Jim's girl had brought her along for moral support, she had picked the right person.

After a verbal bashing I won the right to know her name – Vickie. She was more than a match for an increasingly intimidated group of boys from Ward Evans. She wasn't even stopped by Jim's sharp observations about her reading habits and how he needed to rush out for his copy of the Volcano Times before they sold out.

Taking his lead, I added how I'd heard about a sad group of people who went home and read National Geo, to calculate their carbon footprint, in cold and dark energy-saving rooms. I braced myself for a mauling, but she smiled. I was elated. I'd been pardoned. I invited her out for dinner with the boys. All of us, not just me. I wasn't that brave. She accepted.

The sailing regatta

The following days and months went quickly. I enjoyed what time I had in London, and my new friendship with Vickie. While it hadn't gone unnoticed by the guys, it was some time before I acknowledged what a dynamite figure this lady possessed. Not dissimilar to Lara Croft and probably as dangerous, even minus the gun.

She took no prisoners in terms of attitude and confidence. It struck me as obvious that if she loved herself, it could only encourage others to do the same. She certainly walked and talked with pride. She was, for all those reasons, the full package.

Vickie certainly oozed high self-esteem, and not just in a physical sense. It was rooted in her own deep spiritual beliefs. Interested in various religions, she wasn't for any one prescribed type but found her personal system that she happily and generously shared with me. It was loosely based on Eastern history and ancient philosophy.

As time went on and she was routinely included in most social events, some of the boys started to view her with suspicion, maybe because she just stood out or was difficult to label. We managed a few personal breaks, loosely based around business. Vickie and I went to Dubai and stayed at the Berg al Arab hotel, the only seven-star hotel in the world. Built by the Maktoum brothers, who owned United Arab Emirates, it was an amazing monument to Arab success. The hotel was so richly furnished it stood little chance of ever breaking even, let alone returning on investment, but that's not what it was about.

The hotel had a fleet of taxis, Rolls Royce Silver Clouds. Vickie and I were met at the airport in great style. Two of our guys came with us as we'd arranged a meeting with a real-life sheikh, the head of a large financial services organisation. We were there to discuss the possibility of our doing work for their contacts in London.

There are no individual rooms at the Berj, they're all suites with a personal butler, and it was he who instructed me on greeting our guest in a traditional and respectful way. I was practised in how to seat the party, where I should sit, and that it had to be me as chief executive to pour the traditional tea – an act of servility and humility.

I love that these old courtesies are maintained in today's world; so many of these traditions are gentler, respectful and dignified, exercised across all class barriers. It struck me that humility always triumphs over pride in the end and so it was here.

They were respectful and generous in return. The meeting seemed to go well, but we had been warned that when they said: "I see" or "That's agreed, then", it referred to their understanding and not an acceptance of a contract. Dealing with them would require patience and time, not something in great supply at the Ward Evans Group.

We returned to the UK with lots of stories to tell more in keeping with *Lawrence of Arabia* than the truth, but it added to the mystique and crazy rumours that swept around about our company, its people and our activities. More revenue was being written and our new business fees alone were starting to climb over £750,000 per year. Importantly, we were retaining what we had put in. The sheer size of the business was considerable, and accolades from outside the industry were starting to come in.

We were one of the fastest growing businesses in the UK for three years consecutively, something we were particularly proud of as this was across every sector, including IT and the like.

I was named and pictured on the front cover of a business magazine with the headline: 'Exemplar of Entrepreneurial Vigour', complete with the inevitable shot of the Aston Martin. I think translated it meant: 'How did this dickhead get this car and can you believe how much business he's doing?" I was nominated for York's Business Personality of the Year.

We were the third largest independently-owned insurance brokerage in the country, and we had our eye on being number one. The company had been going for just seven years and had come from nowhere. The two above us had been in business over twenty years each, and their success was a result of mergers and takeovers. Ours was fighting over every client one by one and winning in the market place. It was a marvellous testimony to the hard work and dedication of our sales executives that we could build the business in this way, brick by brick.

Financial Services was doing very well, as they got their business from contacts on the corporate side, and we learnt that certain aspects of that market were driven by cost - just like a car insurance policy. This wasn't really recognised or, if so, it was certainly undersold.

If you had life cover, it cost you a certain amount every month. It was cover that simply paid out if you died within a certain time. You didn't give a bugger about which insurer you used, so long as it paid up and was around to do so. It wasn't about investment track record or anything complicated. Just how much to cover for X years at Y amount, and if you could get it cheaper, you would.

But no one seemed to realise that they could because it was tagged onto the pension arrangement. Usually called death-in-service benefits, but there were other types as well. Because this cover was associated with pension arrangements but not tied to it, most people didn't understand and were reluctant to change around.

Surprisingly, many brokers weren't investigating this as a competitive product that had a cost, which could be won or lost just like any other commercial business. We did, and cost savings were made that we then recommended they pay straight into premiums for their pensions, which earned us money in terms of commissions. More of the money the client paid was going into investment, rather than protection, which had still been secured at the same level but for less money.

Bish, bash, bosh – sorted, as Jim would say.

It was a win-win situation, with a simple premise that we weren't trying to sell more of this or that but simply reorganising what a person or a company had. It was better for them as a consequence and earned us a great deal – good news all round.

Tom was our main director in Financial Services. His main claim to fame was that he was related to one of the guys from Chas 'n' Dave and he was another gentle giant, standing six feet tall and with a ready smile.

He was one of life's butterflies, always flitting from one subject to another. He had great ideas, but was a hard man to pin down. His infectious charm seemed to carry the day, and he was well-liked, a natural winner in front of clients. He could also play the piano, so was a welcome addition to our nights out – if there was one to be found, he was straight at it.

A guy called Declan quickly joined Tom. The prevailing view about most guys who work in financial services is that they seem incapable of handling their own finances. Maybe it was just a case of 'cobbler's son' syndrome.

Declan seemed to embrace this idea and, in contrast to Tom, always had a worried look on his face. But he did lots of business, and his charm seemed to get people on his side – apart from my mother, who famously remarked once: "There's more to him than his face suggests!"

I knew what she meant. Declan was a man who looked well-mothered, with pasty white skin and easy charm. He always looked on the verge of a major illness, a sort of poor man's Eamonn Holmes from GMTV. Clients loved his laconic approach to business and he was perfect, as nobody wanted to feel stressed or pressured when talking about their financial affairs. Pressure was something both Tom and Declan seemed incapable of.

He headed north whilst Tom supervised the south, and between them they built a vibrant team. We had made the connection that if we couldn't save you money on general insurance, we'd introduce our financial services boys and they would.

It was like fighting a battle with another battalion in reserve, if they were needed.

It's amazing that, in other brokerages, it was common knowledge that the two different sectors never spoke to each other although working for the same company.

During the sailing regatta, the Financial Services guys would inevitably be on one of the sponsored boats with a pension insurer, with the general insurance team on the other. There was a lot of good humour and cat-calling if the two boats came into close proximity.

Someone thought it funny to shout as loud as he could in an affected accent: "Declan – Ken Dodd's dad's dog's dead!"

To which Declan would reply: "Eh? What you saying? I can't hear you. Who died?"

To which everyone on the boat would shout again: "Declan - Ken Dodd's dad's dog's dead!"

I still don't know why this is funny but try shouting it out; it had people rolling around in giggles. Or maybe you just had to be there. Either way, Declan was the sort of person who would carry this information around with a slightly concerned look as if he wanted to do something about it. He wore a worried expression all day and evening, until he eventually asked: "Who died again?"

When our first regatta came around we had lots of potential sponsors for each boat, some from general insurance and some from financial services. The boats were a beautiful sight moored up at Challenge Business headquarters, all nine of them being fifty two feet long. We made sub-banners and flags for each boat, and managed to produce Ward Evans sailing shirts for our guests, each team in a different colour, immediately defining the boat and moulding each into a fighting, competitive crew. The professional skippers had the helm for the start of each race, which would be from Southampton to Cowes, but had to give it up after the first minute from the starting gun. Other than for intervention on safety grounds, each boat was then in sole control of the team. The atmosphere was competitive when these vast crafts turned into the starting line with full sail. It was one of the most exciting things I've seen and I could understand why anyone might get the sailing bug.

Each boat jostled for position. There were time penalties for those who crossed the line too soon, arguments and complaints radioed to the referee's dinghy. But it all calmed down as the competitive urge consumed us all.

These occasions were immensely enjoyable and the Ward Evans Sailing Regatta was a hospitality day that insurers didn't want to miss. There was even talk of the winning crew achieving automatic entry into the Commodore Cup, although that never happened. Many of those who came as guests went on to take up the sport, and each event was topped by an evening barbecue at the Royal Corinthian Yacht Club.

Chay pulled strings and we were made most welcome – it's hallowed ground for sailors and we were lucky to be allowed to set foot in the place.

Hotel bills were avoided as everyone slept on board, which I'm told was rather like camping and needed to be approached in the same resolute way – exciting, but you wouldn't want it every night! I never knew as I found an exclusive little hotel with very few bedrooms and lots of hot running water.

The owner had numerous photographs of famous people on the wall, and my secretary arranged for a signed photo of Chay and me rowing The Needles to be placed alongside the Branson Blue Ribbon Challenge. Given our deal this was both poignant and fun, and Mum loved it.

I used to invite her and Dad to join us with a couple of their friends. They liked nothing more than waving us off on one side of the Solent and waving us in at the other. To see my mum engaging with some of the biggest insurers at these events was amazing. She'd delight in showing some of the older guys how to jive and was the sort of experience only ever repeated at the embarrassing wedding that everyone in the family remembers.

I was also seeing a lot of Vickie. The more I got to know her, the more interesting and surprising she became. There was much more to her than a few quick one-liners, and we had hours and hours of conversation about her beliefs, values, and life. She was very spiritually aware and always encouraged me in a gentle way to question my own. She constantly brought me crystals to keep about my person, books to read, incense to burn. I think the guys were wary of her because she wasn't the normal city girl and some of her views were contrary to the hedonistic lifestyles that had come from our own collective success.

In retrospect, they wanted that to continue and I was having too good a time to listen to Vickie's concerns and wise words.

I think they were scared I might cash it all in and head off with her to trek across India or similar. To go and find my true self. Well, if the Beatles could go through this rite of passage why shouldn't I? And my teacher was a whole lot better looking than theirs.

The guys thought I might have more earthly reasons to be with her, but either way I could hardly believe my luck. She was one of us, and wherever the boys and I went, my beautiful Yoko came too, spreading peace, happiness and love to all.

CHAPTER 5

Buying the boat

The financial year-end was usually a time of celebration. It came around again all too quickly and we were still flying.

We'd posted year-end profits of around £400,000 and, in accordance with our policy, we again retained it within the company. We didn't pay dividends and the money was reinvested for cash flow and to help fund further expansion.

As directors we were drawing out on PAYE something approaching a million pounds between us all, so when that was added back in it was obvious the business was making healthy money. We thought we were now safe to get the boat we'd dreamed about.

At the next Southampton Boat Show we determined to go down mob-handed, and after kicking a few 'tyres' put our name down for a Sunseeker Superhawk with a specially-extended bathing platform. It was a strangely serene moment, signing the forms. It was also a bit like buying a luxury car – the further up the chain you go, the less you get for the basic price.

You think you've got the boat, but actually you have the shell. The owner of the Sunseeker agency took us below in the biggest boat they had there and cracked open a bottle of champagne. While this was happening, a commercial manager came in with loads of forms and looked us up as though measuring us for a box.

"Right, down to business," he said. "What power engine? Two or three? Fitting out? Navigation? Lighting? Stereo? Air con? Life vest? Dinghies? Flares? Insurance?"

We called a halt, saying: "Give the details to James – we're off to the Guinness tent." We saw Chay, too, who promptly called us mad fools and told us to go and cancel the order. No way, we said.

"Well if you're determined, enjoy it. It'll cost you more than a collective divorce. You should have asked me first. There are only two days you really enjoy buying a boat like that, lads – the first is the day you buy it, the second the day you sell it," he scolded.

"Now if you wanted a proper boat, not a margarine tub, you should have looked at one of my beauties. That's different – a real investment, and best of all once you get it out to sea it's free. They don't charge for the wind, you know."

A few weeks later we got a call from the Sunseeker agent.

"We've got your boat, lads. Where do you want it?"

Now there was a detail we hadn't considered. We kicked the inevitable jokes around: "Have you got a roof-rack, Pete?" "Maybe it'll go in Jim's garage."

It was beautiful, though. A Ferrari of the ocean. Extended to fifty feet, three big engines and more dials and twiddly bits than we could poke a stick at.

James researched where we might put it; we all had a preference for Majorca, at Puerto Portals. Wellies Quay. It was the place for us.

After a few days we got a call.

"Hello, guys," said James. "Boy, do we have a mooring or do we have a mooring? How can I say this...? Well, who would you pay money to moor next to?"

We came out with a list of names. Jim said Rolf Harris because he liked his songs, and I made a mental note to have a word with him later.

But every suggestion was met with a no from James, until I told him to get on and "just bloody tell us".

"Well…. We are moored on Wellies Quay. Next to Cabaret of Angels."

"And what's that?" we asked.

"Only Peter fucking Stringfellow!" said James, excitedly. "Holy shit – imagine his guests!"

Deep Water Bear had arrived, and we were on the next plane out.

Palma and Wellies Quay

We arrived at Palma in double quick time. We took only hand luggage to avoid waiting around baggage collection, and took a taxi straight to the boat.

There was our gleaming, beautiful Sunseeker Superhawk, ready to help us in the serious pursuit of wine, women and song – or at least sunbathing and a bit of dolce vita.

Fifty feet of perfection, all kitted out, topped with the British ensign flapping proudly. Not for us Panama, Gibraltar or any other flag of convenience. We were proud that this was earned in London, and therefore it should be registered there. VAT paid, which in those days was the exception rather than the rule. The purchase brought us into contact with another set of lawyers.

It occurred to me that my previous observations of chartered surveyors and their mutuality of interest could be topped by the legal profession. Prosecution, defence, purchasing, selling, contract-maker and contract-breaker. These boys occupied a whole marketplace of mutuality – everyone got a slice.

The process included the lease of the mooring. For an astonishing £30,000 per annum we got a piece of concrete where we could tie up Deep Water Bear, an electric cable to plug us in to power and an elaborate hose for fresh water. That was it.

We looked at buying a mooring and were equally stunned to find prices ran into the million-pound-plus mark. Most moorings cost more than the actual boat. If ever there was an example of the adage 'location, location, location' this was it. And that's ALL you got. The deal was completed through gritted teeth.

We soon tired of just sitting on the boat. Many a laugh was had at our expense when Jim would tell people in the nearby bar: "I'd watch out, mate. We got pissed at a boat show and the next thing we know we were given the keys to this bloody thing! What the hell are we going to do with it now?"

We eventually decided to arrange with Sunseeker to go through a course in order to be awarded the International Certificate for Operation of Pleasure Craft. It was a world of strange, floating, flashing lights called cardinals and bishops, navigation and how the hell to call for help. After three days of training and exams we all passed, other than Jim.

He decided not to bother, which was an unspoken relief to all of us. We'd seen what he did with fast cars; a fifty foot boat didn't bear thinking about.

We found it easy to get Deep Water out of her moorings, but getting her back in was rather more difficult. Neighbouring boats would keep a lookout and politely move out for half an hour when news got round we were heading back.

"Why are the rest heading out as we're coming home?" wondered Jim, but it didn't take long for us to understand.

Where and how to anchor up was also a problem. These things, to our amazement, do drift around a bit and where you left it may not be where you find it after lunch. Often we'd sit down to eat only to see Deep Water Bear float into view, heading directly for a multi-million pound floating palace. As one, we'd jump up from the table and, to peals of laughter, try to start the outboard motor on the dinghy – or, in some cases, even dive in and swim like hell before it could cause serious damage (to our pride, as well as other craft).

Restaurant owners were surprised at first, thinking we'd done a runner, but were relieved to see us return half an hour later to finish our meal and settle the bill under the careful eyes of watching boat-owners who contemplated the day we might not make it back in time to avert disaster.

Word got round and we learned first-hand the meaning of the phrase "to be given a wide berth". Nearby harbours and bays might be packed, but there was a hundred-metre radius around our boat.

We needed a skipper, it was clear, so Sunseeker introduced us to Greg. Sighs of relief went round the port.

Greg was described as being as mad as a hatter but a safe pair of hands for sailing, so he quickly fitted in and became a trusted member of our team. The unexpected side-benefit was that, as friends with Greg, you had a passport to be friends with half the island. Everybody knew and loved him – especially the ladies.

He was, it has to be said, a devastatingly handsome man, even from what we could see. Everywhere we went, people would shout hello and ask how he was. Girls would stop him everywhere. We needed to put this to good use.

Jim was philosophical as ever: "When you get to sixteen years of age, you have to make a decision in life if you're no oil painting. You can have mates who are better looking than you, or mates who are uglier. I'm happy if they're more handsome, as they attract the birds and I pick off the weak ones."

Striking a Buddha pose, he continued: "It's like on the gaming reserves. Animals like us don't go for the fittest zebra. We watch carefully as the main lions, the strongest ones like Greg, get the stampede going and scatter the crowd. Then we lazy, ugly sods keep an eye out for the old hobbling buggers. It's market forces at their best, pure Thatcherism."

"I don't think she had this in mind exactly, Jim," I interrupted, but he was on a roll now. Nothing could stop him sharing his view of life and courtship.

"There are plenty of beauties out there and occasionally while going for the weak ones you bump into a beauty!"

I considered Vickie. She would take a lot of pulling down, I thought.

Jim did get his fair share of beauties, and to be honest we looked at him, and then one of his many girlfriends, and it didn't seem right.

He shared his wisdom: "I call it my bumblebee philosophy of life. It's an aeronautical design fact that a bee shouldn't in theory be able to fly. Its wings are too small and its body isn't designed for it, it's too round and heavy. Next time you see a bee, take a look, the academics are right...."

"What's that got to do with you and pulling beautiful women, Jim?" we asked.

"Well, just as no one told the bee it couldn't fly, no one told me I couldn't pull, so I just go out there and do! That's the secret - don't let anyone tell you that you can't do something!"

You couldn't argue with Jim in that sort of mood. In the meantime, Greg was our skipper and proving devastatingly attractive to the women. The package was further enhanced when we had a Ferrari 355 F1 Spider brought across as a little getaway car. Greg looked after boat and car very well. The opportunity wasn't lost on him, and it was nearly too much for some girls. Even Mum, when she came out with Dad, would

sit there saying: "You know, I could take you home with me, I really could!"
"Shut up, Mum!" I'd say, as my father would tut and smile. Greg's charms weren't
even lost on my then-12-year-old daughter. But he wasn't affected by the attention –
he remained a real lads' lad.
Jim observed that on this occasion, he wouldn't mind feeding off the crumbs of this
rich man's table, and we all knew what he meant. When you employed Greg, you
effectively got his whole family. His father visited the island many times; his sister, a
hairdresser, was always in attendance for a quick trim; his brother also travelled
across about once a month. Another lucky bastard, also good looking with a shock of
curly blond hair, and sporting with it as he was a former UK jet-ski champion. We
came to know them all, and their friends, and every day was different.
Not unnaturally, Greg went out with a walking, talking, live princess. I mean a real
princess, not just a girl who looked like one – although she did, with her chocolate-
box looks.
It was like a real-life fairy tale. The princess and her brother holidayed on the island,
and we'd take them out on the boat occasionally. I sometimes pinched myself to see if
I was dreaming about the company I was keeping.
I met her mother, a former top model from years gone by and a champion water skier.
She still had the legs and wasn't much older than me – I had to put dangerous
thoughts aside. My breeding might let me down, and I could get into proper bother if I
wasn't careful. The princess's dad was there and he held the top job, if you know
what I mean. I didn't want to mess with that.
We quickly got into a routine of late starts, a little sun-bathing and then taking the
boat around Puerto Portals to a famous restaurant named Tonies for beautifully-grilled
fish, freshly caught that morning. The only problem with Tonies was that we had to
moor up at a little nudist bay. It was difficult to get to without a boat, which was why
it was so private. People made the effort to go there and men and women of all ages
would lie there naked. We were fine with this, but Mum was outraged – we'd go there
deliberately to see her various responses and faces.
"I don't care what you say, it's not attractive is it, love?" she'd tell anyone in earshot.
"If it was me, I'd just put it away!"
We were moored on Wellies Quay and Mum would get confused and ask if we were
going to Willies when she really meant Tonies. We never corrected her, but we knew
what was on her mind!
If my parents were with us we'd book into the Marina Hotel, just up the hill from the
harbour. It was clean, cheap and cheerful. Mum got into her routine, bringing her
travel kettle and digestive biscuits. Any idea of romantic cuddles would be interrupted
with a banging on the French doors in the morning – more alarming as they opened
onto a balcony usually three or four floors up!
I opened the curtains to see Mum leaning over, half-climbing over the balcony with
two cups of tea.
"Here you are, love. I knew you'd like these. Got you some biscuits as well. Bet
you're glad I brought the kettle, aren't you? Got to get up early to beat me, old love!"
We'd eat in the best restaurants. One in particular, Flanagan's – the favourite of King
Juan Carlos of Spain when he's in town – was difficult to get into unless you booked
well in advance. But inevitably, when we met my parents downstairs in the hotel
lobby, Mum would say: "Your dad and I have decided we're going for a walk. You
get on and we'll you later."
"What about the restaurant?"

" You get on… Your dad only wants a sandwich." He'd give a resolute smile, knowing there was no changing her mind.

When we met up with them the next morning, I'd ask what happened and she'd tell me, with a smile and knowing look: "Bugger off, none of your business."

My father would tell me, when pressed: "Your mum found a Scruffy Murphy's down the road so she was happy there. Met some lovely people."

" As long as you enjoyed yourself," I said, shaking my head. "What did you have?"

"Soup and meat and potato pie," Mum answered. "It was just like Marks and Spencer, and before you ask I don't know about the soup. It was brown. I don't like my food being messed with."

What could you do? In future, each evening, we'd turn left to go to the port and they'd turn right to Scruffy Murphy's. They were happy.

Days on the boat

We'd had a good lunch at Tonics. If Mum was on the boat we could keep her away from Scruffy's and soup followed by steak and kidney pie. Afterwards we'd have some quiet time, maybe reading or swimming, and liven things up with music before heading back – usually something inappropriate.

This time, we'd kept to ourselves that we were meeting the princess's parents who were moored up round another bay. They were leaving the next day, and Greg had asked if we could touch base with them for an hour. We'd all been invited for cocktails.

Eventually, I had to reluctantly inform Mum of our intentions.

"Mum, get ready to meet royalty."

"Where the bloody hell do you think we're going? I'm going nowhere dressed like this!" she said with finality.

"We're going to meet Greg's girlfriend's parents."

"Bloody hell! Tom! Tom! Get your trousers on. We're meeting royalty. Me in my flip-flops and all, bloody hell. I'll have to change. Greg, slow the bloody thing down."

She disappeared in a flurry of expletives, occasionally shouting at us to either slow the boat down or stop it from rocking.

She returned from the cabin sporting the biggest, reddest lips ever seen – they'd have shocked a Parisian whore.

"I found this colour downstairs," she said as we flew along the water.

"Holy shit!" I thought, but avoided any more conversation that might cause trouble.

"I can't get it straight with all this bloody banging around! Are my lips straight?" she continued.

"They are until you smile," I said.

She shot me a look; this was serious business. "It will have to do."

The boats were tied alongside each other and we were introduced. It couldn't have been more relaxed, and everyone was friendly and charming.

After a few drinks, Mum cornered the princess's mother and sat with her, while my father talked politics to hers. (This should have been a bit of a no-no.)

Mum, who never usually touches the stuff, was quaffing lots of champagne.

"Well love, I expect you don't get any time for yourself, being royal and all. I couldn't do it, love, I really couldn't," she said, as though it was a lifestyle previously offered to her and which, after consideration, she'd rejected.

She continued talking while casually lighting up a cigarette on the boat. That's another real no-no and I shot her a look of horror, to which she characteristically reacted with a shout that reverberated around the boat.

Strident and now confident, thanks to the alcohol, she said: "And you can bugger off with that bloody look, I'm catching the ash in my hand, aren't I? I'm not daft! They think I'm daft you know, love. They wouldn't even stop to get my lipstick straight!" Everyone laughed. She's one on her own, is Mum.

Everyone had a great time. Cocktails and champagne were drunk late into the evening until we landed at Flanagan's and enjoyed real VIP treatment.

"Go on then," Mum said without invitation. "We'll give Murphy's a miss tonight. What sort of food do they do here then? I don't want anything fancy," she told the manager as he hastily arranged tables. "I had some lovely brown soup at Scruffy Murphy's. Do you do anything like that?"

Fun and games

We'd originally looked to moor the boat in the South of France, an obvious and very glamorous place. We were persuaded against it as a boat our size had few interesting opportunities around the local coastline.

Majorca had many coves but it was a small island; we were keen on taking Deep Water further afield.

Greg gave it a lot of consideration, and having talked us out of Algeria and the like as our sort of fast craft was a particular favourite for drug running, we decided on Minorca as our first small adventure. Nothing much could happen to us there.

Johnny and Patrick, our IT Directors, were flying out later and went directly there. When the call came, it was to report on all the hot spots.

"What's it like, Johnny? We're due to set off in the morning. We'll be with you after six or seven hours." We were full of excitement and expectation.

"It's shit, Mike," he said candidly. "It's just so quiet. Full of families and retired couples."

"OK," I said in a rather unconvincing voice. "See you over there."

"You are coming, aren't you?"

"Well, it might have to be Plan B," I said. It didn't seem sensible to spend seven hours at sea just to pick those two up.

"What's bleeding Plan B? I didn't know we had one! What are you saying, Mike – that you aren't coming?"

"We don't have one, but when I tell the boys what you've said, we will."

I put the phone down and talked to them. "Ibiza," said Peter. We told Johnny.

"Jesus, how do you expect us to get there? We're in bloody Minorca!"

"I'm sure you'll manage," I said. "I'll let you know if we change our minds again - some of the guys are talking about Barcelona."

"Bloody hell, Mike. It was always impossible to tie you down before but you're a moving target with that boat. We should put a tracker system on you!"

"See you in Ibiza, or maybe Barcelona!" I teased.

"Be in Ibiza," he said, and rang off. He'd be on the next flight and would enjoy himself once he was there, I persuaded myself.

We set off from Palma the next day, arriving after just a few hours, and were surprised to see Johnny just an hour or so later. We gave him a round of applause and he won some Brownie points for that. Johnny was ever resourceful.

We weren't booked in anywhere so had to do some creative thinking. Various options were discussed; we could stay on board at a push, but it would be a bit uncomfortable with seven of us. And impossible full stop with Jim, unless he slept above deck. Someone suggested we get a couple of joints while we mulled it over - nothing too heavy. It shouldn't be hard in Ibiza, so Johnny and I volunteered to go looking.

We climbed the old town at around eleven in the evening as people were starting to come out for a mad, bad, crazy night. We planned just to walk in and ask for what we wanted; it seemed straightforward – this was a lively place after all, we'd read lots about it. Determined to not let the boys down, off we went with a determined spring in our step.

Halfway up the hill we found the first club open at this early time. We went in and, having been forced to pay the entry fee, stood around conspicuously and asked to speak to the manager.

We got straight to the point, and he was taken aback by our audacious request - we were clearly Englishmen abroad and lacked tact and diplomacy. It didn't happen like that, we were told, but a club further up the hill would suit our requirements.

We continued, chatting about what a miserable bastard the guy was and occasionally stopping to admire the beautiful view. The night dropped quickly to an inky black and, staring out to sea, we could smell some man-made substances mixed with the musky floral scents on the cool night air.

"It's around here somewhere," said Johnny.

We walked further up the hill and he suddenly stopped outside two large doors, with a counter to the left, a small bar to the right and stairs leading to God knew what. It seemed lively enough as the dull beat of urban music hit my diaphragm.

We paid a guy dressed in a leotard and bunny ears. He looked at us, we looked at him; the spell was broken when he silently held his hand out. We handed over a £20 note and decided not to ask for the management. We'd sort it ourselves.

"Did you see that bloke in fishnet stockings?" Johnny asked casually.

"Yeah, some mad buggers on this island, aren't there? I haven't been clubbing for years – last time was when *Saturday Night Fever* was out and I was dressed in a white suit! I guess anything goes nowadays."

We pushed our way through the heaving crowd to the bar and ordered two Jack Daniels and Cokes.

I was starting to get a bad vibe when Johnny, on polite enquiry was advised to go downstairs and ask for a few joints. We got the impression people were beginning to stare at us and it put us on guard. We'd better stick together.

The stairs led to a dark, dungeon-like place full of heaving bodies, intermittently lit up by a strobe light pulsating in time with the music.

"Noticed anything peculiar, Mike?" asked Johnny.

"No, but I don't feel safe here for some reason. It's a bit wild, isn't it? Go ask them to put on some Beatles," I teased in an effort to hide my nerves.

"Looks like a bloody zoo, lots of people dressed in such an extravagant way, but I'm not up on all this clubbing shit. I've nothing in my wardrobe that could blend in with this lot! But we should have got dressed up a bit – they're all done up to the nines and we're in our bloody yachting shorts!"

"They're all fucking men, Mike! That's what's bloody wrong! It's a fucking gay club and we're dressed like extras from Wham!" There was panic in Johnny's voice.

I'd never felt so self-conscious in my life. Our top-of-the-range yachting gear, with what were fast becoming too-little and too-tight shorts, contrasted with the heavy-duty leather nightclub gear everyone else wore. It was obvious once the penny dropped that we'd been set up for our impertinent questions by the manager at the first club. And now I could see videos of a graphic nature around the dance floor, and they weren't of some romantic film.

"Let's just make our apologies and leave," I said. Our daring and different American college campus look stood out, and Johnny in particular was attracting admiring glances.

"What's wrong with me, then?" I said in fits of nervous laughter.

"Come on, Mike. We should have known when we met the bloody rabbit!"

Johnny was starting to lose it. For the first time in my life, I thanked God I wasn't the good-looking or youngest one. The only thing to do was rip the piss out of Johnny, who didn't appreciate it – especially as he realised that his dyed-blond and spiky hair didn't help.

"Well, come on, it's not their fault is it?" I teased. "I mean, take a look at your shorts – lime-fucking-green? You dress like a slap ho tart. You've always been an attention-seeker, that's your problem. Is this why you die your hair blond, eh? Wait until I tell Jim and the boys. Shall I say I left you with a few friends and you'll be back later?"

Johnny looked pale. We went back up stairs and the rabbit looked at us with accusing eyes.

"What's wrong with you two lover boys?" he asked.

"Nothing," I muttered, like a naughty schoolboy, "We're just leaving mate… er, love. My mate's not well."

"Not through this door you're not, lovely! You just came to gawk and take the piss, is that it?"

"No!" we protested. "We just got off the boat and..."

"And I'm Danny la Rue," he interrupted, dropping the slightly effeminate accent. "You need to go through the exit downstairs. This is one-way only – just like your arseholes," he shouted at the two naughty boys standing in front of him with bare, quivering legs.

This is how it must feel when a lady in a short skirt walks past a load of builders. I tried not to sound frightened: "No problem. My mate and I'll go back downstairs and find the other exit. Come on, Johnny."

Where was Jim when you need him? He always settled arguments for us – but, then again, the sight of a twenty-stone man in tight shorts might have sent them over the edge!

"It bothers me that they've got us trapped in here," said Johnny. "Let's get out, forget the joints."

I stood at one side of the dance floor and Johnny volunteered to search for the other exit. That meant walking through a dark floor full of gyrating dancers, so I was staying put.

He came back a few minutes later, ashen-faced.

"Fuck, I've just had my arse pinched and been asked to dance!"

I couldn't stop laughing.

"Well, it's not funny," Johnny continued. His humour had long since disappeared. "I told him you're my boyfriend and you're the jealous type!"

I could see a leather-clad Village People type glaring at me.

"Jesus, hold my hand and let's get out, Mike."

"You can piss off!" I said. "I leave you for a few minutes and you're already flirting with another man!"

"Screw this, I've had enough!" He had a new determination. "That entrance where the rabbit is has a fire door next to it. When I hit that door, run like fuck down the hill.

We're leaving whether Bright Eyes likes it or not!"

He didn't give me time to complain. He went straight up the stairs and my eyes met the bunny's. For the first time I knew what it meant about a rabbit being caught in the headlights. There was a moment where the world stood still; his eyes met my eyes; his ears twitched and so did mine. Then there was an almighty crash; Johnny had hit the fire door and was shouting for me to follow.

The bunny had a frighteningly loud voice that was now clearly Liverpudlian: "Oi, you little bastards!"

The rabbit had become rampant. He vaulted over counter and chased us down the hill, shouting and swearing.

We could hardly run for laughing at the sight of this bloke in a black leotard with flapping bunny ears galloping after us, while friends, families and lovers stared in amazement. These were the days before the likes of Trigger Happy TV – I wish I'd thought of it after this experience.

"Bloody good job he was wearing his high heels!" Johnny said, gulping for air between fits of laughter.

"Don't you talk to me," I said, "Don't think you're out of the shit, love; I want to know what happened on that dance floor!"

We arrived back at the boat still trying to catch our breath while the guys poured some long gin and tonics. We told our story amid hilarity and general piss-taking, before attention turned to what we'd do now.

Johnny and I said all we could – that there were a load of crazy bastards out there intent on partying.

"But I'm not going up that bloody hill while there's a rampant rabbit about with a Scouse accent!" said Johnny. "At least not without Big Jim – you were bloody useless, Mike!"

"We need a few cars," said Jim. "A place to go, a place to drink. That's all. Bish, bash, bosh – simple."

Peter spoke quietly. "I know a great club, best on the island, Amnesia. I've read about it. But they'll have closed their doors by now, it's a busy place, so we'll have to think about how we can get in."

"Mike has his black Centurion American Express card – 24-hour personal service and all that. Let's phone them. It's what it's there for!"

Johnny considered the possibilities, "Go on, Mike, you're always going on about how good it is and how you can get in everywhere anytime with it. This is a real test. Give them a ring."

I was a founding charter member of the Amex black card, one where you were invited to join, having shown clear assets of over one million pounds ex-domestic property. I'd been given a personal manager who'd make the right phone calls and get tables in restaurants that were in other circumstances fully booked. They'd been impressive in the past. But this was a different matter, sitting on a boat in Ibiza.

Peter piped up: "Tell you what, you just give the security answers. I'll do the rest."

I phoned, answered a few questions and went above deck leaving him on the phone. He reappeared a few minutes later looking pleased with himself.

"We're in," he said, smiling. "They're sending limos for us."

"Shit, Pete, what will that cost on my card?"

"Nothing, Mike – it's part of the service."

The card was good, but not that good.

"What the hell did you say to them, Peter?"

"Well, I just happened to mention we were a pop group, on a night out from Palma, moored up, and could Amnesia send some cars…."

Shortly afterwards, Amnesia's PR guy was on the phone, desperate to say hello.

"Bloody hell, what will we do when they get here? What'll happen when they meet us?"

"Who are we supposed to be? Anyone I know?" said Jim

"That's the genius," Peter said, "It's The Verve!"

"And who the bloody hell are they?" asked Jim, taking an interest now he might get a few free drinks out of it.

"Glad you asked, Jim. It's brilliant, even if I say so myself. They've just had an outstanding hit with *Bitter Sweet Symphony* from their album *Urban Hymns*. Great record, it's being played everywhere."

"Yes I know," said Johnny.

"Well, what more do you want?"

"Get on with it, Peter. What do you mean?" I asked.

"Well, no bugger knows what Ashcroft looks like do they? Or any of them, come to that."

"Who's Ashcroft?" Jim said, proving the point. It was true – their music was fantastic, but they tended to shun publicity.

"So tonight, Matthew," Peter continued, "we're going to be…"

Amnesia

Within an hour, two limos turned up at No 1 mooring. We invited the Amnesia PR people on deck and poured drinks.

I went below to talk to Jim.

"This is working too well. We could get into real trouble here. We only wanted entry to the bloody club!"

"I know, Mike, but they've seen the boat and are convinced. I'll have a word with them," he tried to reassure me. "I'll tell them to address all concerns to me and for them not to fuss or hassle us – that we just want a relaxing time."

I think this made things worse, as the more Jim protested about not wanting this or that the more convinced they were that we were The Verve and wanted to supply us with pampering and free hospitality.

We were taken by limo to Amnesia and escorted to the Super VIP area. The main VIP area was roped off near the bar, but through that was a second roped-off section overlooking the dance floor.

Dancers gyrated about thirty feet up on ledges facing the crowd and then come down to sit, dance and entertain the VIP guests. It was a wonderful circus of characters, colour, music and drink.

Every time we went to the toilet, a security guy would go before us and one behind us. A bottle of Jack Daniels arrived, along with one of vodka, one of Cristal champagne and assorted soft drinks. We'd ordered nothing, but everything was made available. Patrick got the worst end of the deal as we'd explained he was our sound guy so they were particularly keen to show him their massive sound system.

The night went on. We danced within the VIP area – the management didn't want us to join the crowd where they might lose us, although that was what we wanted.

The night's excesses continued into early morning. We sat with the most beautiful female dancers who promised to be our new-found friends and invited them back to our recording studio in Palma. Fact gave way to fantasy as we had the biggest party, and I remember drinking some Coke that we thought had been thoughtfully provided to keep us upright, what with all the alcohol we'd consumed.

I eventually woke up on a bench in the middle of the town. It was the strangest feeling. I didn't know where anyone else was and staggered back to the boat as the others also returned from different directions.

"Where the fuck have we all been?" I said. "What the hell happened?"

"One minute, lights on; next minute, lights off. We all got back at various times; none of us can remember what happened. You're the last one, Mike," Peter told me. "I think I know why it's called Amnesia."

When we all felt well enough, we met on deck for an orange juice. We huddled around in shocked, subdued silence, each with a raging hangover.

Jim summed it up: "It's simple, I reckon. Either they found a picture of Ashcroft – or that fucking bunny turned up!"

The Grand Prix

We were never that much interested in joining any of the posh London clubs. We felt one of us would ultimately commit an indiscretion and be asked to leave.

So social nights took us to our usual late-night destination of Dover Street Wine Bar, where they always looked after us and Jim didn't look out of place as he stood among the big guys outside who controlled the door.

But we did join Monty's Club, on Sloane Street, as a client who organised all the Grand Prix balls was a member and insisted on meeting them there to talk. We loved the account for obvious reasons so joined without question.

It was a great place to network and the staff were relaxed and friendly, which suited our style. It was one of the first places run by Jamie Oliver.

When I joined, because my principle address was in Yorkshire, Peter and I explained to the membership secretary that we'd be away most weekends and therefore wanted their cheaper package, for "country members".

Every time we visited, one of the guys on door control would stop us and ask if we were members, to which one of us would reply: "Yes, I am a *country* member!"

The doorman would move aside and say: "Yes, I remember!"

It never failed to get a laugh and we'd bet on how long it would take one of our guests to figure out what the guy had said. They'd break out into sudden laughter after about five minutes saying, "Bloody good that, 'I'm a *count-ry* member' and him replying 'yes, I remember!' I've just got it!"

Being close to the Grand Prix guys gave us access to the Paddock Club and pit lane, and we bumped into some of the Formula One drivers. We agreed to try not to be too impressed when meeting them at parties and the like, but I think Jim took it too far one night when, slightly irritated by a particular driver who was lording it up, he threw his keys at "the car jockey" and asked him to park it.

They took it in good spirit and we were delighted to be on Eddie Irvine's boat, the Anaconda, when he came third in a Jaguar at Monte Carlo. That was the team's best finish, and Eddie's best at that circuit. He did it with his mother, father and sister on the boat to watch, and it was touching to see this success in the family at firsthand. Eddie was renowned for his party lifestyle, so it was a good place to be when he got this great result.

The other guy we bumped into who could party a bit in those days was Chris Evans. Peter and I met him, along with sports agent and broadcaster Johnny Maguire, on a flight to the Hungarian Grand Prix, and also when Chris was a guest of Eddie Jordan's in Budapest. We got on famously and had a great time, singing and dancing in the hotel bar and disco. We took the Mickey, insisting he didn't go near the turntable. We never lost an opportunity to point out to Chris that, in this town at least, he was nothing more than a 'ginger whinger'.

He was a great sport, one of the boys, who returned our style of humour in spades. He invited us to Virgin Radio to see the show when next in London, where we bet him that he stand on his head on the chair whilst broadcasting to the nation. He did. I, for my part, did my famous Jimmy Savile impression to Madonna's *Music* which we all promised would one day be recorded.

We saw what it was like to be in possession of a famous face but agreed that, despite the obvious benefits, we were happy being a crazy gang with enough money to do what we liked without hurting anyone. Chris had – no doubt still has - constant attention, with people shoving paper in front of him to sign without a please, thank you or hello. Sometimes this extended to camcorders while trying to have a normal conversation – it would have driven us mad. But wouldn't it be great to be famous for just a day?

The business contacts that came through association with the event company were amazing. I've no doubt that if we'd continued our sponsorship at Jordan we would have got the cost back in extra business.

No one could have worked harder for sponsors than Eddie Jordan, even if he could be stressed out at times. He always visited the Paddock Club and gave us a debrief of the race afterwards, spending time with his supporters whoever they were. The Jordan contingent was full of Irish support and, whatever the result, the place never failed to kick off a party.

We also regularly crashed into the bar at Claridge's and often found Gordon Ramsey there. We eventually met as he was chilling there one night, I presume while he was preparing to open his restaurant there.

I mentioned that he couldn't be an absent chef in all his places for long and expect them to be a success. If I was paying eighty quid a plate I wanted him to at least over-see it, even if he wouldn't deign to cook it. Seemed a fair enough argument to me and I didn't mean it to sound anything other than the comment it was. But maybe it was unfortunate timing, because it was like lighting a firework.

Jim suggested we move onto a less-inflammatory subject, like football, but it was too late. I got the full might of Gordon's venom, as regularly seen on TV. It was quite a privilege to be on the end of it and it felt almost like a reality TV contest. I got a few jokes from Billy Connolly, charm from Jamie Oliver, a few drinks from Chris Evans, Michael Palin's cutting wit and a great party with Eddie Irvine. Now I got a complete and comprehensive bollocking from Gordon Ramsey. Everything was right with the world and God was in His Heaven.

The short version was that he disagreed with my well-constructed critique of his overall business strategy. I was called all the names under the sun, and a few that didn't belong to this world. Delivered, it has to be said, with an evil grin and he suggested I never, ever even TRY to get a table into one of his restaurants.

I told him it was too late as I'd eaten in most of them, and he might have known that if he'd been where his executive chef, Marcus Wareing, had been.

This didn't placate him, and Gordon turned to Jim, who was trying to keep things a little more jolly. He gave him an open invitation to any of his restaurants as long as he didn't bring "that prat" with him. I promptly banned Jim and all employees on expenses from all his restaurants and said we'd go hang out with Marco in future. We all left with smiles on our faces. It's not every night a man like Gordon gives you a dressing-down and he was, it has to be said, the absolute best at it.

Peter Stringfellow

We were extremely busy at work, but one advantage of having the boat in Palma was that it was cheap and quick to jump on easyJet and be there in no time.

We'd seen Peter Stringfellow a few times. He made us most welcome and was polite and kind. He was always surrounded with the most glamorous ladies but as this was normal life for him, he didn't seem to notice – or show it, if he did. He described it as his "personal reality"; Jim said he wouldn't mind living in his parallel world.

For us, of course, the women were sensational - people nearly fell off boats trying to get another look. This always provided an interesting diversion as we were moored up next to him and he did comment that the girls he knew hadn't exactly missed the Ferrari or the boat, which wasn't the largest there but might have been one of the quickest. (And, skippered by us, one of the most dangerous.)

"I see your car everywhere on the island," said Peter once when he invited us to dinner at Stringfellow's in London.

"I bet it's Greg more than me behind the steering wheel," I said.

"Don't worry about that, Mike," Peter insisted, "I know about ladies, and the one thing they all find out soon enough is who owns what!"

I was thinking of the mileage, but it was interesting advice from a specialist in that area. Advice I should have paid more attention to; it may have made life interesting, but it was also very dangerous in the relationship stakes. I was honestly happy with Vickie, and one beautiful lady was more than enough. And more then I deserved. Vickie made it clear in a very calm way that one mistake of that nature and she would be gone. She saw the boat, the flash lifestyle and the Cabaret of Angels moored next to ours. Her eyes narrowed and she visibly froze. She was marking territory. It was the same when I looked into getting a housekeeper for the new place I'd recently bought, Woodland Grange Estate.

"I think I'll get a little Polish girl, someone who'll say 'Ohhh Mikey,' with a finger twirling her hair and 'How can I ever repay you?'" I teased. It never happened.

Peter Stringfellow was a fantastic conversationalist and really interesting. He'd been there and done that. He'd met artists, Hollywood stars, musicians and politicians. He'd been rich and then poor after his experience in the States. When he opened in Los Angeles he took bookings from mega stars who then sat in his restaurant eating nothing and drinking nothing. It was well documented that, as a consequence, he earned nothing.

Back in the UK, he could walk into a restaurant or club and work out via a table count exactly what the club was earning or could earn if managed properly.

He asked if he could borrow the boat for a French pop video being made for his then-girlfriend. I consented, and he mentioned as a backdrop there were a few dancers coming out. He was having a celebration dinner that I was welcome as a thank-you for the loan of the boat and, occasionally, its mooring; I thought of Vickie and decided against it.

I think Peter and my skipper, Greg, were astonished. I don't know many people who'd turn down Peter's invitation to dinner when he's in that company.

I took the easyJet back on the day of filming and, as I settled down to a pizza that evening, Greg texted me. He used two words: "Beaver Espania!"

CHAPTER 6

Storm clouds

I was in one of our management meetings on the east coast at Ravens Hall when a call came through from my estranged wife. Although separated for some time we remained on good terms and I was always encouraged to keep in regular touch with my children.

My six-year-old son, Oliver, had a mark on his leg which had turned into a cyst. It was starting to look ugly and needed to be removed. The surgeon took it out in a routine operation under local anaesthetic. Surprised at just how deep-rooted it was, he sent it away for analysis.

We didn't know he'd done this because he didn't think it was necessary to tell us. It was routine, a cyst or boil that was gone, and just procedure.

Now he wanted to nip round to talk about "certain matters". I wasn't there and Sue hadn't mentioned it – she had her parents with her and through it was part of the service.

The consultant came to the point quickly. Cancer had been diagnosed. They couldn't be sure what type – there are many kinds of Hodgkin's/non-Hodgkin's lymphoma, and they couldn't categorise it yet.

But Oliver needed to be in hospital quickly for further tests; the cells were cancerous and he needed urgent treatment. Furthermore, because the 'cyst' had broken his skin, they were extremely worried about the spread of the disease. This effectively made the cancer Stage Three – the worst of whatever the eventual diagnosis would be.

Shock, disbelief and fear overwhelmed the family. Fear for Oliver, the family, my life, of the unknown.

I told Sue I'd be back next morning. I needed to compose myself, think things through, and cling to the last moments of normality. She was with her family and I was — well, I spent so much time with my colleagues, they'd become like family to me.

I called Peter and Jim into a room and told them the news. There were tears and ashen faces followed by pledges of support in whatever way I wanted it. The company, its power, people and money were available, at my disposal to do whatever was needed, whenever we knew what that was.

I told them to tell the other board members and a few of us separated from the rest while we sat in quiet contemplation, trying to make sense of it all.

What could anyone say? There are no words I could think of and nor could they. I needed to get back and talk to a specialist, demand answers, have alternatives, make plans.

We said confidently that nothing, but nothing, would stand in the way of Oliver getting the best treatment in the world. I didn't know how good the UK and the NHS would be, but our collective demands would be high and if they could not be matched then we'd go wherever necessary.

I left the next morning advising James, Jim and Peter to continue with the conference. It seemed strange to think that while on the road back home things were continuing in the warmth and joviality. The familiar world, the known world. Where was all this going to lead?

I arrived at the family home to shocked, cried-out faces and red tired eyes. It needed a physical image to make it real for me and here it was.

My pain was small compared to his mother's pain, one so dedicated to the unrelenting love expressed with every action in ordinary, everyday life.

Oliver hadn't been told at that point that he needed to go into hospital, so he'd been sent to school in order that normality reign as long as possible.

I so wanted to see him, half wondering if I'd be able to see the illness that had escaped my attention, and there it would be, clear for the world to see now the penny had dropped.

Just six years old. A lively, beautiful, cheeky, blond-haired little boy. I wanted to do nothing but cuddle him, but had to be careful – if I was over-emotional he'd noticed, and start to worry.

Lucky, we'd always been a tactile family. I still kissed my father, so when Oliver was picked up from school it was smiles all round, albeit the hugs were a little tighter, a little longer. I looked into his eyes; bright blue, shining brightly. This wasn't a little boy who had just been diagnosed with cancer. Surely it was a terrible mistake?

I heard that conference finished early and everyone returned home in subdued mood, to cuddle their own children and spend time with them.

Sue and I had a heart-to-heart and agreed that any differences would be put to one side; emotionally, at least, we'd be there for each other. We faced an uncertain future, and try as they might no one could appreciate the sheer fear and panic that threatened to spill out in every moment that was not checked by a determination to see this through in a united way.

We needed to lean on each other. Whether we could was uncertain, but we had beautiful extended families and each would play a part in our own and our child's survival.

We were to meet Mr Lewis at St James's Hospital in Leeds. He'd taken more samples from the specimen and had a team of people working on the exact identification of what form of cancer this was through a process of elimination. A process that effectively told you what it wasn't, not what it was.

Just a few years previously they'd split this type of cancer into two main sub-sections – Hodgkin's, and non-Hodgkin's. This had been refined to over forty different types, each with its own protocol, complications and prognosis.

Oliver, Sue and I arrived at St James's. I'd spent well over six months in the same place at Oliver's age with rheumatic fever. It scared me to be back. The place always frightened me and lived in my memory as one of fearful abandonment. It was as if I had never escaped – it had eventually caught up with me and claimed my life back as its own.

In those days of pre-enlightenment, parents couldn't stay in hospital with their child. This is probably why the feeling of abandonment never left me, or many other little children who endured long admissions, no doubt.

It wasn't boarding school; most of us could neither move nor get out of bed. Some were paralysed and traumatised with their illness. Every second day or so I was in floods of tears as my mum and dad said goodbye. I had a sister, and decided they'd put me there because they loved her more. I even accused them of it. To think of the pain they must have gone through trying to care for their child in that restricted way increased my own and heightened my emotional sensitivity in adulthood.

This wouldn't happen with Oliver. If he was there, so would we be. Wherever he was treated, we'd be with him.

We were introduced to the family liaison manager who would help us, act as our bridge between the real world and the one that engulfed us, and Mr Lewis came to see us. He was a big bear of a man with a short beard and a gentle, careful, reassuring nature. I guessed that he must see many parents in our position and wondered how he could ever have a happy day. How could he, dealing as he was with life and death at such a young age, the mouthpiece, if not the instrument, of a cruel God?

Your child will live. Your child will die. It needed courage to be willingly involved with something like this, where inevitably one would get close to the child and its family. Some had to be losers. He couldn't win every time.

We were invited to see Mr Lewis in the cancer day centre before going onto the ward. We took a deep breath and reminded ourselves that we had to be strong for Oliver. We opened the door and entered a world that grabbed our souls. A world of children in various stages of progressive illness, some going into treatment and some coming out. Bald little things, bloated and pale from the effects of chemotherapy.

I could see Sue shaking, physically shaking, fighting to hold back her tears for her little boy. I loved her more at that point than ever before. What we saw was shocking. This was our new reality. The hospital couldn't protect our child or his parents from it, and nor did they try. We needed to come to terms with it, to have some acceptance and understand that this was where we were, this was how it was. For some time, and with an uncertain outcome.

We glanced around furtively as Oliver went to play with new friends. If he saw a physical difference with these bald little children, he certainly didn't show it. Children who are perfect strangers are drawn to a toy box where, within minutes, all boundaries break down. They share the toys and their play, whatever their appearance, background or language.

We parents sit with arms folded, talking in a quiet hush. Each blessing the poor little souls around us, wondering whether they are going into hell or coming out of it. Somehow, it still felt like an enormous mistake. We shouldn't be here; they've got it wrong. This doesn't happen to us, it happens to others; to other children.

Diagnosis

Oliver was diagnosed with one of two types of cancer. Anaplastic lymphoma or large T cell lymphoma. They don't test for large T cell – there was no point, it was always fatal.

About forty children a year in the whole of Europe got the disease so there wasn't such a demand for research as with childhood leukaemia and it seemed very little was known about it.

Because the cancer had breached the skin – the largest living organ – I guess they had to class it as Stage Three, although the surgeon who took the cyst from Oliver's leg caught the disease early.

I wanted to know all the facts, mortality tables, everything at once. Sue wanted to know why this disease had chosen her little boy to feed on.

We were put kindly but firmly into some sort of holding circle of gradual disclosure, familiar to anyone who's had to face really bad news. Lewis said there was no point talking about mortality rates as, if it's one in four, then three survive but it doesn't help the one that doesn't. Those sorts of calculations were discouraged, but I still made them through whatever information I could lay my hands on.

I got the impression that the internet was regarded as more hindrance than help as the information flow couldn't be managed or explained in a professional way. But not to investigate was impossible and I searched to see what it was all about, what the options were, trying to gain comfort from the probabilities.

Sue was in floods of tears, not quite believing what was happening to her little boy. Lewis had to patiently explain that this wasn't a question of why or a judgement sent from on high. He told Oliver in a kind yet truthful way what was happening and why his mummy and daddy were upset. We were very grateful for this kindness.

Of course, it needed to be said as it could cause even more distress to Oliver if he failed to understand some of the basic reasons as to why suddenly his life had changed in such quick and dramatic way.

I don't know what we would have done without Lewis's steady hand and generous heart. We came to rely on him a great deal. What right do we have complaining about life when these life or death dramas take place every day in hospitals up and down the country?

There's no evidence to suggest why children get this type of disease. All that's known is that it's a western disease. Perhaps it's that kids nowadays don't play in the mud or eat dirt like we used to, and antibodies that should be there to protect their immune systems don't grow as strong and resistant, leaving them prone.

Think of the entire chemical blasting an average kitchen gets now with one squirt of whatever – biological this, disinfectant that. The chemicals may obliterate all germs and may be industrial strength, but it's not how grandma used to do it with carbolic soap and water.

Or maybe the disease has a correlation with pesticides. Research was taking place about the proximity to farms and fields. So few children got this type of disease that analysis was slow.

I asked why we couldn't establish whether it was large T cell lymphoma and they wouldn't give me a direct answer. So I surmised that they don't bother as it's a sentence of death, which brings up moral problems about treating children with expensive chemotherapy drugs, giving hope when none exists.

Sir Chay got to know about this unfolding tragedy and was asked by one of my colleagues to talk to someone in the medical profession as to where we should go to have the cancer treated.

He was extremely kind and concerned, and his extensive list of contacts brought advice from the chief executive of Nuffield hospitals. Oliver was in very good hands at St James's in Leeds and with Mr Lewis, who was very highly regarded. He should stay there.

I had talked about taking him and a small entourage to Philadelphia state Hospital, or Texas University Hospital, but given the advice received decided he'd best stay put. This was a lot better for him – at least familiar people could come and visit him. We weren't going to be able to buy ourselves out of this situation.

A hell full of angels

Oliver was admitted to the children's ward. He was in a small, private side room for a few days, as we all tried to get used to our new environment. It was better for us adults but not much for Oliver, who wanted to speak to and meet the other children of his age on the ward.

Presents from employees and well-wishers started arriving soon we had mountains of toys, which Oliver was delighted with. This needed monitoring as he spent five minutes on one toy, and five on the other, and some were left completely unopened Pride of place went to Buzz Lightyear, the latest 'must have' that said: "Alert, alert" when anyone entered the room. The doctors and nurses smiled indulgently even when they'd heard it a hundred times.

My PA arranged a surprise collection from our employees and toys were piled in a room at the office. Oliver heard about it and, while he might wonder what all the fuss was about, he was happy to take them and put other thoughts to the back of his mind. We agreed Oliver would have one new toy per week on a Friday night, and after a few weeks it should be donated to the ward's toy room for all the inmates to enjoy.

Oliver's health needed to be assessed for the aggressive bout of chemotherapy that would attempt to purge him of the dreadful disease. What really scared me was the realisation that every cancerous cell had to be destroyed.

It's not good enough to get most of them – they all needed to be poisoned and cleared. Leave one out of the millions – possibly billions – that were there, and the cancer would return. It was frightening to think of the odds of them missing one rogue cell. Heart and liver were tested, as they'd be under enormous strain; physiological tests were completed; general health assessed. There was counselling for Sue and me whenever they had time. We felt we didn't need it, certainly not as much as some of the other parents there; we were fortunate by comparison with some. Horrendous stories reached us of parents being dismissed as employers couldn't accommodate their time off or the emotional consequences of that person's unwanted journey through this frightening, painful time.

At least we were okay financially. But to think of someone's pain and add onto it a financial burden would have completely overwhelmed me. It did, for some; there were more broken souls in that ward than just those belonging to the children.

We soon understood that we could and should stay with Oliver as much as possible and camp beds were rolled out when he was transferred after a week to a little bay accommodating eight beds. We'd pull the curtains around, trying to live in our own little world, both lying on Oliver's bed to watch television, play games, talk and sleep. Thank God for Patientline, I thought, as we had a little portable television and telephone line on an arm pulling from behind the bed. What unremitting boredom would there be without this connection to the outside world? The service was given for free in the children's ward, a generous gift. These children were in for the long haul and so were their parents.

Eventually we had a pre-treatment discussion with Lewis about the type of chemo Oliver would receive. Malcolm had done his homework very well and consulted with many specialists. There was a massive team behind him, not just in the UK but across Europe, where best practises and research information could be made available. Oliver would be given a toxic mixture of Vimblastin and other stuff that I can't remember or recognise. It was a French protocol. Effectively, Oliver's bed was in St James's in Leeds, but his treatment would be as if he was in a specialist cancer hospital bed in Paris. This filled me with joy, hope and relief.

Whether it was better than any British protocols I don't know, but the French were known as being ahead of the game in the treatment of certain cancers. And we weren't going to be restricted by geography with regard to the treatment given, victims of the cancer national lottery we'd heard about.

It was obvious this team would do its best, irrespective of money and budget considerations, and the good old National Health Service would be there when we needed it. Irrespective of camp beds and crap food Oliver was getting the best, as any child – irrespective of outside considerations – should expect and deserve.

Lewis said the chemo would almost certainly have side-effect; a blow, but not in comparison to the simple matter of life or death. It's not surprising just to what degree priorities change in these circumstances. Why is it we have to be confronted with these awful circumstances to gain wisdom into what's important in life?

Then when the threat fades so does the hard-earned understanding. I later learned what a high price we have to pay for wisdom and self-knowledge.

Malcolm also advised that the amount of chemo Oliver would endure was as aggressive as it could be for his tiny frame. He was only six, after all. Lewis explained that he needed a very precise amount of chemo to hopefully do the job, while at the same time, he had to keep Oliver irrigated with fluids to ensure his kidneys, liver, heart and other vital organs would not be damaged. However, such treatment might scar his heart so they needed to keep an eye on that too with regular cardiographs. He'd need X-rays to watch for tumours, but when and how also needed precision as the chances of those causing cancer as they investigated the possibility of a tumour was a consideration. He would certainly lose his hair and his appearance would bloat, and he may be violently sick. Some children sail through; some literally can't stomach it. But his hair would grow back in time, we were told.

His chances of survival were never discussed while Sue was there, but I'd deduced for myself that Oliver's chances were less than fifty- fifty over a five-year period. That's of course if it was the lesser anaplastic lymphoma and not the fatal large T cell. Malcolm privately shrugged his shoulders. He explained it was hard to say, and in any event what was the point of the calculation? They'd do all they could.

If Oliver survived, it would be no particular comfort to the parents of the children who died. One thing was for sure, Malcolm explained, their first chance of stopping this cancer dead in its tracks was the best chance. That's why Oliver needed very aggressive treatment. There would be little left in the bottom drawer should this cancer return.

Living with it

I tried to continue with corporate meetings and running the Business. Sue and I had determined that Oliver would never stay at the hospital by himself, and we reassured him about that. However long this took, and whatever the circumstance, he would have one of us there playing or sleeping alongside him.

It was agreed Sue would spend every two nights at the hospital to my one, and we soon became institutionalised into the regime, folding up the camp bed in the morning, tests and eventually chemo, and bottle after bottle as Oliver was constantly on fluids.

The nurses were easily identifiable as two groups – those who were dedicated and genuine carers, and those who'd sadly been ground into disillusioned drug dispensers. It seemed that those who joined the profession to genuinely care for their patients had slowly been driven to despair by too much bureaucracy and now had simply no time for the primary function of caring.

It's so non-PC to raise a questioning voice about these angels of mercy, but this hardly serves their interests or those of the patient. It's certainly a debate worth having, as we're all clear about what sort of health service we want when we have to call on it. But by then it's too late to complain.

I saw disillusioned nursing staff who simply should not have been at the hospital any more, and others who made me wonder what kept them there as their gargantuan efforts – sometimes in their own time – went largely unacknowledged and certainly unrewarded. If nurses could be so detached and hard-hearted towards these little inmates, what chance would a ward full of aged people have?

Fortunately, there were enough loving and caring staff there to keep spirits high and they squeezed that part of the job into every day – even if it meant doing it in their own time and at their personal and emotional expense.

One of the happiest sights was seeing the 'jolly trolley' at around five o'clock every evening, when a nurse would push a trolley full of sweets and become a veritable Pied Piper, leading a cheery bunch of children who tried their best to follow. Mobile drips would be everywhere and there was even the occasional skateboarding contest as children used them to speed up and down the ward, both feet on them and hanging on tightly.

Such was the ingenuity of these youngsters who could still play in the face of such terrible circumstance. It was inspiring to see. The sweets were always welcome and a useful monitor of how a particular child might be feeling at that time.

The need for nurses to be allowed sufficient time to express their caring ethic was never clearer than with the poor children whose parents couldn't – or didn't – get into hospital to see them every day.

There was a heartbreaking case of a woman who brought in her young daughter, diagnosed with some form of leukaemia. She stayed for a few days and then left, never to be seen again, leaving the child to her fate and her emotional well-being to the hospital.

We learned she was mother to seven children and her husband had made a hard if pragmatic decision that his wife could not afford to spend that time with just one child and should remain at home to care for the others.

It was rumoured that they went to some lengths to move house, and to forever forget the poor little mite holed up in the ward.

Either way the child didn't get any visitors, and while social services did their best, the heartbreak in those wards wasn't restricted to the simple battle against illness.

It was inevitable that, with the random nature of cancer, all walks of life were thrown together and we were all on the same journey. Businessmen who tried to steal into the corridors to make a call and catch up with the office rubbed shoulders alongside known street-walkers and drug-dealers.

Sometimes the food brought in to supplement Oliver's diet was stolen from the communal fridge. Just because we were in a children's ward, it didn't stop real life crashing in from time to time.

And in the middle were the most important people – the children, in a yo-yo state of health depending on either the progression of the disease or the effects of chemo, with attendant bowel problems, and general ill-health.

It was an unreal place. Cries and screams in the middle of the night. Loneliness and despair, interruptions of tests and more tests, bed moving in the early hours when a child got too ill to stay in the ward.

In the morning, Oliver would ask in wide-eyed innocence: "What happened to Joe? Where is he?"

Eventually he stopped asking and never mentioned it.

Words failed me. My life's experience hadn't prepared me for this. I simply didn't know what to do or say, or how to react. This was a crazy world, and I began to wonder where I really was – in London with its clubs, bars, women and wild nights, or this island of despair.

I found myself taking a deep breath before going to see Oliver. I wondered how he'd be and, much as I wanted to be with him, something inside me was telling me to back off. Apparently it's a common feeling when someone you love is seriously ill and there's the chance of a tragic outcome – you're scared for yourself and your own emotional well-being.

But it just made me feel guilty. I was plain scared. We all were.

All change

I spoke to someone who'd lost a daughter in tragic circumstances. He explained what real emotional pain was like for him.

"It comes in waves, Mike. One minute you're okay, just a dull ache that you learn to carry, but then in a moment you'll be swept away, overcome with grief. Then, as suddenly as it comes, it goes away again. The problem is that you live each moment with the knowledge that it will happen again and again, at any time, and everything is slightly tarnished by that. You're likely to feel guilty for laughing or enjoying yourself again, if indeed that's even vaguely possible for you to imagine."

I found his account deeply moving; it resonated within me. That's how I felt – one minute I'd be conducting a meeting, the next I was in floods of tears.

The guys found it alarming at first and naturally tried to comfort me, but I didn't want that. I asked them to ignore it, and within moments it disappeared.

I wasn't getting much sleep either. I was either at the hospital or exhausted in the Yorkshire flat, trying to pay attention to my other two children. The extended family was helping a lot, but I still needed to be their dad.

Any possible chance of romance with Vickie evaporated due to my neglect of her. I was moody and sullen, I had nothing to give. She understood and was beautiful in that, making it easy for me to let go at the expense of her own happiness.

Maybe her insightful personality saw that there was nothing I could give her, and equally she asked for nothing. The parting was a gift to me, a precious one.

I was already emotionally wrecked and couldn't cope with more trauma. The directors, on the other hand, acknowledging these uncertain times, heaved a sigh of relief. They didn't want any fundamental revision of my life, or theirs. We were all on the gravy train.

I couldn't go forward and be involved in operational control; I needed to pass the torch to someone else.

I talked to Peter and Jim together, offering both the Group Managing Director role to effectively control the three main companies and one or two of the 'concept' companies we were trialling at the time.

Peter didn't want the responsibility and Jim said he didn't feel capable.

We discussed selling. We thought we could easily get between seven and ten million pounds – the three of us would never have to work again.

We also knew we'd got a fantastic sales team in place to take advantage of the Ward Evans Atlantic Rowing Challenge that was just over a year away, and in terms of new business we were putting on something approaching one million pounds of fees in our corporate venture alone, with excellent retention on existing clients.

We were putting capital value on the company of £1.25-£2 million per year in extra value. The financial services side would benefit in correlation to the growth achieved on the general business, so that was moving forward at pace too.

Ward Evans Direct had just moved to its own office in Leeds so that it could attract additional telesales staff, so we were geared up there for considerable expansion.

But we decided to keep the business. We had too many ambitious people in there to sell it from under them, even if I had good reason to do so. I'd stay on as chief executive and James would be offered Group Managing Directorship.

He was overjoyed, though saddened his appointment came in these circumstances. He did, however, have his own thoughts and regime to put in place, with a nod of recognition that Jim and Peter were untouchable. They would not stand in his way and would assist him in all he looked achieve. After all, the position had been offered to them and they turned it down.

CHAPTER 7

Buying the estate

My domestic life was in chaos. Aside from the Harrogate flat and the hospital, there was the occasional mad dash to London, where I could try and lose myself in the bright lights.

I was frantic with worry over Oliver. I tried to keep positive but as soon as I allowed my mind to drift, it went to 'what if?' scenarios. The term 'living nightmare' took on a new meaning. I only had peace while asleep – when I could sleep.

I was a stranger to both my belongings and emotions. It felt like my outside didn't match my inside. Nothing was permanent. I desperately needed a base that meant more than bricks and mortar; somewhere I could relax with the children.

When Oliver got over all this, I wanted somewhere they could run and play. A beautiful house came up for sale, close to both the family home and the York office. Without thinking about it too much I put an offer in, and within six weeks had secured it and moved in the contents of a couple of suitcases. That was all I had.

Everything else stayed at the matrimonial home. Maybe it was guilt, but I didn't want to touch anything there other than the suits I had.

The purchase happened so quickly, I hadn't even walked the land. So it was with both apprehension and excitement that I took long walks around the 185 acres of low-lying shooting land with its three lakes and five flighting ponds, formerly owned by the Duke of Norfolk.

In walking, I tried to make sense of where my life was heading and the realisation that what seemed certain never really is. The only constant was change. In fairy stories, adversity pulls people together to form a bond of love, to take on the world.

I thought that might happen to Sue and I, but in reality we were ships that passed in the night. She was at the hospital; I was in the office, with the children, in London; I'd be at the hospital, she'd be at the family home. The only time we were together was in front of Lewis to hear the next terrifying instalment of what would happen.

All relationships under strain have a time-critical period in which to heal, where it's make or break. Ours went by, unrecognised and unacknowledged, as all thoughts and emotions turned to the more important issues of Oliver's treatment and eventual rehabilitation. There were no real fights or raised voices, just a walking, nervous exhaustion as we made our own lonely ways through this nightmare. Living apart became the norm, and I guess buying another house was an acceptance that this was no temporary situation. I needed to lay down plans for the future.

"What the bloody hell are you doing, buying this?" Jim asked.

"Putting roots down," I said.

"I'd have bet on an apartment in London, above Langan's or somewhere!"

"It's for the kids," I explained, which was half-true. I had a vision of Oliver and me, flying around on quad bikes with animals, horses and ponies in attendance.

"I just want to settle," I said to Jim, who was still shaking his head.

"You need help," he told me.

"I'm onto it," I said, "I'm interviewing for an estate manager to look after the place."

"I meant a doctor."

I'd decided that cooping myself up in a bachelor flat was absurd when I could have somewhere to walk and relax, fish and be at peace with the world. And what a place for the children to run free and visit.

James got on with running the business and, with the rest of the board, decided it would be a good thing to consolidate our offices in York and Leeds under one roof. Within a few months we headed for two floor and ten thousand square feet of high-rise modern office block in Leeds.

Chris, our internal financial accountant, had done a splendid job with him, two other ladies and a part-time staff. He decided he was too much of a home-bird to move to Leeds and I understood his decision.

The company was moving to a new phase, and it was the right time for him to go. Chris didn't like big business; he moved on to do audit work with small accounting practice in York, and James and the rest set about finding a replacement.

We'd had the same auditors for years and they knew our systems and procedures, so with their assistance such a change shouldn't be too traumatic.

I found an old colleague who'd worked as second-in-command at the previous company with Chairman Neville, and after some deliberations involving another Porsche and share options we welcomed our new group finance director.

The idea was that he would oversee all finances and split the team into internal and office departments. Within six months we had some twenty people working in our finance department. Looking in from the outside I thought this was a bit alarming, and James was as concerned as I was.

Malcolm, our non-executive director, helped James mentor our new recruit as he was a chartered accountant by training and could offer guidance. In addition, our existing auditors sent someone to assist with new programmes and procedures that we were told were necessary for additional growth.

We were expecting to expand considerably and the Atlantic challenge was just months away; we hoped to capitalise on that exposure. This meant everything – people, systems, management information – needed resourcing in order of priority. So the sudden explosion from around four people to what eventually amounted to twenty seven wasn't just for our existing requirements but also for new challenges yet to come.

In this context it seemed sensible enough. And between James and the rest of the boards, there were some seventeen directors with over two hundred people in the company – that was sufficient brainpower to work it all through. After all, they were being paid well enough.

Dark days ahead

I was happy and relieved to give up operational control. I couldn't concentrate on the detail, never my strong point, and didn't like to micro-manage the business in the first place.

But it was moving fast and needed constant attention, and I just wasn't up to it. It was also obvious that I'd be spending a lot of time at the hospital with Oliver, so my lack of physical presence at board meetings would be an issue.

James made the point that if he was to do the job as Group Managing Director, he needed to be allowed to get on with it – there's a difference between allocation and delegation. I agreed. The company had been built around my fairly strong personality, so James would require absolute authority to cut through that and introduce the new regime.

He knew about the alternative, which was to sell, but why give up all this work to another major international when we were close to being the UK's largest private insurance broker?

This view was shared by Peter and Jim who, despite all the money they would have got, didn't want to think about either working for anyone else or taking early retirement.

If selling wasn't an option, I was advised that the money I received back from the company should be equal and equivalent to having the money in the bank, which seemed fair enough. So if my personal shareholding was worth six million or so at the time and interest rates were five per cent, I should receive around £300,000 in either salary or dividends.

From a monetary point of view, continuing the business was dependent on my being in the same financial position as if I had cashed it all in. I didn't care which of the companies it came from and in what form.

So long as that formula could be maintained, I'd have no need to sell and nor would Jim and Peter. This was important for all directors and middle managers to know; they needed to understand the rationale behind the thinking. It was logical, honest and straightforward. If a crisis of confidence were to sweep the company, whole teams of people could walk out in days and the business could quickly be ruined.

At that time there were plenty of envious open arms from competitors should there be that crisis. They needed to know the company was in safe hands and that my personal problems were not going to immediately result in a shotgun sale that ended with them working for a company they'd enjoyed taking business from for seven years.

It was okay having a personal, charismatic leadership style but as Churchill found out, it's a one-trick pony. I felt a change of leadership would be a good thing as it would broaden the appeal of the Business to potential employees and its customers.

We had a product providers' dinner at Rudding Park in Yorkshire, an annual thank you event. It had been nothing other than a celebratory and information-giving dinner for all insurers to announce our financial figures.

We always believed in freedom of financial information and always issued full reports and accounts showing highest salaries and such, so that everyone understood exactly what was going on. We were proud of our results and this transparency separated us from other brokers.

Thank you dinners were pretty rare in our industry. Broker entertaining insurer wasn't exactly traditional. Most establishment types thought that if they wanted the broker's business it was up to them to wine and dine. We saw it differently – without insurers' support we couldn't write the new business we were piling on or keep it at renewal. We needed them.

It was a good time to announce both my resignation and the new corporate board. Other than James, who was Group Managing Director of all the trading companies, the only other senior person from the old Corporate board was Peter. He agreed to remain in charge of insurer relationships, and played a very important role in keeping stability and continuity. Big Jim agreed to see if he could bring some entrepreneurial vigour to Financial Services. The stronger the connection between general business and financial services, the more would be transacted.

More than thirty of the insurance world's great and good were there for dinner when I made my speech, and another 30 around the bar to mingle and talk after the formal proceedings.

The evening was a great success, with the highlight being a street magic show by Paul Xenon – absolutely amazing at close quarters. No one seemed to mind my resignation; some had heard about Oliver and appeared to understand.

I was happy the company was doing well and was in safe hands, and felt that with everything going on in my personal life I needed time out to be with Oliver and consider the opportunities the new house and estate would bring.

It was lovely to see over a thousand pheasant chicks arrive at Woodland Grange and put into the numerous pens. The estate manager had also ordered 250 ducks to feed on the various flighting ponds.

The place seemed to come alive, back to its natural order. It was such a relief to walk around the fields and woodland, hearing the sound of the wildlife animate the environment.

Pheasants, woodpigeons, deer and ducks roamed free; we even had the occasional green woodpecker. That first year we put a thousand chicks down and I never got around to actually shooting them; I liked them around the place. The neighbouring farms were quick to point out that I was going against a kind of etiquette as all their pheasants buggered off to my land where they had plenty of food and were safe. Come to think of it, as I walked around the rides and pathways I had thought there were a lot more than a thousand birds kicking around! They also looked a lot fatter than they should – some appeared to have trouble flying at all, they were so well-fed.

It wasn't an easy time to enjoy such trappings, but Woodland Grange did give me an escape and I found myself retiring there more and more.

It was lovely to tell Oliver about the times we would have once he got out of hospital and many evenings were filled with my listening to Oliver's plans for the pheasants, fish and cattle. We both wanted to escape from our immediate surroundings and this, through our planning and imagination, was the way to do it.

It was strange how cocooned we felt with the curtains around us, watching television or just lying together. It was if we were on a sea and didn't know where we'd be washed up or when – safely to shore or crashing to a rocky end? Whatever it was, I wanted us to be together. But only Oliver could take the poison, the pain and the sickness. As much his mother and I were there, only Oliver could physically battle for survival.

He went through chemo with enormous and genuine courage, hardly complaining. He was getting so many drugs he had a portal fitted to the main artery on his neck, allowing immediate and pain-free drug administration. Oliver was nicknamed 'Lightning' in hospital as he took his oral drugs so quickly.

It was amazing to see this little boy showing such courage in the face of adversity. The chemo was taking effect, though, and he was at his worst one particular night. All his hair had fallen out, other than a few persistent clumps, and his head was itchy from dry, burnt skin that appeared tissue-like. He looked so exhausted and his weight was falling alarmingly as the chemo suppressed his appetite. The usual rounds of steroids were used to try and bolster his strength.

In the inevitable cries and dim light one evening, I looked into his sleeping, moon-like face. He looked like a little lost alien. Not of this world, and not long for it. The nurse's torch that checked on him at regular intervals looked like it could shine straight through his transparent body. He had just lost a friend in intensive care and, while it wasn't talked about, he knew his little buddy had gone forever. He knew that he'd had cancer, too. I wondered if Oliver ever made the connection.

Oliver never spoke about it, but I felt that there was wisdom in him beyond his tender years - a knowledge born from this experience. It was the first and only time I felt I was going to lose this little boy. Sobbing quietly I felt overwhelmed with hopelessness, fear, and panic that there was nothing that I could do for him other than be there, as his mother had too, night after night, day after day. It was a credit to her that throughout this she would never leave Oliver alone, and he never was out of her sight other than when he was with me or his grandparents.

I found myself on my knees by the camp bed, silently begging God to spare Oliver. I wasn't particularly religious, but it was the only thing to do, and it felt right and humbling. I was embarrassed that I hadn't turned to God before – why should my prayers be answered now? But it was a prayer for Oliver so maybe, just maybe, He would listen.

"Take everything away," I pleaded. "But preserve and sustain this little boy."

Every parent I know would gladly change places with their gravely sick child. There is no pain like having to watch your innocent infant go through such trauma.

A nurse came in and asked if I was okay, and I told her I thought I'd dropped a bottle. I'm sure she didn't believe me, but busy as usual she left. She'd probably seen all manner of strange behaviour in that ward.

It was hard for the nurses, too, being underpaid and over-worked and then seeing this day after day. They couldn't afford to get too emotionally involved with any one of their young charges. But, inevitably, the best did.

I got back into bed, ashamed that I'd called upon the Almighty, when I'd never really paid any attention to Him when things were going well. I had no moral right to call now, didn't even really have the faith. But I needed Him, and so did Oliver. It was a final and sincere hope, an act of desperation.

My eldest daughter, three years older than Oliver, came home inconsolable one day. Word had got out that her brother had cancer.

Children can be most cruel at such times, as well as understanding beyond their years. One had come up to her in the playground and had taken delight in imparting news to the effect that she'd heard her parents talking and they said Oliver was going to die.

"Your brother will die of cancer," she said pointing a jabbing finger.

My daughter was distraught, to say the least, and so were Sue and I. But the headteacher took strong and decisive action, with the assistance of the family liaison officer.

The latter arranged a workshop for the whole of daughter's year. It was about the various types of cancer and its effects; it taught them that it was indeed serious and many children did die, but it wasn't an automatic death sentence.

The children were asked how they thought it affected Oliver and Charlotte, and their immediate family, and did they think there was anything they could do to help?

It was another tear-jerking time. The kindness that was then showed to us all was a blessing, and one that I will always remember and be grateful for.

I'd come to realise the value of the family liaison officer and the merits of a good school that listened. My daughter had a few days off while this was going on and I took her skiing in Courcheval. It was so difficult for her, with Sue and I breaking up and her brother in hospital. And it's very easy to ignore the wants and needs of your other children when you're focused on the one in hospital, or your own personal sadness. She'd been ignored a great deal and needed her own time, with Sue and me separately if not together.

Thank goodness for our extended family. My mum continued to steer her own path, smuggling in the fish and chips frowned on because of some health and safety rules or other. She put them in her coat as she swept around the ward, eventually taking orders from other little children for this Friday night treat.

She also undertook her own private investigation into who was nicking Oliver's milk. She hadn't forgotten the case of the missing slippers.

"They have to get up early to beat me, old love," she'd say. Now she really had someone to pursue, someone to beat, someone to get up early for. In this crazy strange world, some days everything seemed quite normal, as if it was all meant to be; a cruel but beautiful piece of the jigsaw.

The estate manager and the poachers

Lou, the estate manager, was in his early thirties and a kind, gentle, new-age sort of guy who'd spent a lifetime around horticulture.

His parents were farmers and land, planting, animal husbandry and building things from nothing was second nature to him. It was important we got on as he'd be around the estate more than me, and I'd have to trust him implicitly while I was away.

He protected the estate as if it was his own, and we talked about the possibility of him building something a suitable distance away from the main house that would be allowed under an agricultural licence. In many respects, therefore, we were both dreaming about what it could mean for our families long-term.

I'd been in and out of the hospital or whizzing down to London, so Lou had to keep a sharp eye out for when I landed. When word got out I was back, he'd shoot over for chat.

"Mike, I know you're not too bothered about this shooting lark and you've got a lot on your mind, but I've seen some pheasants that have been shot at night and not collected."

"What do you mean, Lou?" I asked in genuine surprise.

"Well, we've got poachers. Could be anybody. Everyone knows you put a load down and haven't shot them, you're hardly ever here, so either these are people who want them back - drive them onto their own land – or just people who want to sell a few brace."

The idea of strangers roaming the land at night scared me.

"Well I sure don't like the idea of people knocking around in the dark. For one thing it's getting dark bloody early at the moment and my kids are around, and for another I've just seen the bloody *Blair Witch Project* and it's scared the shit out of me!"

Lou considered this.

"Well, I can do a few night checks, but whatever you do don't confront them by yourself. It's dark out there and these guys have got guns so you might hear them but you won't see them, and more importantly, they won't see you. They could easily mistake you for a fox, a deer or anything. Best leave it."

I tossed and turned in bed, wondering what the hell was going on out there. Lou kept checking and told me they'd been back.

I went to the pub, pissed off at this violation. I wanted to spread the news. For all I knew, these guys might be in this pub laughing at me. I talked loudly, saying I knew about the problem and that we had a team of people guarding the woods, money no object, etc.

I had a few drinks, got annoyed, and repeated that everything was under control. Then I had a few more. Proud of myself, message delivered, I went home in a sour mood.

I shouldn't have believed my own line about being safe as houses out there because, fortified with hard talk and hard drink, I decided to underline my assertions by getting on the big red quad bike and driving around the estate, making as much noise as possible. If anyone was out there, the buggers would know I was too.

This was silly. In the darkness, despite the headlights, I felt completely alone. The beams disappeared into an inky black.

I took off down a little path into the woodland, remembering that Lou had said to make as much noise as I could if confronted by poachers, to make out I was there mob-handed, and to head back to the house and call him urgently.

Then I saw a flicker of light.

I turned the quad off and squinted into the darkness, waiting for my eyes to become accustomed to the night. I was sure I saw lights, and I realised I was scared stiff and well away from the house. But sooner or later, I'd have to turn the engine back on to get back and call Lou or the police. And they'd hear me, maybe go for me.

As I sat on the bike, all my bravado drained away. I couldn't see their lights now; maybe they were as scared as me? They were sure to have heard me approach.

I sat there, wondering who would make the first move. I waited, and waited. There was nothing I could do, so I took a deep breath and turned the quad back on.

There, in the darkness, I saw it again – lights moving, slowly and quietly. I could see torches moving. I inched forward slowly, the engine purring under me.

What should I do? Turn around and go for help or continue towards them? I couldn't see behind me and I didn't know whether I could manoeuvre the quad around and get back. If I followed the path, I knew I'd eventually come full circle back to the house and safety. I had to decide – fight or flight?

Adrenalin surged and I could hear my heart pound. Who were these people? It would take me ages to get back to the house. I wasn't going to walk, they'd surely seen me and I was certain they'd heard me.

They must know the difference between a quad and a deer or a pheasant – they wouldn't shoot me, would they?

I had to fight. I turned the quad bike straight into the direction of the lights.

"Right you sod!" I shouted at the top of my voice. I pretended I was with a group of mates, yelling as loud as I could, the noise ringing and echoing through the dense woodland. Pheasants roosting in surrounding trees flew and called in alarm.

"John, you go left; Jim, get the guys and go round the back..." I tried to sound convincing.

"Come on!" I screamed at the top of my voice, hurtling towards God knew what, doing a poor imitation of Charge of the Light Brigade. I was astride the big red quad, one arm waving like a lunatic, one on the throttle. I was getting closer, but so were the lights.

Shit! They weren't backing off, they were coming at me!

I needed more speed. I'd go straight through the middle and keep going until I got back to the house.

"Don't stop," I told myself, "and when you get there, keep going and crack off home. Get more help, just disperse them. Don't look back. Too late to turn round. Keep going, faster....."

"Come on!" I shouted. I hurtled forward, into the lights. Then I hit something. I wasn't hurt, and it was a strange sensation. I flew the air; the quad had stopped and I'd been catapulted off it, cartoon-like.

This was novel. What happened now? I waited for the pain, more bemused and fascinated than scared.

Splash!

I was swimming. Then the quad bike hit the water in front of me – thank God it didn't land on top of me! But I was swimming and dripping wet in a blue-striped Gucci suit. I got to the side of the lake, realising what had happened.

"You bloody stupid idiot," I said to myself. There were no gangs of poachers roaming my lands, preparing to take me on. I'd just seen my own headlights reflected in the water.

I trudged back to the house, dried off and crashed into bed. The next thing I knew was when Lou and the housekeeper burst through the doors looking anxious.

"Thank God!" said Lou. "I did the morning rounds and saw the quad floating upside down in the lake."

"We thought you were dead! Drowned or something," said the housekeeper, looking relieved that she didn't have to find another crazy house to work in.

"No, not quite," I said.

"Poachers?" asked Lou.

"Drink actually... Let them have the sodding pheasants."

Lou shook his head. "I see you found the new path down to the lake then!"

Oliver's homecoming

Oliver's treatment was finally coming to an end. I'd heard much talk about courageous children battling these sorts of diseases, but I think sometimes the word 'courage' is misplaced.

It suggests that there's a choice where none exists. You either get on with it or you don't. I learnt in my time on the ward that real courage is shown in the way you choose to conduct yourself within that battle, the one all inmates go through. I saw a lot of courageous children being good-humoured, uncomplaining and, in some cases, tragically accepting their fate with nothing but a serene disinterest.

Oliver was courageous. He took all his pills like 'lightning', thus earning the nickname. He did it without masking the taste with orange juice or chocolate, just got on with it. He never complained about the poison running through his thin body, or made a fuss when he'd snag his line against an object attached to his main artery. The very idea made my stomach turn and head dizzy. He just took it in his stride.

His body had withstood as much chemo as it could and now stretched before us was a world of tests, waiting and x rays. In short, a world of remission.

Oliver had been in hospital for what seemed like forever and his treatment delivered routinely. Once given, there was nothing more to do. You can't just 'top up' chemo for good measure.

But administration in the hospital was surrounded by bureaucracy, and delivery at the sharp end was often slowed down by faceless individuals pushing paper behind the scenes. When I mentioned to the hospital administrators that we were leaving, we got what, sadly, is very much a standard response.

"What, Oliver is due to leave today?"

"No," I said. "Oliver is leaving this morning."

"Well, Pharmacy needs to know," I was informed, "and they are very busy!"

"Are you seriously telling me we have spent all these days and nights here and nobody knows we're off today?"

"I'll go check," said a nurse who was with the administrator.

"Get dressed, Oliver," I said. "Your mum's waiting for you at home, and so is your family."

"They'll get to you soon," the consultant doing exit checks told me.

"No," I said, still grateful for all the help, treatment and advice he and his colleagues had given. But Oliver's needs were more important than any words of gratitude.

"I'm sorry, but we are gone, mate. Oliver has spent more time in here than any little boy should ever have to. He is not staying one minute more. If pharmacy can't sort it out right now I'll send a taxi." I marched out with Oliver padding alongside me.

The consultant, bless him, got the drugs himself. "I'll be crucified," he said. "I'm not supposed to do that."

I looked at him. It wasn't his fault. What frustrations must these people feel who work hard and want the best, only to be let down by faceless bureaucracy?

"Good luck, mate," I said. "I'm grateful. I really am." I meant it.

I took one look back and, with a few tears in my eyes, said a silent prayer that we wouldn't be back again. Oliver took his first uncertain steps out, clinging to me as he felt the wind around his balding head sprouting the first signs of new hair.

He pulled a baseball cap on and we walked hand in hand into the bright, cold day. I glanced across at him; he was looking around, seeing things anew. Of course, he hadn't been out in the fresh air for so long to see all those things we take for granted. He caught my eye, and smiled.

"You still got the pheasants, Daddy?"

"Yes, at least a thousand. You'll see them soon enough and you have to find names for all of them!" I said as we climbed in the car and set off home.

It was a special day.

It was strange taking Oliver back. Sue came to the estate to greet him. She, like Oliver and I, had become somewhat institutionalised. Hospitals are awful places; no one goes in with a singing heart.

But when you've stayed in one for some time, it's a safe environment and you get into the routine. The world outside, by contrast, was frightening.

This was coupled with a feeling that when chemo was being administered, we were doing something active; remission was a passive experience. We could only wait, watch and hope.

We had to forget about it, count the time down to relative safety. Get the probability equation into safe figures after five years. A waiting game, and hope it wasn't the other type of disease.

No one is ever cured completely of cancer; remission just becomes permanent. This required a change of thinking for me.

Before I'd needed support; now I craved distraction.

There was plenty on the cards. I might not be operational but I always got automatic copies of all directors' e-mails, and could listen with interest to the dialogue that was going on, jumping in with my two penn'orth when I thought it was appropriate.

It was like changing the steering of a fast-moving vehicle; too hard or sudden and it goes off the road. But once you had a short, medium and long term objective, you didn't need to redefine it every week. I had to occupy myself with something else.

James had done very well on the face of it. Business in all sectors was booming, and it hadn't escaped him that with Oliver coming out of the hospital, I might want to climb back into the driving seat. He made his views clear quickly and, indeed, it would be unfair of me to call the shots and try to return things to how they were.

I didn't want to, anyway. I hadn't missed the pressure of running a big business. I wanted to enjoy myself, digging out a few more lakes, buggering off to London and Palma, and generally swanning around.

I'd headed the company for seven years, and grown it to an award-winning business. James had taken up the challenge and not only continued its success but enhanced it.

I was looking forward to seeing Oliver and his sisters enjoying building dens and the like in my acres of woodland.

"Daddy, you've got a footballer's house," he said when he saw Woodland Grange. It was the finest accolade he could give.

"Wait until you see this, Oliver!"

I pressed the remote control and the large, wrought-iron gates opened as if by magic. Lights automatically lit up the long drive.

"Wow, Daddy, you've even got TV cameras! What are they for?"

"They're to protect our pheasants," I said with a smile.

His granddad was there, and he had a present to share with his sisters. Granddad had bought them a shiny blue quad bike.

Oliver saw it hidden behind bushes as we played a find-the-present clue game. His lovely nature came out when he immediately turned to say thank you, rather than run straight to the bike. But it wasn't long before he was flying around with one sister on the back and one on a metal tray that he tied behind.

"Do we have fish, Daddy?" the children asked.

"Too right," I told them. "A long time ago they were all documented when the lake was dredged and now they're a lot bigger. There a good few carp in there of over twenty pounds, you can sometimes see them in the sunshine."

"Oh boy!" said Oliver.

I pinched myself. One minute in hospital, the next sitting on the patio with my children, overlooking the main lake with my parents, and even Sue had found a boyfriend. Everything was beautiful; everything seemed to be turning out well.

'Strange how things can quickly change,' I thought. There's always hope.

"You know, Dad," I said. "We've said it before, but it really doesn't get better than this, does it?"

Dad shook his head. He seemed distant, lost in his own world, as the kids came in and out of view. Taking it all in. Probably saying a silent prayer of thanks.

In retrospect, maybe he was thinking it was too good to be true.

And nothing lasts forever.

Launching the Atlantic Challenge

The Atlantic Challenge rowing race loomed, and before that we needed to perform a naming ceremony and launch a fifty-six foot sailing boat that would be part of the safety team for the rowing boats making their way across the ocean.

The boat was painted in Ward Evans colours and new logo and, since the launch was close to my son ending his treatment, the directors of Group Plc agreed it should be called *Oliver*.

The launch, in Southampton, coincided with the last sailing regatta before the race – skilfully negotiated by James. It was a beautiful day and there were around a hundred people there as nine boats, including the Ward Evans sailing yacht, were moored in readiness. Oliver never flinched as he went up to the boat to name it.

I said: "The determination of these people sailing cannot be under-estimated, each on a personal journey greater than that of crossing an ocean, each facing their own challenges with fortitude and courage. But the most courageous person I know amongst all the people I have been privileged to meet is my little boy, Oliver, who battled against cancer without any safety net, and without complaint.

"The challenge wasn't one that he asked for or welcomed. But when the time came, he met it square on. He stepped up to the mark.

"I'm sure those who use the safety boat or need to call on it during their long and perilous journey across the Atlantic will be comforted to know it's around should it be required at any time, and I hope they might spare a thought for the little chap whose name is on the boat, who has travelled his own journey, and has reached the safety of his family and loved ones.

"In considering this, think also of all the other little people in hospitals up and down the country, who face their own challenges with the same courage and determination, day in and day out, often with no land in sight. All the competitors have chosen their challenge, the time, the type, and the place, but these people fighting cancer do not."

With that, Oliver was invited to smash a bottle of champers against the bow and there wasn't a dry eye in the house as he said in a loud, clear voice: "I name this boat Oliver!" to applause and smiles.

It was a very special moment. Chay and I hadn't much time as the boats left their moorings. I had almost forgotten I'd agreed to do the Row Around The Needles.

The Royal Corinthian Yacht Club

After agreeing to do the row, I learned it's quite dangerous to sail close to The Needles due to the strong and swirling currents.

But we'd agreed, as it would provide the best backdrop photo opportunity, and hopefully the papers would carry it. If not for me, then for Chay, and with a bit of luck we'd get on the television – especially if something went wrong!

It was an honour to get into the same rowing boat as Chay – it's not often you can do that with the living legend who made his name as one half of the first two-man crew to row the Atlantic.

Chay was, of course, a natural despite his advancing years, but I was less certain. We were strapped in, but the lateral movement of the boat made me feel I could fall out at any time. I'm told there's a picture of me with one of my oars the wrong way round – detail wasn't my strongest point.

In fairness, the pictures looked good and made Meridian TV. The *Oliver* was twenty five metres away and a helicopter hovering overhead had to be told to move as you could see the down draught, it was so close.

Chay said it was nothing like when he did his world record, but I was leaving nothing to chance. Every creature comfort was just out of sight of the photographers and TV cameras – I knew I could order a gin and tonic and have it on the rowing boat within minutes. It was only a photo opportunity after all, I had to constantly tell Chay when he kept chiding me for rowing like a sissy.

But the Royal Corinthian Yacht Club awaited, and I was soon on dry land, showered and changed, and mixing with guests and embellishing my tales of derring-do while Chay looked on, shaking his head and smirking.

"Whatever happened on that rowing boat stays on that rowing boat, okay?" I told him.

"All I'm saying is, despite your crises, I knew I'd get you home, mate."

Chay smiled, taking it in good humour. But in order to burst my bubble, I think, he came up halfway through my story of waves and swirling currents and interrupted:

"You could still get someone important to launch the Challenge you know."

"No thanks, Chay," I said, Peter listening to every word and agreeing with me.

"We've spent enough, and it sounds like more money to me."

"Its only bloody money, man!" he said with a cunning smile on his face. He had something planned.

"Well, I'm looking to get some real publicity for the BT Global challenge, because I know how to do it. You know, I knew your little company was too small for this type of global sponsorship; you have to have vision, invest in your brand. You say no, Mike; I say yes." he said warming to his subject. Seeing he wasn't making an impact, he walked off but turned around and, for dramatic effect, added: "You know – I'm talking about getting Blair," he said, giving this declaration sufficient gravitas and effect by pausing as he stood there, ready to receive our gasps of appreciation.

"I hear he's a bloody good dancer, our Lionel!" Peter said, quick as a flash.

Chay shook his head, acknowledging the laughter of those in shouting distance, before returning to the bar.

"Fucking idiots!" he said, settling for another gin

The race start

The Ward Evans Atlantic Rowing Challenge started in Tenerife and headed three thousand nautical miles to Barbados, following prevailing trade winds.

A small contingent and I flew across to start the race as sponsors. We immediately came up against problems, not least that the local harbour master declared one of the reserved harbours from where the boats were supposed to be launched as unusable. This was a small detail that should have been sorted by Challenge Business.

It didn't make for a smooth introduction but Chay just looked for another harbour and moved everyone there within twenty four hours.

When questioned he merely said: "We can all sit around talking about it or we can do something about it. So let's get on."

We could get the competitors to move, but not the bars and restaurants. For the poor owners this was to be their big pay-day week, and the circus was about to up tents without a drink being served.

This led to a bit of a Mexican stand-off between them and Chay; they'd waited and geared up for three years to entertain, feed and water the competitors and the spectators who were due there for the race start. It amounted to their Christmas, and while it was a difficult decision to move the race start, we apparently had no choice. It seemed an outbreak of a PR war could spark at any time. Rowers were pissed off, as were the bar owners, and relatives who'd flown to see the start didn't know where the boats were.

In addition, the Iraq conflict looked like it was going to kick off in a big way. America was cranking up the rhetoric with Iraq and the UK was right behind. If the Tornados started to fly, we had it on good authority we'd be in trouble with a race that we could hardly delay.

Jim said: "Come on, Mike, they can't blame that on us!"

"No," said the tech advisor of the race. "But if America and the UK go in, then we happen to know that all the GPRS satellite navigations systems will go down and you'll have between thirty to fifty rowing boats heading in all sorts of directions across the big blue…. Some won't make it."

Marvellous. No harbour to launch the race from and a chance that all the navigation equipment would go down in the middle of the ocean. Weren't we in insurance?

I could see it on *News at Ten*, boats everywhere and nobody knowing where they were, rescue services being stretched to breaking point.

"Well," Peter perked up, "How the hell do we know that? It might not be that bad. Who knows what's going to happen?"

A few of the tech guys from Challenge Business laughed.

"Well let's just say this; you don't get electricians built like those brick shithouses, do you? I thought you lot at least would have twigged by now," said one, pointing to two men-mountains in the distance. "All I'm saying is, they're not sparkies!"

"Then why would they say they were?" Peter asked what we were all thinking.

It soon became clear that these polite jovial giants were Special Forces. It was obvious once it was pointed out, but the guys that big Jim had been enjoying some Green Fuckers with did look most unlike any electricians I'd ever seen.

"Crikey," I said, "Come on then, I'm the bloody sponsor – any other military around?" I asked.

"Couple of guys may, just may, be from Delta Force. That's about it. I don't know for sure. We don't ask too much in these circumstances, it's just not the done thing."

"Not the bloody American plumbers, the bastards!" Jim added his humour to the occasion. "I've spent a few nights trying to out-drink those buggers. Didn't seem interested in quoting on my new bathroom suite either!"

Chay mumbled that all competitors had the sun and the stars, and that's all they needed. He gave what amounted to a sermon about how it didn't matter when you were out there on the blue, staring at your little brown toes.

"That's what's it's all about, you know. Once you're out there by yourself, staring at your toes, ask yourself would you want to be anywhere else in the world? That's why people compete. It's to get away from all the trappings of technology and modern life. Just you and the stars. That's all that's needed."

This romantic view didn't stop our PR company having a complete fit. They, after all, along with Challenge Business, would have to do crisis management when the boats got lost in the Atlantic.

"There's a hell of a lot of water out there, Chay," said one.

"They just might be staring at their toes a little bit longer than they thought if they get lost. They might turn into burnt chipolatas," Peter stated.

It was obvious that this crisis wouldn't upset Chay with his lifelong mantra of "They say no, we say yes".

Our poor PR guys, trying to avoid a calamity, continued to try and find a solution.

"Well, excluding the obvious electricians and plumbers, Chay, some of these teams are teachers, husbands and wives. They're not going to know, as they have been training per your tech spec. They rely on what they thought was standard issue in the boat, GPS. And if we don't get them home to Barbados their toes may be all that's left of them!"

"Don't worry, boys," Chay said, "I'll invite them on a crash course for anyone who doesn't know how to navigate. Shouldn't be out there if they can't navigate anyway. Wasn't like that in my day."

Apart from the obvious distractions, there was an unreal ambience around the place. Each crew checked out the others' boats, some doubting the other's assets, others being tremendously helpful and kind, assisting hands-on where they could, trying to get the kit together. Each vessel had to go through a tech inspection before it was allowed out and people were working hard to finish.

"I was talking to the competitors and they feel a bit guilty about having to move their boats to a different start site," I said. "To cheer things up, let's have a big do before they go. We can issue drink vouchers. Hand them out to competitors and have them redeemed only in the bars along the original front.

"That would guarantee that only participating bars got the business, as we originally planned. Might get us some goodwill back as well."

This was put into effect and a great time was had by all, with the possible exception of the harbour master and Chay looking daggers at each other all night.

There was no formality, just families and friends milling around a strip of bars, beers flowing and music playing. All exceptional people, courageous, individually unique, and adventurous. It was another great night, a unique experience of bringing together pioneers from across the world. We had competitors from New Zealand, Australia, America, Italy, Russia, France, Sweden, Finland, the UK, Ireland and, as I proudly pointed out, God's own county – Yorkshire.

They all possessed that quality of spirit, challenging the norm, wanting adventure. Every conversation was sprinkled with what each would do once they got this little trip out of the way.

I heard people say: "I have to be back in two and a half months because I'm off on a solo across the Pacific. That's six thousand nautical miles; this is just a warm-up."

And: "Have you heard from Johnny? I keep seeing him around town pulling six heavy tyres behind him whilst he jogs eight miles a day to prepare for his trip to the Pole."

We Ward Evans boys walked around with our mouths open at these stories. We were truly with people from a different league. It was easy for us to forget that they'd be out by themselves, facing thirty and forty foot waves for up to three or four months.

The next night, Chay arranged a barbecue for competitors and guests.

"Cost me nothing, this, Mike," Chay said, proudly pointing to the assembled crowd.

"They wanted the bar takings and I said yes, if they did the sausages!"

He made a small speech, which the competitors largely ignored because they blamed him for moving the launch venue. Chay, irrepressible as ever, saw things differently. The stage was well away from where the bar was, so most people turned and looked, then went back to talking to each other. Chay, undeterred, got on with it and came to our table proud as punch afterwards.

"What did you think of the speech?" he asked us.

"Have you just given a speech, Chay?" replied Jim. "I admit I heard a noise but I thought it was just the neighbours complaining!"

"Bastards!" Chay smiled, "Got me on that one. But it cost me nothing all this, you know," he said still with a smile on his face. "Any fool can make money. It's keeping it that's difficult!"

The actual start of the race was a bit of an anti-climax. The day before, America did initiate action against Iraq and the GPS systems went down as predicted. I wondered if some of the guys heading out might just prefer to be going home to God knew what on active service. But they were all off and gone, though it alarmed me somewhat.

"Shit!" I said, "Look! How come they're all off in different directions when they're heading for the same place?"

"Don't worry," Chay patiently explained that they were separating so they could get on with the job. "They want to be out there alone, that's all. They'll be fine."

I flew home, and kept in regular touch with Challenge Business's central office. The GPS systems were switched back on via satellite after a few days.

Apparently, there were some very shocked rowers out there when they found out their exact locations So much for sun and stars.

CHAPTER 8

Getting back

Back in the UK it was difficult to settle into anything resembling ordinary life while thoughts turned to the boats making their slow, precarious progress across the ocean. Reports came back almost immediately of various competitors in distress who had to give up for one reason or another.

One of the most striking was a husband and wife team where he, a six foot three giant of a man, could not stand being in the small boat in the dark. It freaked him out. He explained it was the noise of the waves and not knowing in pitch black from which direction it would hit the boat, and the constant jolting from one way then the other. It showed that no one could really train for the actual experience of being out there. We had nothing but admiration for him. He'd given it a go and had the courage to admit that it wasn't for him. For his wife, it was everything she dreamed of and she positively relished her time alone, the peace, solitude and excitement. He told his wife to carry on and she did so with enthusiasm, immediately capturing press attention and everyone's good wishes, as she continued to row herself across three thousand miles. It made great copy, and was a welcome human-interest factor for promoting the race.

The chap who left the rowing boat was obliged to board another, albeit larger, craft – the safety boat – and spend many more days at sea as the boat continued on sentry duty. It wasn't allowed to interfere with the competitors as this would rule them out of the Challenge, and any rescue would mean the rowing boat was burnt at sea.

This caused a great deal of emotional distress, as the material embodiment of someone's hopes and dreams would be in flames in the blackness of the ocean, not to mention the £25,000 it cost to build and equip the rowing boat. This had to be done so the boat wasn't a hazard to other craft that might wander in that general direction.

My life had become a lot more relaxed, if mundane. I got down to planning the landscaping of the Estate and looking through the many and exciting plans that Lou had for the place.

There was discussion about getting planning permission to build wooden tourist chalets, special breeding of animals, maybe increase the deer population and open up fishing to the public. It was a relief to concentrate on that area of life.

Every weekend the children came over, usually with my parents. The youngsters ran free and built dens and special quad paths, while Mum struck up a relationship with the housekeeper. Seeing them was rather like interrupting school kids behind the bicycle shed with their cigarettes.

"What are you looking at?" she'd say. "We've cleaned this bloody place top to bottom and we're having a well-deserved ciggie. No one can bottom it like me, old love!"

I used to look and shake my head. Anything that needed doing seemed always to go via my mother.

"If it was me..." Mum would start every sentence, without pausing to establish the fact that it clearly wasn't for her. Eventually, we took great delight in mimicking her.

Mum was happy there and Dad loved messing around on the lake with the children and the dogs.

Oliver's hair was growing back and he no longer felt the need for the usual uniform of young chemotherapy patients – the baseball cap. Everything in this rather grand and extensive garden was starting to look rosy.

Business seemed to speed along as ever. The companies seemed solid, if a little more mainstream, which was inevitable as we were established now and had a lot of clients to protect from competitors. It seemed a simple case of doing the same thing and very little else.

James was a master at cross-selling opportunities, like getting extra benefits onto client portfolios. The secret, he used to say, was to make a pint out of a half-pint glass. He certainly knew how to do that.

"You'll be getting some of those insurance war medals if you're not careful!" we ribbed him. James was justifiably proud of taking the reins and continued to expand the business with increased profit growth year upon year.

I settled into a small office on the estate that was perfect for me. I'd get up and, over a coffee, look over the emails that came in for my attention. Not that there were many; James was on the ball.

I'd taken the liberty of being silently copied in on all emails relating to the directors in the group holding business, as I was still interested and wanted to at least keep abreast of the dialogue, even if it was just listening in.

It worked for me, and through a series of what was kindly described by others as 'positive interjections' – or interfering, depending on your point of view – I believed I could keep general strategy on track.

I could and did leave the details to others, who were certainly earning six figure salaries and share options for dealing with it. The rule of thumb was that if it was new, I needed to look at it. If it was about doing the same thing better, it was James.

Having read and answered my e-mails, I'd have breakfast and meet with Lou. I loved to walk around the woods with the dogs, seeing the physical as well as seasonal changes to the beautiful estate. It really was stunning, and you could tell the month simply by looking at the vistas.

Then I'd change into suit and tie and go into Leeds, if I wasn't heading to London. Sue had found a steady boyfriend and he moved into the matrimonial home, which pleased me as I didn't like the thought of her there by herself. Maybe her happiness and new life helped appease any guilt I felt over our original break-up.

Either way, the world right now was a good place to be, and God willing would remain so. The rhythm and pace of life calmed me; it was like selling the business, but not quite letting go. I still had my family of corporate people and was regaining my actual family among what was on offer at Woodland Grange.

On the business side, James and his team came up with an excellent idea. Many of the clients were on finance agreements, effectively spreading the cost of their commercial premiums. It was felt we could make hundreds of thousands of pounds by buying the money in at one price and selling it out at another, effectively replacing the finance carriers.

The turnover of the business was well into the tens of million and many clients wanted this service, because if they were using our finance arrangements they weren't eating into their own bank facilities. A couple of appointments with James and Malcolm and an assortment of accountants that we now had internally soon got a credit line from the bank. I saw it just as another string to our increasing collection of bows.

James ran board meetings with almost military precision, having a private secretary to document everything. I didn't want or need to go to any other than the one I called for Group plc, the non-trading holding company.

The only cloud on the horizon was that the relatively new group finance director was having a hard time with account reconciliation and getting a handle on things. He put this original problem down to the sheer increase in volume of business. He'd ask his team about the balance on one account and in the morning it would be one figure; then, after checking again later, it became another. It was impossible, given the short amount of time between collecting the two figures. I asked Malcolm's view, as well as seeking assurances from James.

Malcolm said our system of accounting was groaning under the weight of transactions and he and our IT director, with the auditors, would work on another system that would cut account reconciliation time on the thousands of transactions that were happening every week.

Privately they said they wanted to look hard at the financial director as they weren't sure if he could cope. He walked around with a permanent worried look on his face. Other than that things seemed to be under control, with the occasional breakout of confusion and some chaos. But everyone was working hard, so it was agreed that only I and one guest would fly to Barbados where the first rowers were coming in. The publicity would be great.

Even with this prospect, it was hardly the party that we'd planned; there were rumours Chay wouldn't turn up either. That bothered me, and I needed to investigate.

Meeting Holly

Having just finished a long shareholders' meeting in the London office, I was too easily persuaded to have a few 'sharpeners' in a Japanese wine bar called Timusue Army, near Tower Bridge.

It wasn't a natural choice of venue for the Ward Evans boys, and you could imagine how Big Jim felt in that setting. He looked slightly bewildered, scared to move and somewhat self-conscious as a thousand Oriental eyes watched his every move. To them, he was a giant.

He tried his best to move in a slow, careful and deliberate way; otherwise, his sheer size would knock a drink over or crush someone. He'd turn left and right, apologising and causing havoc at the same time. The golden rule was for him to stay still - usually at the bar.

But the place had value as it was near-as-damn-it underneath our London office, next door to the spit-and-sawdust pub that Jim preferred. His usual protestations that it wasn't exactly the Dog & Duck could usually be overcome with a few green bastards at half-price during Happy Hour; for us it was just different to the usual places.

So we popped in for a quick drink. Some of my colleagues were going back to Yorkshire, but Peter, Johnny and I were staying at Butlers Wharf. Jim mooched behind us before taxis were called to scoop us up and take us on somewhere.

We burst in talking animatedly about the day's business and there, in a group with some colleagues, was Holly. They all looked stunning, surrounded by assorted men who hoped to catch their eyes. They looked like moths around the flame, all hesitating before crashing and burning when their advances were refused.

Johnny, always confident, had a Jack-the-lad attitude and volunteered to ask them to join us. They reluctantly, but surprisingly, agreed after some 'magical' words that Johnny said were secret, known only to boys who'd grown up on the streets of Manchester and were 'mad for it', in the words of Oasis, his favourite band.

He knew I'd been on my own for some time now and wasted no time in telling ladies about it. I felt like an overlooked second hand car that stood unloved and unused, being hawked to the nearest unsuspecting potential owner.

Johnny did his best to introduce me to women, but sometime they really didn't fit the bill. As Jim once put it: "He wants a playmate, not a primate!"

"Have you seen some of his ex-girlfriends?" Johnny would retort.

But it was an act of kindness, and different to Jim's approach of picking the weak ones off from the 'herd' when they got separated from the rest.

"Always get your banker, Mike – the quiet girls on the periphery. They'll be grateful for the attention. Then move on to the attractive ones – that way you can always come back to your banker, who'll be hoping for you to return later on," said Jim.

"Of course, you can just charm women, Mike, if you want to take the more steady, longer-term view. In that case you need a different approach."

" So how do you do that then, mate?" I foolishly asked. Jim's eyes glazed over as if he'd seen a beautiful vision, and of course we all settled down again while he shared his philosophy of love and courtship. You never knew where his conversation was going so you didn't want to miss it.

"Well, you can play the deaf-mute act," Jim said seriously. "It works every time. Have you never tried it? This is what my brother John and I do, anyway, and it works for me. We often go in the Punch & Judy in Covent Garden, it's always heaving in there with women on the lash.

"I take hold of Brother John's hand, and in we go. The thing is I've always got to be the deaf-mute, as John reckons I've got the face for it." Jim pulled an expression that only a simple man built like a brick outhouse can effect and maintain.

"What happens next, Jim?" we asked impatiently. He certainly had us captivated.

"Well, my brother walks up to a bunch of girls and starts talking to them - just ordinary chat, how are you and the like, while still holding my hand, and I continue to look the way I'm supposed. The conversation naturally gets around to me, still smiling away without a care in the word, then me brother tells them I'm a deaf-mute from birth and that he takes me out on occasion. Just to have a good time, few drinks, meet a few girls, because it's healthy for me to get out as much as I can.

"They usually smile at me and I give them my pleasant look back. They usually ask if I can understand everything and are generally very nice to me, more so than if I was 'normal', that's for sure. When the ice is broken, John tells them that even though I can't hear the music I'm a bloody good dancer. He says you just need to tap me once on the shoulder to start dancing and two taps to stop."

He went on: "So John taps me on the shoulder and I'm off like Michael Jackson – moonwalks, everything!" Jim gave us his moves and 'happy happy' simple face, twisting and turning while maintaining the expression.

"Two taps and I stop. Well, the girls love this and queue up to start tapping me on the shoulder. I feel the beat, and I'm off! Then John asks one if she'll take my hand so he can get everyone a drink and passes me onto her before she can say no. She'll see I'm a little uncertain so generally says something nice and that John will be back soon. I get a bit concerned and grab her hand more tightly. Anyway, John pisses off out of the place leaving me with her! Bish, bash, bosh – sorted!"

We were in hysterics. "How long does this last for, Jim?" I asked.

"Well all night sometimes, depends whether I fancy the girl. Usually when they realise John's gone and they get over the shock they make me dance and buy me drinks all night. I'm quite a turn for them. But I won't let her hand go. Usually one of them takes me home. It may be unusual but I'm telling you I've had a lot of success with the deaf-mute routine. I've met a few that way, mate. It might work for you, Mike, looking at your face..."

"Cheeky bastard!" I said, to laughter.

"Mind you, they don't half kick off in the morning when they hear me on the phone asking for a taxi to take me to the office!"

Jim did concede that the approach might not be for everyone; it was almost impossible to get right, unless you were Big Jim. There had to be something better than that approach, so Johnny's direct in-and-at-them with a smiling face and who-gives-a-damn attitude was, at the very least, a refreshing change.

The girls had been persuaded somehow to join our table and made it clear that it was just for one drink. I sat next to Holly and, to my complete surprise, she and I talked and talked and got on well.

She held me in the gaze of her brightest blue eyes. She was slim, tall and elegant, she had a devastating broad smile that was nothing short of hypnotic.

Her natural blonde, curly hair fell below her slim shoulders and tapered down her long, elegant back. Her poise and demeanour was one of sophistication. This lady clearly thought she was classy and encouraged others to think the same. Her accent was of a soft Irish lisp that Jim identified as Scottish.

"Well, I knew it was Celtic honey, that's what I mean," he said trying to recover his position. "Aren't Scottish people wet Irish people anyway? Something about history there, Mike," he said. Actually, Jim was by far the most educated person amongst the group. He just hid it well. Moving on quickly, I instinctively went to hold her hand.

"Back off!" she said, "I hardly know you. You don't touch my hand, or anything else for that matter, certainly not in the near future! I like to get to know people first!"

I excused myself for a moment as Jim enthralled us with yet another inappropriate Irish joke and the strangest Irish accent that only a born-and-bred London boy could muster. I went to the bar's kitchen area and asked if they had any disposable gloves I could borrow. I put them on and returned, holding Holly's hand with my gloved one.

"I can see I'm going to have to be careful with you," she said, warming to me.

"I believe in safe admiration," I said.

Her standoffish demeanour mellowed and I managed to get her number. I called her later and asked her to dinner at Langan's the following evening; she agreed. I could have done cartwheels down the street, I was so pleased.

She was stunning. Originally from County Tipperary, she escaped Ireland at the tender age of 17. I say escaped because she left the small town as soon as she could to venture into the big wild world. She was sick of small-minded, gossiping neighbours who knew everyone's business and craved the anonymity and potential of a large city. She studied physiotherapy at a London university and now worked for a major private hospital, specialising in knee injuries.

She was also five foot eleven in stocking feet. We laughed about her feet being the same size of mine, and she explained she was always discouraged to wear heels because of her height. I managed to locate a beautiful pair of black Jimmy Choo shoes with four-inch heels in her size and sent them with a note saying she should be as tall as she was beautiful. From that point we were pretty much inseparable. The guys liked her too; she didn't challenge them and lapped up the lifestyle.

I'd planned to take my eldest daughter skiing in Courchevel for a few days. Just for some one-to-one quiet time, as a lot of obvious attention had been paid to Oliver. We had a lovely time, and I accepted Sue's instructions that under no circumstances should I leave Charlotte alone. Not that I would anyway!

We took business class to Geneva and then caught a helicopter to Courchevel. Snow buggies were waiting to take us to a wonderful hotel. We dressed for dinner every night and sat in the cocktail bar, her just ten years old in lovely, flowing dresses.

We soon got into a routine where she asked for 'the usual' – lemonade served in a champagne glass. I sipped the real stuff. It was a wonderful time.

The eve of my birthday fell while we were there and I was passed a note at dinner that simply said: *"Your wife called. We said you were at dinner. She didn't say anything else."*

We laughed a lot about that. "You'd have thought she could have wished me happy birthday!" I said.

Charlotte called her mum every day in any event to keep her up to date with the holiday. When she was asleep in the room we shared, I stayed on the balcony overlooking the snow-capped mountains and had lots of time to think about the new lady I'd just met. I called Holly every night and arranged to meet her at Silverstone on my return for the British Grand Prix.

I'd been invited to the Grand Prix Ball, thanks to our client with the contract for arranging these events. The director of the group was also related to Eddie Jordan, so we were in the Paddock Club as their guests. Arrangements were made for Holly to meet me there via helicopter; it all went to plan other than the weather, which was so bad it nearly brought the circuit to a standstill. Many choppers were grounded and cars were sinking into the mud.

I was asked by my friend, Charles, whether I fancied an immediate trip after the race to Paris to see France play Brazil in the World Cup final. Some people had given back word because of the weather and he had a few places available. For me it would cost nothing.

In any other circumstances, I would have given anything to go, but these days weren't ordinary. I declined as I had something more important happening; Holly was turning up and I had my own very special day planned. Charles walked away shaking his head, saying: "Some days, it's just unbe-fucking-lievable!"

But Holly was special. She had to be, to give up a World Cup final ticket. Eventually she arrived, looking every inch the natural beauty she was, statuesque in the Jimmy Choos.

"Ho, you're more handsome than I remember you, sweet," she said, knocking me off stride completely. I didn't know if that was a compliment or not, but it certainly broke the ice. She really did capture my heart very quickly. I fell in love and became perhaps a little infatuated with this exotic creature. I was interrupted by a colleague to say we were due to chat with Eddie Jordan before the race started. This was an exciting prospect as well as an unnerving one, as I knew bugger all about racing.

I was furnished with what seemed like a dozen different type of security passes around my neck and was told how things get a little bit more exotic at each level. The girls got prettier, the tension increased. I was told that if I got to the very core of Formula 1 racing it would be good manners to bring a screwdriver.

I wondered what that meant, until I saw the girls milling around the paddock. They must have known as much about Formula 1 as I did. The penny dropped. That's what they're called, the paddock girls – screwdrivers. Because most of them do.

In the garage itself, the mood and the nonsense was left outside. This was clearly a place operating at the highest level. There were about forty minutes to go and the weather was driving everyone mad with its wild, changeable conditions.

I'd heard speculation on the television about what sort of tyres would be on the cars, so thought would be an ideal topic to talk to Eddie Jordan about.

I came face-to-face with him. He looked agitated and stressed and clearly didn't know why he was wasting his time with someone like me. I sympathised, but I was Charlie's client and he wanted the best for me.

"Eddie, this is Mike from Ward Evans. He's sponsoring an international rowing race, but you never know – he might be interested in Formula 1 in the next few years."
I could see this didn't impress him; he was very, very distracted.
"Hello, Eddie!" I said. Not wishing to fall into the same trap as I had with Michael Palin, I ventured with a knowing look: "Well, what do you think the weather is going to do during the race?"
He looked at me as if I was mad. "How the fuck do I know? Go ask the fucking weatherman!"
And with that, he was gone.
"Must have been a bad time," I was told, "Sorry about that, lot of stress you know. He does get worked up, don't worry, it wasn't you."
I didn't mind; nothing would spoil this day.
"How did it go, darling?" Holly asked.
"Okay," I lied. "A little brief, but okay."
That evening, after the race, we shared our first kiss on the bridge overlooking the gardens at Le Manoir Aux Quat' Saisons, Raymond Blanc's wonderful place.
We were one of the few groups that had managed to book a private dinner there after the race, along with the West McLaren team who had just won the race courtesy of driver Mika Hakkinen.
We had a great party and returned to the hotel slumped in the back of Mercedes, a little worse for wear.
"Let me help you take your trousers off," Holly said when we arrived at the room.
"God, I must be pissed," I thought.
But it sounded encouraging. This relationship was going places.
It wasn't long before Holly was a regular feature in my life. The highlight of my week was seeing her long limbs unfold from the first class carriage at York Station while I stood at a vantage point on the bridge by the clock.
This was true, romantic love.

Arriving in Barbados

In response to some gentle probing word came back that Chay needed to attend to other business and wouldn't be there when the first team was due in.
I couldn't help wondering whether he was waiting for what promised to be a larger PR event. The lone female rower from the UK was getting a lot more attention in the press at home and was much more useful to us than the New Zealand boys who were clear favourites, ex-world champions who were storming home again.
Not too exciting for the UK, unless you lived or did business in New Zealand where they were treated as heroes.
There might be a month or so between these two boats coming in, and because we didn't have a budget for both we had to decide which one we'd attend. We were obliged to be there for the winners of the Challenge, no question.
But it wasn't turning out to be the big occasion we'd hoped for. There'd been a lot of publicity and column inches during the race, but the finish was promising to be something of a non-event.
I had one PR agent who flew over to Barbados called Ash. He was there to look after media reports and was kind enough to keep me informed of developments. While working under stress, he maintained a calm, "What's the worst that can happen?" view. I'd also asked Holly to come along. Ash made the connection that the Prime

Minister was MP for the parish where the boats were due in at Port St James.
The three guys who owned Port St James were also eager to help and were
tremendous hosts, so Ash put a cheeky request into government to see if their PM
would present the winner's prize.

The answer was yes, which was a real boost as we took off for Barbados. Chay had
already decided to send the managing director of Challenge Business; he himself was
out of the country, no doubt pitching for another deal. I was still very fed up with this,
but there would be enough egos on stage.

I got a call at Sandy Lane where Holly and I were holed up; a nicer place could not
exist. The hotel was completely bulldozed some years before and completely rebuilt
to the meticulous specifications of its two Irish owners. It had a reputation for
exacting standards and opulence.

A particular attraction was the beach that was combed more each day than my hair,
with specific machinery to give a pristine appearance. The sun loungers were laid out
with a flag at the side; all you needed to do was stick the flag in the sand and there
was a waiter to do your bidding. It was heavenly. I wished I could be there for the
lone rower a month later, not just for the winners. We also got a good discounted deal
after working our international sports event pitch – that it was 'good for Barbados'.
Holly and I immediately caught up with Ash, who was already beavering away as best
he could on his own. I was still very dissatisfied with Chay and, perhaps for the first
time, regretted that napkin contract. I made my views quite clear to the Challenge
Business MD, even though I knew in my heart it had bugger all to do with him. Once
Chay's mind was made up, nothing and nobody would change it.

Meeting with Ash, and the Challenge Business guy we settled down in the aptly-
named Monkey Bar. I couldn't resist the opportunity to say exactly what I thought.
"Three bloody years in the planning and we didn't have the right harbour to launch
from, and Chay didn't put it in his diary to fly over for the boats coming in, eh? Bet
he's here when the lone rower gets in with all the press interested in a young,
beautiful women rowing across by herself. Couldn't he have made two trips?"

"Sorry, Mike," the Challenge Business guy said, shrugging his shoulders with a
resigned smile. "You know Chay..." And he gave me corporate crap about not
expecting the rowers in this early, the busy diary and commitments of a Knight of the
Realm. Ash intervened. He knew today was the big day and the end was nigh.

"Listen, the rowers are an hour away. We have a few TV crews turning up,
confirmed. And, surprisingly, lots of press reporters. The PM will arrive, greet the
rowers, shake your hands, and HE will be the first to speak. Mike, I want you to be
second. Okay with you? Okay with Challenge Business?"

We agreed.

Ash wore a look that indicated he had something up his sleeve and seemed very
pleased with himself. The conversation ended with a plan to meet on the stage next to
the landing area by the Port. The Challenge Business guy looked relieved the
conversation was over. It was obvious he wasn't looking forward to making polite
excuses. Something I thought he just might have to get used to with Chay's approach
of 'my way or the highway'.

As soon as he'd gone, Ash pulled me to one side, smirking. He clearly had something
he wanted to tell me. He looked around conspiratorially and, satisfied nobody could
hear, continued: "You know Chay likes speeches, don't you?"

"Too bloody right, whether people listen or not!" I said.

"Well, he was never going to leave it to someone else so he's sent his own across for this guy to simply read, the cheeky bugger. It means if the press pick up on it, it's still attributed to him, so he gets the publicity without even being here."

I was getting angrier with the clever, media-savvy bugger. Not for nothing had we nicknamed Chay 'the Silver Fox'.

"I figured that would happen," Ash continued, "so I loitered around the Challenge Business office out here."

"Yes," I said wondering where he was going with this.

"I've nicked his speech straight off the fax. No one knows, no one's seen it, and it's good! It's all here, word for word. You read it in your own name – that'll teach 'em!"

" Bloody great idea!" I threw the strained, strangulated speech that I'd struggled with over and over, desperate to strike the right note, and grabbed the fax from Ash. It was a lot better. Chay had been doing this all his life and knew what to say.

"But won't this guy simply get another copy?"

"Of course," Ash said with a gleeful look. "But you'll say it word for word first – that's why I insisted you go before him. What's he going to do, repeat it? I don't think so! The first time this MD guy is going to know about it is when he hears it from you, with the cameras running and the PM listening. He's hardly going to kick off, is he?"

This minor victory really made the finish for me I was overjoyed about getting one over on them, and the speech was very good, I had to give Chay that.

The rowers came in to well-earned applause from a surprising number of people. The crowd had grown as word got round about the finish, and lots of locals and tourists turned up to applaud. It was nothing less than the competitors deserved.

They came in as smoothly as if they'd been on a park lake for twenty minutes. They'd cleaned themselves and the boat and looked remarkably refreshed. I wondered if it might have been better if they'd turned up grubby and on their knees. But these guys were true champions, who had held the world record before and had broken it again.

"You know," I said to anyone listening. "These guys have just broken a world record, and made it look easy. You would not believe the state of some of the people who will get off these boats at some point between now and three months time. Some can hardly walk, lots of them will be dehydrated and need immediate medical attention." he PM arrived. Within minutes, the niceties over, the camera lights came on and we were on stage.

The finish of the race

The Prime Minister turned up in a big black Mercedes complete with outriders and standard sunglasses that made his protection team look like something out of *Miami Vice*.

Excitement ran through the crowd. It was hard not to feel it and I was glad to be clutching someone else's speech. His name was Owen Arthur and he was very gracious with an easy, practised charm. He first said hello to the customs guys, which I thought was a nice touch. They worked for the government after all, so I guess the PM was their chief exec.

He made everyone feel at ease and had a few laughs and jokes with the winning team. The PM took a natural lead once the lights went on, familiar with the attention. He praised everyone, saying how good it was for the island and the parish. Just how well-liked he was was clear, as both a person and a statesman. Thankfully, he hadn't nicked any of my – or should I say Chay's – words.

In a few minutes, it was my turn. Cameras turned on me. Nothing quite prepares you for being stuck in the gaze of a few TV cameras. I'd been told to talk to the camera, not the crowd. Treat it as a person. But that was easier said than done; trying to calm my nerves, I took a deep breath and off I went, speaking slowly and carefully.

I thanked everyone, and praised all. I talked about world records, and human endeavour. I mentioned the name Ward Evans probably more than I should have, then concluded by asking everyone to remember those still at sea, going through their own personal challenges. When the lights went off, when we were at home and the cameras long gone, some small boats would still be out there for a few more weeks. They'd battle away on that great sea, eventually coming home to no celebration save their own satisfaction of a challenge met, an ambition completed.

The words were obviously familiar to the MD of Challenge Business, as his face went white. The penny had dropped. He looked as if he might faint as his head bobbed up and down, looking at the paper in his hand, mentally striking out words already said. I handed over to him with a smile. He'd figured out it must have been something other than coincidence. I'd even apologised for Chay's absence.

He stood up and slowly said: "What can I say? Mike has said it all." Everyone clapped and agreed, little knowing how literal he'd been.

I was off with my newfound confidence to have a quick chat to the PM before he left. I had one last thing to do. While the going was good, I decided to invite him to an informal meal I was holding for the winners the following evening. To my astonishment, he was interested and asked where.

"Shit, I have nowhere booked – I didn't think you'd say yes!" I told him.

He laughed and told me to book it, he'd be there; and then he was gone.

It was tremendously exciting. Ash had his PA's number, so, armed with that and the promise of a great night out for the winning Kiwi team, I was off, never to see the Challenge Business guy – who'd hovered hopefully around, perhaps waiting for an invite – again. I felt a little unkind – it might have been nasty and it wasn't the guy's fault, but I was still pissed off with Chay. He might have later pointed out: "It wasn't on the napkin, Mike; I just said I'd try."

Holly and I walked to the Lone Star restaurant, not too far from Sandy Lane. The hotel restaurant was closed on Monday evening so we needed somewhere off-site. I spoke to the manager and asked for a table for eight the following evening.

He smiled, and with a dismissive flick of the book said: "Certainly, sir! We're booking for late January at the moment."

I said I needed it for the following evening, I knew this would be met with rejection, but I had rehearsed this in my mind time and time again. I wasn't going to rush it; the moment was one to savour.

"I've told you, sir, we're fully booked," the man said, getting quite exasperated with my impertinent insistence.

"Have you heard about the Ward Evans Atlantic Challenge?" I asked not caring if he had or hadn't. "Well, I'm the chief executive."

I knew this alone would cut no ice. Why should he care?

"I'm sorry, sir, there's nothing we can do," he interrupted with a forced smile. He was used to turning away celebrities; an overpaid insurance salesman wouldn't cut it.

"Please let me finish," I said, effecting patience and calmness. "It's a shame you can't fit me in, because I'm having a private dinner with your Prime Minister."

This brought him up sharp. "Really?"

"Really," I said trying to look as if it happened all the time.

"Please wait a minute, sir."

The owner, an ex-cowboy actor who'd enjoyed a colourful career in Hollywood, appeared as if from nowhere. He also knew my name.

"Hello, Mike," he said. "How has that event of yours gone? I've been following it with interest. We all have. It's good for the island."

Then with a flourish: "Which table, Mike?"

With a sweep of his hand, everything was at my disposal.

"I'll take the one on the rail; please ensure it's private."

"Certainly, Mike, I'm looking forward to greeting your party personally. Please send on my personal regards to the PM."

It was such a moment. I've rehearsed something like that in my life and felt elated but, like lots of things you've dreamed about, it was over in a minute.

The feeling of importance was addictive, though. I loved it and wanted more. I got back to Sandy Lane and trapped the manager, who was always around. I positioned myself so that he had to stop and say hello.

"I've had to book a table at the Lone Star tomorrow, with your Prime Minister, because your restaurant isn't open here," I said in a matter-of-fact way.

The manager was an Irish guy whose origins weren't that far removed from Holly's. He had a professional charm about him and had certainly looked after us during our stay. Probably thanks to Holly, who even in that esteemed environment bowled everyone over with her looks, charm, and lilting Irish accent. When I introduced her to one of the three super-rich guys who owned Port St Charles, a guy named Busy, he took one look and said: "You got a sister, beautiful?"

"I'm sorry about that," the manager said. "Leave it with me; we should sort this out right now for you."

"Why?" I asked.

"Well, for you and your guests I'll get it opened for you personally. We've not had the PM here since this place was rebuilt; we'd love him to come."

Bloody hell. Best place on the island and he hadn't been. It made me realise how honoured I was that he'd said yes to my garbled invitation. I also thought I could get used to this life just a bit too much.

"No," I said. "It's fine, really. I've booked Lone Star and they've gone to a lot of trouble."

He didn't need to ask how I got in. There was obvious competition there.

"Well, be sure to bring him back here for a nightcap," he said.

I can really understand how people could get seduced into this unreal life. What fun could you have with a mate like this in every country? It then occurred to me how, actually, some people do.

"I'll bring Prince Michael next time, we could have some fun if we arrange a pass out from the princess," I said, and thanked the manager for his concern.

I really could get used to this.

Dinner with the Prime Minister

The following day came as quickly as Christmas to an eager child. I tossed and turned all night, waiting. I'd rehearsed what would be said and how to keep things light and interesting.

"Mustn't cause insult, don't get pissed, well at least not before the PM..." I repeated to myself. The nightmare kept recurring in my mind – what if called him Arthur Owen instead of Owen Arthur? Those names seemed too familiar. I could just call him

Prime Minister, and then with drinks shorten it to PM.

Having made self-congratulating phone calls all over the place to anybody remotely connected with me, and some who weren't, I quickly realised I had no content for any reasonable conversation to have with him at all. Holly, who was typically unflappable, reassured me but just to be safe I had the PR guy run through the latest press cuttings and get his biography faxed through to me.

I flicked through the info while sitting on the beach. This guy's life story captured me, even with my capacity for missing the point; he was a real walking, talking, local hero. He trained as an economist and then buggered off home to Barbados, got into politics and was elected when the country was just about bust.

He said that he only had a few million in the treasury at the time; this meant nothing to me, but I was fascinated with the figures involved. It was a giant game of real economics, an enormous Monopoly board. Except decisions were made that really affected people's lives, and I was in awe of the guy.

He used the Trinidad economic model, whatever that was, and here he was years later, in charge of a dynamic tiger economy in the Caribbean. A man of the people, he expected no favours, was frank and fearless in his dealings. The population loved him. He kept being re-elected. And what a colourful character he was. Devoid of pomposity, he told it as it was. No wonder they'd open up restaurants for him. And that's another point; he would never use his position to ask. The more I read about this man, the more I liked him.[1]

Press cuttings speculated that he'd been a little put out by our royals. It seems Barbados has been left out of the tour once too often, yet they were part of the Commonwealth. The star guys of the royal circus, William and Harry, hadn't yet made a visit and this had reportedly pissed him off.

I seized on cuttings relating to the possibility of the country coming out of the Commonwealth, seeking a newfound confidence, a free spirit to go forward without anyone's protection. And if that were to happen, who would blame them?

As far as I could see, the only royals who had a history of visiting the place were Prince Andrew, who was otherwise occupied   before he married, and Sir Cliff Richard. The latter would have done the deal for my mum, I thought. She'd have us stay in the Commonwealth just for Cliff, who had a home there. She wouldn't be able to see what the fuss was about. I made a mental note to cancel my pretend Prince Michael invitation at the next event and got scared thinking about the damage I could potentially cause getting drunk on this night out.

It was something about the thought - being careful – that brought me down to a blind panic about our other laid-back Kiwi guests. It's all right talking myself into political diplomacy, but I'd forgotten why the dinner was taking place at all. These two big buggers had just stepped off a rowing boat having eaten, shitted and pissed on the thing for forty-odd days. They were Kiwis and didn't give a bugger for protocol. This was going to be only their second night on dry land, and they may just kick off a party, let off some steam, and who could blame them?

I got Ash to put word out to the guys to be on time and to enjoy themselves but the

---

[1]   Owen Arthur was educated firstly, at The Coleridge and Parry Boy's School and then later Harrison College, Barbados and then the University of the West Indies - Cave Hill, Barbados and Mona, Jamaica where he earned a BA in economics and history (1971) and an MSc in economics (1974). After graduating, he held positions with Jamaica's National Planning Agency and the Jamaica Bauxite Institute before returning to Barbados and joining the Ministry of Finance and Planning in 1981. (http://en.wikipedia.org/wiki/Owen_Arthur#Early_life_and_education)

heavy stuff was to happen after the PM had left.

"How do I bargain with them, Mike?" Ash enquired.

"Tell them I'm in negotiations to do the race again and I want them to be able to defend their record."

Whatever the reason, I needn't have worried. The Prime Minister turned up in a black Mercedes again, with only one outrider and a personal guard who stood at the top of the stairs keeping a close eye on things. The PM was in his casuals and clearly intent on a good, relaxed evening. The Kiwis were late, but they had just rowed the Atlantic. I'd have been in hospital.

I got straight into the PM while the Kiwis got straight into Holly. She could handle herself very well and expected the onslaught.

"Boys at sea, you know," she teased.

I rattled through my join-the-dots knowledge of Owen Arthur's biography and he seemed genuinely pleased that he could talk to me about the economy. I teased him about the possibility of a republic.

"Sounds good to me, PM," I encouraged. "Mr President. Now that's a real title!" I dared to say, imitating Big Jim's pull on these things.

We had a great time. The cowboy came over in a very dignified way and greeted us all, once seated. The manager was a great laugh and the whole restaurant clearly knew he was there as requests for introductions came over.

I'd read he was estranged at that time, and I thought as he did the whore's tour of all of the tables what an unbeatable line was uniquely available to him: "I'm your Prime Minister; may I join you for drinks?"

He was charm itself and sufficiently relaxed to be slightly indiscreet. Some of the stories were jaw-dropping.

He once had dinner with Michael Winner, who I had noted from press cuttings had teased him about what could be done with 'the grey man', our Prime Minister, John Major. It was reportedly alleged that he'd suggested jokingly that it might help if he had an affair to liven things up.

Somehow, this got back to the Sunday tabloids and all hell broke loose, with many bruised egos. The off-the-cuff comment, were it ever attributed to the PM, was getting a massive overreaction, disproportionate to what had been said, and in what context. Diplomats were woken from their slumbers on both sides of the Atlantic. It was only years later that we realised how such an innocent comment was bang on the mark, when it became known that at that precise time, John Major was busy having it away with Edwina Curry. No wonder the reaction – I bet the secret service was alerted too! Everyone got merry; it was a relaxed evening and friendships were made. I asked him to have a nightcap at Sandy Lane, but he declined: "Government as usual in the morning." And with a smile and a wave, he was gone.

Postscript: The PM got married in 2006 and went on honeymoon to Birmingham. How much more man of the people can you get?

Inland Revenue

Our remaining time in Barbados was spent relaxing, in spite of a phone call to say that it appeared we had "forgotten to pay the Inland Revenue."

"How can you forget to do that?" I wondered. That was a lot of money when you had two hundred and forty people in the company. It was described as a glitch, but the guy's stress levels were way up and he was beginning to look shaky

I was reassured by James and Malcolm that they were on to it, and that the new client accounting system would soon be in operation. We had so many new staff in the finance department that the group FD confessed he didn't even know all their names. If that was the case, how did or could he know what they were doing?

I tried to relax, put it to the back of my mind. James and some other Plc directors had spoken to the Inland Revenue, and we paid the late bill. No penalties.

When I got back to the UK I called a meeting, more strategy than anything else. We had some new products in development and I wanted to kick them around. I found the group FD was away on sick leave. It seemed to me, as to others, that this wasn't a bad thing, as he was not unnaturally very protective about his staff and what exactly was going on in that ever-growing department.

Now James and Malcolm, along with an army of other accountants and account clerks, could get stuck in to find out what the problem was.

Over and above that we'd called the auditors in and one of their senior guys was left with us on a consultancy basis, regardless of cost, so when the financial year-end came the following month, most of our records would have already been audited to their standards.

It would then just be a matter of ticking the boxes to get to the final profit figure. The auditor and his assistant had known our account inside out for some nine years at that point and had conducted all our previous audits so they were well versed in our systems. We also had one qualified accountant in each of the three companies, a staff of twenty-odd others within that department, and a group FD, who its fair to say was struggling. We also had Malcolm, our non-executive, who himself was a chartered accountant.

I wasn't unduly worried, but was anxious that we get the audit out the way, things in order, new systems in place, and frankly the possibility of another group FD if our existing one continued to unsettle us.

One good piece of news was that the lone female rower, Deborah Veal, came in in a very creditable time given she had done it by herself and, because of the human interest story, she got a lot of publicity. Debs paid our company the highest compliment by posing at the finish on the boat with a single oar held high above her head. She had the presence of mind to turn the oar towards the camera so that our name could be seen emblazoned clearly across it.

She was exemplary and knew that if she wanted to be sponsored again, she needed to show just what a true professional she was, Business and pleasure. The picture, with Debs looking beautiful and composed, made the front page of *the Sunday Times*. We simply could not have got better.

It was the Christmas break and I was looking forward to time at Woodland Grange. Holly had arranged to come up, Peter had organised a great party for the New Year, and I was having the kids and my parents across. It was going to be a great time and, while I had nagging doubts about the accounts situation, I wasn't going to let anything spoil the here and now.

What would be the point? We'd get to the bottom of things very soon.

"When the office returns to work, I'll get hold of James and tell him to get the finance department into gear. I'll also ask Malcolm to get more closely involved," I reasoned. I tried to relax. But like anything that has yet to be resolved, every quiet moment was attacked by this anxiety. I came to despise this down-time always damaged by pressure and stress. It needed sorting, and quickly.

CHAPTER 9

Christmas at Woodland Grange

The Christmas break was wonderful, when I wasn't worrying about the finance department problems that had only just revealed themselves.

The whole family went to the local pub, where the proprietor gave out oodles of Christmas cheer. He was open only for a few hours and gave free drinks to all the regulars. He had a special surprise for Holly and me – a bottle of Krug champagne. Every month I would buy Hols a bottle as a special treat, and it was nice to have our custom appreciated and rewarded.

The proprietor was keen to ensure there was no favouritism: "I buy all the regulars their favourite tipple; this is yours."

The pub was homely with no jukebox or gaming machines. There were three rooms – one to the right, two to the left. Each was decorated in warming colours, no garish electronics here. The husband-and-wife team planned to hand it to the next generation, their two sons, with one serving top-class food in the kitchens and the other looking after front of house.

They cared for the business, were close to the profits and looked after their customers as well. A rare thing in that industry, as pub after independent pub seemed to inevitably go to the large, multi-national catering and beverage chains, losing for ever their character and history. Instead they became plastic bars with formulaic food – bullet peas and corn garnish.

We were lucky to have this as our local. Word was that if the pub ever closed the property prices would drop by ten per cent due to the lack of demand for houses within walking distance.

We returned to the Grange for a relaxing Christmas lunch – me, Holly, Mum and Dad, and the children. Even Sue and her boyfriend turned up to say hello.

Later, we went for a walk around the estate and I realised, among the tranquillity, that I had a depressingly large mortgage on this beautiful place. Something had to be done about that.

It was as though when you love something that much, you become fearful that it can't be permanent and someone or something will take it away. Instead of enjoying the walk, I had a shudder down my spine. Sue still lived in the family home and was welcome to it; I saw it as the children's home and there had been so much disruption in their lives that they needed stability.

But I really did want to put roots down here, settle and grow old. Put this country pile into a trust for the children and make it a place where they all could live. I woke up to the fact that I'd lost interest in the business; I wanted out.

It pulled in a load of money each year for me, but it wasn't enough to pay for this. I needed to sell the shares and capitalise on its outstanding success – cash my chips and walk away from the gaming table.

Words I'd previously heard were like a great weight on my shoulders, a bloody great albatross that waited to be acknowledged: "How do you know if you've been successful or not when you're still at the gaming table? Bank it, and then count it!"

It was the first thing I wanted to deal with when I got back to the office.

Sometime around New Year, James and I met with Malcolm at Pool Court in Leeds. I needed to get a few things off my chest and wanted Malcolm's clear view of things. "Malcolm, what's going on with our group FD?" I asked directly.

"I can only guess, Mike, but I feel he may be overwhelmed with everything – that's the only explanation. Accountancy isn't complex and nor is your business. It's not as if you're in manufacturing or something, with complex stock control. Your accounts are easy. Any accountant worth their salt should be able to take over the reins and within, say, three months, it should be all sorted." I wondered if this was a fair comment, but certainly wanted to believe it.

"He scares me," I said. "One minute he says one thing, then the next day another. I wouldn't mind if we had some consistency. Putting it mildly, it's bloody worrying and I've had enough. Going into our ninth year of business we shouldn't have these sorts of worries.

"It's my fault, I brought him in from my old place and thought he could do the job, but he walks around like a ghost quoting figures that make no sense. When pressed, even he says he doesn't understand it. What's going on?"

Malcolm warmed to the subject. "Sometimes the account balances are wildly out. Sometimes there's a massive surplus, sometimes a massive deficit. It changes within twenty four hours, which proves the whole lot's wrong. There can't be such fluctuations."

This made me even more nervous. It was clear James and Malcolm were as worried as I'd been but hadn't been that vocal previously perhaps out of loyalty.

"Either way," Malcolm continued, "whatever he's saying it's got to be wrong."

"It's got to stop and we have to get a grip on this quickly. We'll have to apologise to him and tell him it's not working out," I said.

James agreed. Malcolm was obviously relieved we'd come to that decision.

We were all concerned it might take too long to get a replacement. We'd have to break the news to the group FD, who was still off sick. Having said that, he'd shown no signs of wanting to come back and frankly, the way things were looking, he wasn't going to. Well, that was a no-brainer. We all agreed we'd offer a generous redundancy package. That would protect his reputation, and ours.

"Hold on," I said, "Doesn't that mean we can't employ anyone else to do the job?"

"No," said Malcolm. "Each company has a qualified accountant anyway, so there's no need for a replacement group FD. I'll do that job as his replacement. That way we can call it legitimate redundancy and I can spend one week in four pulling the information together from each head accountant. It's enough.

"Listen guys, you don't need or want another group financial director. If you employ another one it will cost a fortune in agency costs, take ages to get them on board and you'll have to deal with the politics around the current one, which could get very nasty. Lots of bad publicity and to be avoided at all costs. I'm happy to take it over."

Turning to me, Malcolm looked me in the eyes. "At least you know who you're dealing with, Mike, and you can sleep at night."

What wouldn't I give for a safe pair of hands? I was paying the existing group FD over £100,000 a year and what seemed to be the standard management Porsche.

"How much, Malcolm?"

"I'm not doing it for the money, Mike, but I will be flying over one week in every three or four, probably more to begin with. What do you think?"

James and I agreed an arrangement of £50,000 per year. It would be a considerable saving on what we were paying currently.

I was relieved. This was a good result and a sure-fire answer to the problem. I decided to leave my views about selling until we got it all in place and had an audit following our financial year-end. I wanted Malcolm and, importantly, James, on side. There was a lot of work to do, and I believed they were the only guys who could do it.

We'd always made profit, starting in year one when we made £150 pounds. We were very proud of that. Sure, we earned a lot, but we banked a lot as well. After that, for the past eight years, we'd made increasingly more even though we were known in the industry as one of the highest payers across all grades.

Over and above that, I'd always believed in freedom of financial information. We could have chosen to submit to Companies House a limited small firm's accounts that restrict information in the public domain. But we wanted to be transparent from day one, and always gave the full version that included director's salaries. We had nothing to hide. We were proud that we could pay these salaries and still make good profits. Any financial analysis would automatically add senior directors' salaries back into the profits for a valuation that proved the worth of the company.

As long as we were transparent and honest, we also felt the Inland Revenue would leave us alone. We'd long ago abandoned business expenses as a concept, as we'd already been through a one-off speculative Inland Revenue investigation and it seemed they were targeting successful companies.

No one likes to go through that so we resolved a few years previously to pay ourselves well and put everything through PAYE. In 2000/2001, we made and retained over £400,000 profit. This year, we believed across all companies we were targeted for something approaching £600,000 in year nine, and our long term forecast was a million in year ten. All of this would be retained in the company.

The policy of never paying dividends was more than compensated for by having a high salary in each of the three companies. That was our approach and the auditors seemed happy enough.

In year ten, James and I agreed that making £1,000,000 clear net profit was very achievable, which would be a fantastic celebration for that anniversary year. That's if I wanted to keep all the companies together, but I knew in my heart that I'd have sold at least one business before that. I wanted to clear the mortgage on Woodland Grange, get the divorce out of the way and get married again.

It was going to be a busy and eventful new year. Just how much was still unknown.

Engagement

Life with Holly was blissful. We hardly ever argued and, when we did, she put it down to 'scratches'. We suited each other.

She tucked in behind me, always there, elegant, beautiful, supportive and loving. I couldn't believe my luck that this long-legged beauty wanted to be with me and share the rest of our lives.

Some friends cautioned me. "Why get married again, Mike? Take a look around. You have three children and a country estate, a boat, a bloody yacht, a Ferrari, an Aston Martin and a new Bentley Arnage Red Label. Why not live a bachelor's life?

But even with those riches it was an empty life. I loved her, and even considered more children. I decided to do something about it.

I'd mentioned that once I'd agreed terms with Sue I'd be interested in tying the knot. Unknown to me, Holly had been scanning jeweller's shops in Bond Street and had just the thing in mind. We arranged to have lunch at the Savoy Grill – I loved that place, where God knew who had been through the doors. For me, it was like a scene out of a movie - one of those black and white ones where carriages waited outside. The first time I walked into the Savoy, years before, I affected a strident, determined walk – and actually couldn't find the Grill. I'm not sure if it's designed like that deliberately. It's hidden away, immediately to the left and left again by the main doors, shielded with mirrors. You needed to look twice. It's most unnerving to loiter in the foyer wondering where to go.

I was so anxious not to look out of place. You felt you had to keep moving. Most uninvited people or civilians like me who hadn't taken the precaution of a reservation are herded up the stairs by a host of smiling but equally determined flunkies into the "more popular" American bar, a place I found myself many times while still harbouring every intention of being in the Grill downstairs. I felt like the young boy who visits the chemist shop to buy condoms only to keep coming out with toothpaste.

I gave this problem of restaurant reservations some thought. I'd seen first-hand what it was like to have a 'name' with you or to be titled. So I set about buying a ladyship for Holly, organised properly and professionally by a London agent. We put the legal documents together, and sent them to American Express, where Holly held my second Centurion Black card in her name. Sure enough, once the checks were completed, Amex was happy to organise the second name to include the title Lady Holly, and from that time on all doors were open.

She just needed to call American Express and ask them to call whichever restaurant we required, at any time, and sure enough, the table would be booked in "her ladyship's" name. This helped a great deal at places like the Savoy. Access all areas. Eventually I worked it out and became somewhat of a regular - even if I didn't have a table that I could actually call my own like the rich, famous and politically powerful. I walked into the Grill Room confidently with a confirmed reservation and was settled into a mid-floor table - always something of a giveaway with regard to my actual standing, but I was just happy to be served. It was such a regular haunt by some people that Holly and I noticed a couple in their eighties who had a gentle luncheon there every few weeks. They'd apparently done this most of their married life.

It's a fairly well-kept secret that some of the most formidable and exclusive hotel restaurants represent the best value for money for dining in London. The Savoy Grill was not only one of the best and hardest to book, but was also one of the cheapest if you stuck to the standard three-course lunch with house wine. The food was always simple but done to perfection, so this treat could be afforded in any reasonable circumstance. I'd wager a high street sushi bar would cost more.

Holly and I looked on in sweet awe as we saw the couple often. They always dined at the same table and had plenty to say to each other. They brought charm and a quiet dignity, inspiring the notion that everything was possible, that thick and thin were just places to travel to.

I so wanted to be here with Holly when I was eighty. I wanted us to have that intimacy, tenderness and respect for each other, not taking each other for granted, keeping the magic alive and knowing this was the place we'd always return to. Good times, bad times – if we ever felt lost, this is where we'd find ourselves again.

I wanted to get married. Fortunately, so did Holly. We chattered excitedly about what this meant to us both. We laughed, we cried, we did everything they do in films. Circumstances meant we couldn't marry straight away, but commitment was what we both wanted and needed at this time in our lives.

We skipped down the road to Bond Street where Holly had 'spotted' a few rings in the jewellers' stores. She'd been quietly looking for some time and had read that a gentleman would ordinarily pay around one month's salary for his lady, whatever that is, as a rule of thumb. At least, that was the going rate in Bond Street. It amused me as I quietly thought that surely half the people who buy there had inherited wealth and earned very little for themselves. Did the figure include investment income?

It came up in discussion on the way to the jeweller's. Holly didn't want to give me too much of a shock. She mentioned the one month rule.

"Gross or net?" I half-joked. It seemed churlish to talk money. This was the love of my life. I'd only ever been engaged once before, to Sue, who I'd married. So this wasn't something I'd do time and time again.

The assistant greeted Holly like a lost friend – slightly alarming, as I didn't know she'd been in the shop before. As a general statement, 'looking around' didn't mean actually going in, as far as I was concerned. When I looked, I gazed in the windows. Did that make me 'buy-curious'?

We were inside, greeted and seated. This was a serious shop with a security guy on the door. You didn't get that at H Samuels.

"I had this one adjusted to fit your finger, madam," the assistant said.

What? Did I hear correctly? That caused even more alarm. I didn't know what shocked me more – that Holly would seriously agree to marry me or that they knew her size and had adjusted a ring for her. But I did love her assertiveness, her simple Irishness, her charm, beauty and sheer class.

I was besotted; there was no other way to describe it. And she adored me. She was always telling me.

The diamond solitaire shone brightly.

"Darling!" Holly turned to me, waving a finger. "It's £50K, but I've told them I wouldn't ask for that from you so they've reduced it to £42K, Mikey. What do you think? It really is so beautiful! Of course, I know something like this is never entirely owned by one person. It's passed down within the family, the children, one to another. It's a love token that started with our love, sweet. Isn't that romantic?"

It was an antique white diamond. Had it been new, it would have been a lot more. It was sensational and I truly loved it too. I loved the idea that this ring could have been part of another big love story, and now it was our turn, our story, perhaps that of our children down the line. This would be our first great heirloom, something to pass onto my eldest daughter when she married.

The ring was dated at around 1920. All those years of love and life, shining as a symbol of permanence. I turned to the assistant, who I'd just noticed was dressed in morning gear. He didn't need to say a word. He just lifted his eyebrows and smiled with a head slightly tilted. It was a sort of now-or-never moment.

"Okay, well, let's have it," I said.

Cheers went up, kisses were exchanged and I was sincerely congratulated on what an excellent choice I had made - bride and ring. I wondered, if I'd said no, what would he have said then? "You're a shit and she's ugly"? The term 'excellent choice' always sounds so futile; to your face, you never get: "You cheapskate low-life."

There followed a smooth process of celebration; chilled champagne was served and the staff toasted our success as the formalities were sorted – including my Centurion Black American Express card and a call to my bank manager by another assistant while I tried not to listen in.

Minutes later we were out the door, blinking into the bright London lights in the middle of rush hour. Every few minutes we stopped and kissed in the middle of the street, cuddling and skipping to the Ritz

"Let's have more champagne," I said.

"I'm calling my mum and sister," Holly said excitedly. "I'm engaged, Mike! I want to tell the world!"

We crashed into the Ritz, had a drink, and booked a table for an early light supper.

"Go on, Mikey, ask me on one knee!"

"It's a bit late for that," I said.

"A gentleman would..."

I did it. "Holly, would you be my darling for the rest of my life, would you save me from myself, would you marry me?"

"Yes darling," she said proudly. "Of course I will."

Surrounding tables applauded.

More champagne was followed by an early night at Butler's Wharf. I'd never felt so in love and so lucky.

I needed to tell the family. Holly and I agreed we wouldn't have a long engagement. There was talk of two more children, to add to my existing beautiful three. I had so much to look forward to I could hardly sleep.

In the middle of the night, Holly stirred. I found her on the balcony overlooking the Thames, to Tower Bridge and beyond. She looked strangely disturbed.

"I can't sleep," she said, "I'm so happy, Mikey, I really am. But I keep thinking I'll wake up and all this won't be true. I keep getting nightmares that I've lost the ring; I keep waking to check it's on my finger. I can't believe I'm engaged. I'm so happy and yet I'm so scared. I've had nothing as beautiful as this ever happen to me before."

It gave me an insight into how Holly had struggled previously. She lost her father in very tragic circumstances; he committed suicide on the day she was born. He was found in a river and the shock prompted her mother to give birth. She never spoke about it much. She wanted a lot of fuss made on her birthday as her mother found it difficult to celebrate. All Holly would say is that she didn't believe he killed himself.

"How could he leave Mum and me at that time? There was a land dispute, I believe someone killed him."

At the age of seventeen she fled Ireland, turning her back on the gossip that would for ever hang over their family within that oppressive Catholic community. The family was shamefully isolated, just because tragedy fell at their door.

"It was bad," she said. "Mum had to leave me in a cot with a dummy and a teddy to go to church on Sundays. If she didn't, the parish and priest would blame the family."

"What?" I said. "Even though they knew there was a baby girl at home? Bastards."

I knew Holly needed security. I felt for this little girl, lost in a woman's body. She longed for safety, love and tenderness. And I could give it to her. God had been kind again to me. I often wondered how I could deserve all this. But maybe that's the deal – when something is so right and good, you start to worry about losing it.

Financials again

My tranquil domesticity was interrupted by business again. There was some problem with the audit. James and Malcolm were told the client account hadn't married up with insurer statements of what they thought we owed and it needed urgent attention. We called a Group Plc meeting.

"It's a real screw-up, Mike," James said. "The trouble is the whole finance department is screwed with things that have gone on previously. Most of the new recruits haven't been trained. There are so many input errors it's ridiculous."

"How many do you think are incorrect?" I asked, not really wanting to hear the answer.

"Hard to say. But it could be thousands."

"That's a lot of money," I said, shaking my head.

James looked at me. "No Mike, I'm talking transactions. There could be thousands of transactions that are just simply wrong. Christ knows what it all adds up to. We won't know until we get stuck into it."

We all sat back in our chairs visibly shocked, an audible collective intake of breath filling the silence. The news shook me to the very core. I knew things hadn't being going well in that department, but I never thought it was this bad.

"Shit! How the hell has this happened?" I tried and failed to keep my composure in check. "What do you think, Malcolm?"

Malcolm spoke softly in composed tones. "We've had so many new people going through our finance department. It's like they arrive, process a couple of hundred transactions incorrectly, and then bugger off. Or at least, that's what they've apparently been doing."

"What the hell do we do about it then?" I said. I felt like someone had suddenly wrapped a metal belt around it and was pressing it in on me. Stress and tension lay across me like iron weights. I must calm down here.

James interrupted: "I propose that our IT director, Patrick and I write some programme to scan the ledgers. These will throw out a possibly incorrect list where the insurers' premiums differ from ours. That will provide us with identified data that can then be manually investigated. Then we can get a team together to investigate the big ones. Let's face it, the big ones will usually account for eighty per cent of the problem, whereas eighty per cent of invoice queries will account for only twenty per cent of the premiums. So we should be able to make progress if we concentrate on the larger screw-ups.

"Patrick and I will set up a dedicated back room and lock ourselves away in it until it's sorted. Don't worry, Mike."

I turned to Malcolm. "Do we need anyone else?"

He considered. "Well, we have George from the auditors; he's here already preparing our audit. James knows the systems and Patrick can write a programme that will take the manual work out, so no, I don't think so. I think that's been half the problem. We've had too many untrained strangers messing with our systems."

"What about going forward?" I asked.

"Well, while all this is unwelcome, it's timely. Separately, Patrick and I have been working on a new client system, so I suggest not putting any more clients' money through the original system until James and Patrick work it through. I'll set up a separate client account – *No (2)* – for all new transactions from now on. Effectively we suspend the original client account until we get to the bottom of it."

It seemed a sensible solution, the idea being that client account *No (1)* would boil down to whatever the problem was, good or bad.

"Okay, keep us informed, James," I said. "One thing I think is important is that there is no cancellation in the reversing of any ledger entries or any changes whatsoever without getting another whose working with you to also agree it. Where possible that should be Malcolm, who will act with you to concur with your assessment of the changes needed. That way we can ensure no cock-ups and we all know where we are. Agreed?"

"Agreed!"

"Malcolm - you confirm to the finance staff that you're effecting the implementation of account *No (2)*."

We walked out of that meeting with an uneasy feeling, but:

We believed we knew what had caused the problem.

We knew what the solution was.

And we knew how to avoid it in the future.

We were on to it, and that in itself was a huge relief.

Within weeks, it was smiles all round. What was flagged up as a problem with our audit seemed to be sorted with the adjustment of cancelling incorrect transactions and replacing them with the correct ones. Peter and Paul, the very first employee we had, went on a tour of insurers to talk to them about doing some general spring-cleaning of our account, getting old items written off, agreeing this, meeting halfway on that. They were targeted in going for the major agencies and this was well received, as insurers were just as anxious to get their statements correct as we were. We were going to have a new start.

Malcolm and James had been in constant touch with the external audit team and had been working alongside them – when James appeared outside the bunker room, that is. For the next six weeks or so, James and Patrick would work inside a single room, where the walls were littered with list upon list of client names and insurers with various amounts on them. Things seemed to be progressing, but the stress was palpable. Not knowing where we were financially was the very worst of conditions.

"This is like being on a bloody roller coaster," I said to Jim and Peter.

Peter looked ill; Jim and I just internalised it more. Training was immediately implemented with existing finance staff to ensure it didn't happen again. James and Malcolm handled the audit and, after some discussion as to what was allowed and what wasn't, we eventually signed off the report and accounts on consolidated profit at over £600K, in line with original expectations. Malcolm confirmed via email to all Group Plc directors that the report and accounts had been finally completed. This was a huge relief; normal service could be resumed. Malcolm worked with our internal accountants, and various staff to implement his new client account system. I was grateful to James and Malcolm, and Patrick, for sorting the issues out quickly. We didn't want to live through all that again.

The new brokerage account would be used from now on, leaving the old one to eventually, hopefully, boil down to nothing, as old items were resolved and paid.

"It's quite simple," Malcolm explained. "We draw the line; any old invoices go through account *No1,* the client account where all the shit happened and is in the process of being examined and run-down by James and Patrick.

"New invoices relate to account *No2.* Payment goes according to the invoice. Insurers ask for their money, what's left is ours. It's simple business, it shouldn't take long for this lot to work its way through the wash. No more than three months, six at most."

Well that was simple, I thought. Even for someone like me who had a dislike, and no talent for, detail.

The group FD had gone quietly and I was grateful for that. It was a difficult situation and an obvious misfit in terms of personality and position. Nobody's fault including his, other than maybe my selection of him in the first place. It was another lesson learned. It's not just the company that suffers if the employer gets it wrong; it's the hapless employee as well. A wrong decision, like an over-promotion, can be enormously stressful and unfair to the willing and possibly slightly bewildered happy recipient.

I had to be more careful in future. I just needed a contract of employment from Malcolm – we wanted everything formalised to recognise that. Perhaps we'd been too informal in the past. Malcolm provided his own from his own existing company .

"This will be fine, Mike," he explained. "I don't need your standard contract. The money doesn't go to me; it goes to my company. In that way it will be to the benefit of me and my brother, who's holding the fort over there while I'm here. That's only fair for him as well."

It seemed okay to me and James was fine with it. It was signed and filed. I was eager to get back to the Grange. There was digging to do, animals to feed, and plans to make.

I spoke to Sue about my engagement. She seemed happy for me; she'd been co-habiting with her boyfriend for a couple of years, and I was pleased she wasn't by herself. We agreed we'd divorce each other in a non-contested divorce. We'd been separated long enough.

The big thing was that we had joint parental responsibility for our children. No one was divorcing them and we agreed we should take care that they saw it the same way. Holly was spending more time in Yorkshire and got on well with the children. She was like a big sister, making special milkshakes on a Friday evening and doing girlie thing with the girls, while teasing Oliver, who always had another den to build and a secret pathway through the woods to discover on his quad bike. It was like a scene from *Just William*, only in a better setting.

It was time to talk to James, Jim and Peter about my decision to want out. Consolidate what we had, and sell the business, or at least part of it. Walk away from the gaming table with a few chips. It was no longer fun taking business off the others and, frankly, we weren't running it any more.

All roads led to James, and rightly so. He'd kept the ship afloat while I was either digging holes on the estate, in London, or at the hospital. It didn't feel the same and Peter had noticed this too. In fact, Peter felt more relief then sadness about my decision.

Jim took it very well and wasn't bothered either way; money never really bothered him. So long as he had enough, he was happy. "Few beers, Mike, small house, bit of grub, enough for family and friends – that'll do me."

I always loved and respected Jim's straightforward approach to life. "Enough to eat, somewhere to live, someone to love, that's all you ever need. The rest is bollocks." I agreed. Although I still think Jim had in mind the fancy dials on previous fast cars that had just bewildered him.

I talked to James. He had a very straightforward view. He'd put too much effort into this business just to let it go, and even though he himself was a decent shareholder and would benefit financially as a consequence of purchase and share options, he wanted to buy the lot.

"It wouldn't be morally right to trade someone's loyalty as a transferable commodity," he said. "If you're serious about selling I'll head a management buyout. I'm only interested in Corporate, but I know the business and when I strip your expenses out of it, and project profits, I'll have enough gearing to pay something like £6.5 million for the one company."

This was an attractive offer. We could get more, but it would involve a lot of hassle and heartache with contracts meaning the three of us would have to stick around for another year. That would be even more difficult; once you've made the decision, it's not yours any more. Anyway, the three of us agreed we'd set something else up. Not insurance, but something.

After some deliberation and talking to Malcolm, we got back to him. The answer was yes, so long as it could be executed quickly. We agreed the management buyout. He was leading the business and had done for at least two years. So long as he could get it done before the end of the year, it was a deal.

The other condition was that he wanted to announce it. He needed to do this in order to be able to organise things in his own way. Tell staff what he wanted for the future. We reluctantly agreed. It effectively meant that James would be seen as the boss going forward, without actually having paid for the business. But, equally, he insisted he needed this announcement to shape the future in readiness for the handover.

James moved quickly. It was something that had obviously been on his mind for some time, because he was quickly onto the bank, showing report and accounts, and getting funding agreements in principal. I hated being around the place, even for the few days a week I would come in. It wasn't mine any more, everyone talked to James. This was a natural consequence. James was the future; I was the past.

I wondered if a critical mistake had taken place in not insisting on a confidentiality clause, but I'd been persuaded it was unworkable.

"How can I tell people about my hopes and dreams, and why they should stick with me when you're gone, if I can't say what we're both planning?" James asserted.

But it was too late now, the genie was out of the lamp and James, in fairness, was working to our timescales. We'd just had enough and wanted out. Malcolm fully supported this decision and felt his small investment would pay dividends on the sale.

"You know, Mike," he said, "I wouldn't have missed this for the world. I'd have done it for nothing." That was nice, but even his shares were worth over half a million. So it wasn't a bad investment, even if he felt the way he did.

I got a call from Malcolm in May, while I was on the boat in Palma.

"Hi Mike, regarding this account *No (1)*, well, it's still complex but it's boiling down. I think we'll actually make money on what's left."

"That's reassuring," I said. "But it's been operating for some time - we should have a final figure. That account should have had all transactions through it by now."

"Well, I'm sorry to say that any adjustments to the old policies on an on-going basis have been mistakenly put into the *No (1)* account. Consequently, it's sort of been kept live when it shouldn't have."

"Bloody hell, Malcolm!" I said. "Who's responsible?"

"Well all of us here I guess, Mike, but these guys are all working under pressure. James is asking for a lot of financial information for the management buyout at the moment, new people need training, we have a new system in for the new client account *No (2)*. We may need more finance staff...."

"Bugger off!" I said angrily. "We have over 27 people in finance, for God's sake. Isn't it a case of too many cooks? We have gone from three and a part timer to over twenty seven, including three qualified accountants, plus yourself!"

"I take your point, Mike; let's see how it goes. It will be better, naturally, once the original account is dormant and we just use the new system. All new transactions are going through the new *No (2)* account and that should be in apple-pie order."

"*Should*, Malcolm?"

"*Is*, Mike!"

"Good. Let's get the sale to James sorted."

"That's moving along, he has agreement to the funding in principal."

I'd heard from Neville, my old chairman, that selling was a traumatic business.

"It's something you only ever want to do once in your life, Mike," he said. I was beginning to understand what he meant. With all the consultants and accountants and finance staff, the sooner this was put to bed the sooner we'd all be a lot happier. It seemed that the business had stopped and the accountants were smothering us.

Management buyout

No matter how lovely Woodland Grange was, I had difficulty settling. I just knew the next few months would be traumatic, contrasting greatly to the emerald sea and white sand that had stretched before me at SAdam Lane a few weeks previously.

I'd had my fill of accountants, yet found I needed a personal one to talk about the most tax-efficient way to receive the proceeds of the management buy-out.

The long and short of it was that I should put Woodland Grange into trust for the kids then bugger off to Gibraltar for a tax-free year out. Something I couldn't do while owning a house within the UK, but that didn't bother me – I wanted to pass the estate on to the children so this requirement was expedient. I could use Gibraltar as a base and spend a year touring.

I wondered what on earth I'd do on a rock in Gibraltar surrounded by a load of apes shoving peanuts up their backside But the way things were going, I might not notice the difference between that and some of the people at Ward Evans.

I'd seen people make loads of money before only to be miserable in self-imposed exile in places like the Isle of Man. I took my parents there and even they couldn't wait to get home, it was so quiet.

"Don't worry about staying in Gibraltar," I was told. "This is how it happens – go there, stay around and be a good boy for a while. Then hire a car and cross the border into Spain. Then who knows where you are? Could be anywhere in Europe and, if you take my point, that includes the UK – as long as you keep a relatively low profile."

"Bet my mum would know," I thought to myself. She had uncanny radar like that.

A lot of people were crossing the border; this was the time before increased terrorist activity resulted in a tightening of controls. It seemed a simple deal and I was happy with the idea of a year out so everything was commissioned to put it into place. I could return to the UK legitimately for a specified period of time and once the year was over I'd come back, meet up with Jim and Peter, and do something else.

The other two businesses in the group were okay and we could increase the shareholding of the guys running it and let them get on. Arrangements were put in place, foreign bank accounts talked about, all that was needed for Gibraltar.

James asked to see me on my return. "Mike, I have a problem. I've got the management buyout as far as I can. The problem is I'm acting for you as Group Managing Director, and I'm acting for myself as the proposed purchaser of the shares. The facilities guys that are loaning the money want to start doing some due diligence and frankly, with all the shit that happened at the beginning of the year, we're not in a good enough state to suffer their scrutiny. I need someone acting for me, to work on my behalf for a month, to get the accounts in order. We have to separate a lot of the cross management charges."

This was a fair point that I referred to Malcolm. He agreed with James.

"There are a lot of charges that the three companies incur where we do a rule of thumb test and just split it," said Malcolm. "But now James will need definite market rate for things like computer lease, buildings, cars *et cetera*."

"How's our position on the group profit and loss account?" I asked.

"Still on track to do over a million profit," James said with a smile.

That reassured me as we had about five months to go. We didn't need to bring in a massive profit this year, there were simply too many internal distractions, but even we couldn't fuck up a million pounds of carried forward profit in five months. If we made a loss every month for the next five months, we'd still make it a good year. I agreed to discuss with James about his personal help but took the opportunity of reminding him that time was of the essence.

"What do you want to do, James? The deal is to have completion by the end of the year. Otherwise, frankly, it has to go on the open market. We're all making changes, arrangements in our lives. We need it to happen and within a specified time scale." James responded as always with positivity: "Well, I've been to the bank and I've seen Clive..." He was the company's banker, which unnerved me a bit. Who was he working for, I wondered. Was he now James's banker? "He said it's all there other than due diligence."

"What's the problem with that?" I asked. "We have our new client system, it's been working for four months now. Despite the glitch in the old account, and you and Malcolm are all over that, aren't you? That must be close to sorted."

"Well, that's the other point. I want Malcolm here more often to help me with this lot. I can't do it all myself."

It was true that Malcolm had committed to one week in every three or four. He'd promised to sort everything out in three months; we were well past that point.

"You know, James, we've always tried to avoid these sorts of guys. These consultants are like a solution searching for a problem we never really had. Don't you think?"

"He's looking to ensure we don't have a problem, Mike," James reaffirmed.

"Okay, James, get yourself another consultant to help you with the financial situation."

"I've got a guy called David Myles, an independent consultant. He's recommended." I didn't care. I'd had enough of accountants. The whole year was being ruined because we were gazing at our navels instead of driving things forward.

Peter, Jim and I saw it, felt it, talked about it. We were like a boat with its engines turned off; we had no direction and drifted with the current. It felt uncomfortable. The business wasn't sold yet but the staff were, not unnaturally, referring to James as their boss.

We had two choices, we agreed. Call it off and get involved again, or grin and bear it. James had a very persuasive technique when he saw us getting pissed off.

"Look behind you, Mike," he'd say in the office. "You see that bank over there? In that bank right now is *£65 million* pounds of your money. In the next three months, you'll collect it. Stick with it and remember that when you're getting pissed off." James was always a good salesman and he did have a good way of getting my attention. He got his guy in. I waited.

The stress was palpable in Peter, Jim and me. It spilt into our personal lives. We were drinking too much and arguing with our respective partners. I had too much time on my hands as all Woodland Grange plans had stopped until the sale was confirmed. My ideas for the place would be massively different with six million in the bank. We all live up to the limit, particularly if you're not the sort of person to covet money. My mum had a different view. "How much is that in my hand?" she'd enquire, pointing to her empty hand.

"Nothing, Mum," I'd smile.

"And it's in my hand, not yours!"

Holly was excited at going on a world tour for a year. We could do that from our temporary base in Gibraltar, but she also had other things on her mind.

She was 33 and was acutely aware her biological clock was ticking. A year to see the world. We could fly the children out during school holidays to wherever we were, and then settle. Back to Woodland Grange, a new family, a new start, and maybe a new business. Not insurance. Anything but insurance.

I was just getting to sleep at nights when I got a call from David Myles.

"Hello, Mike. I think it's important to see the three of you together if that's okay. Can you come in, and see that Peter and Jim are there too?"

It was about time. Another few weeks that seemed like months had gone by.

"Yes," I said. "Have you called Malcolm?"

"He's on his way over," Myles replied. No niceties there; he was straight to the point. I wanted this meeting. I wanted to meet Myles. I was told he was a no-nonsense, hard-nosed accountant, blunt to the point of rudeness. People took an instant dislike to him because it saved time.

But he got things done, asked the right questions and didn't take bullshit.

"Good," I thought, and wished we'd had him as group FD.

I noticed when I walked in that he was in the boardroom, my boardroom, and had seated himself in my chair. I wondered if he'd hand me a cheque and tell me to piss off. In which case I had to make sure I didn't ruin it; I didn't want to go through this process again. I'd have to bite my lip and shut up.

But it was still awkward. It was rather like a visitor to your house taking over the television remote control. You don't like to mention it, but it sure does irritate you.

I was busy catching up with Jim and Peter when James walked in. Three months from now, we'd be away. We were tired of it. This was our metaphorical airplane that could see the landing lights of the final destination. Even if we turned the engines off, I thought, we could land on the runway simply by gliding it in. We had sufficient momentum, even if it was a bumpy landing. That's how I saw these discussions; bumpy, but not a crash-landing.

What's missing?

The holding company directors filed in and gathered around the boardroom table. There was a distinct lack of joshing, not much small talk. From the looks on James' and Malcolm's faces they'd obviously been briefed already about the content of the meeting, and it didn't look like good news. Myles looked serious and determined. He looked me up and down and I felt obliged to do the same to him. He was on my territory, but somehow I felt like I was on his. The change in the dynamics of power had taken place some time previously, partly when I resigned my directorship, but staff still knew who held the majority shareholding. However, since James had publicly announced the management buyout, everyone looked to him.

Myles was the key to getting the management buyout completed and Peter, Jim and me having our hands on our first six and a half million. So to that extent it was us biting our corporate tongues. A few very brief pleasantries were exchanged. It was obvious we weren't there to collect a cheque, that was for sure.

Myles started: "I'll get straight to the point. I've had a good look at your accounts and it's not looking good. I have no definite information yet on the actual amounts, but I'm confident that the client account is definitely in deficit. That's why the finance team is having difficulty paying insurers and making transfers to the office account. You have a major cash flow problem that needs urgent attention."

This was news to me. "Hold on," I said. "You understand this better than anyone else round the table but you've just hit me with it, so let's take it slowly."

Myles sighed. It was obvious someone had briefed him about me, too, and it clearly wasn't flattering. I retraced our previous conversations.

"Let's take a step back," I continued. "In May, while I was in Palma, Malcolm said we might even expect a small profit from running down the old client account *No (1)* once it boiled down. Peter's been out there with Paul, our oldest and most trusted employee, talking to insurers about writing old items off. I've seen their reports, which were all pretty favourable. They got rid of a lot of old crap, it was agreed, and it was taken off our account. They haven't reported back any obvious trouble. Now you're telling me it needs money putting into it and, by inference, a great deal?"

"Yes," Myles replied.

"The old client account *No (1)* AND the new client account *No (2)*? They're BOTH in deficit?"

Myles pressed home his point. They both needed money injecting into them.

"So you're telling me the new account that was recently set up isn't right either?"

"Correct. That's in deficit as well."

A gasp of astonishment went round the table

"Malcolm...?" I searched. He was quiet, ashen-faced.

Myles went on: "You had a problem with your original client account. The auditors signed off your reports and accounts for the last financial year with qualified warnings. They circulated a letter addressed to all directors giving rise to their concerns about the state of your accounting procedures...You all saw it, didn't you?"

"No," I said. "I'm not a director of Ward Evans Corporate. I knew they'd sent a letter but I didn't see its content. I have an email from Malcolm afterwards saying he was now satisfied that everything was now clean, straight, and in order.

I looked around the table. People were unwilling to catch my gaze.

I continued: "Malcolm and James, with the auditors, declared our targeted profit of over £600,000. We didn't need to make that, it was just a target. Vanity, if you like, to show continued profit growth but the bank wasn't dependent on it; it's a private company. But I believed we had earned that – why bother to declare it otherwise, just to pay corporation tax on it? Furthermore, I'm told we are on target to make towards one million pounds this year. That's my understanding. If it slips, it slips, but we were on for a strong healthy profit as far as I knew. That's the latest information given to me. That's what I, Peter and Jim know. It's all agreed with our auditors..."

I felt I had to get that out of my system. I knew I sounded defensive but I wanted this guy to know I didn't deal with pie in the sky, I'd been told this by guys who were sitting around the table and I was prepared to confront each and every one of them if necessary This didn't seem to have any relevance to what Myles was saying.

"Well, that's wrong," said Myles, grim-faced and determined. "Mike, they and the auditors were effectively working on information your finance team provided. That and the various reversals that James and Patrick effected as a consequence of what they say are incorrect entries." Myles implied something might be wrong in this.

"Yes, I agree," I said, "that and what the rest of the team agrees.

Myles went on: "The profits declared for the last financial year are based on the information your team has provided. They say it's not practical to test all the assumptions."

"Well, all I know is that we pay them extra because we are a regulated business and they have to be satisfied that there are sufficient funds to pay insurers in the client account. How can that be difficult or misunderstood? This was the last financial year that Malcolm and James had taken us through when the previous group finance director had taken sick leave with stress. If it was that serious, why didn't they address a registered letter personally posted to me?" I asked.

"It's in the notes to your reports and accounts, you should have looked. Anyway, let's get to the point," he said. "We can't do anything about that now. That was just the auditors possibly covering their arses. Your original client account is in a right mess, you all know that. You then set up another client account, the *No (2)* account. That used another system designed for volume, put in place by your IT people."

"Yes," I said.

"So the original account could boil away to nothing. Then we'd know where we were. Well, the new account, *No (2)*, is in deficit to more than £500,000, by my guess."

"What?" I exclaimed. "Impossible! It's only been in place six months or so!"

Murmurs of shock, discontent and outrage swept around the table.

"There's a fault in the new system. It adds negative amounts instead of taking them away."

"Tell me they're wrong, Malcolm," I pleaded. "I must be dreaming this."

Jim jumped in: "So, two minus one equals three?"

"Precisely," Myles said. "And you've been transferring it from your client account - *No (2)* - to your office account, where you pay salaries and various expenses."

"Malcolm, what the fuck is going on?"

All eyes turned to him.

"Well, Mike," Malcolm started in a soft whisper, "We haven't had time to effectively test the system. Patrick and I have done our best. After this meeting, we're going to test it to see if this is how it's happened or if it's something else. There's so much confusion about the original account, and James has been going through entries in the back room with Patrick. It's....confusing."

This was no answer at all.

Patrick said he doubted Myles's findings, but would check.

"Seeing as we all did that, Malcolm and Patrick's answer isn't exactly persuasive," Myles retorted. "You need to find money to replace that which you've overspent. And fast. It's effectively operated like a trust account and by rights, if it's in deficit, you have to report it to your regulators. The best thing I can suggest is if you all take a cut in salary until we get it back on track. Draw up a list of redundancies as well. Are you all agreed? It's your company at the end of the day.

"I'll get back to you with my best estimate of the total overspend, but it's well over half a million just on the new account."

"Okay," I said, "get the information as quick as you can."

I looked at Malcolm; he didn't catch my eye. I looked at Patrick, who shook his head; I looked at James, who had turned pale.

We all looked as white as ghosts, I'm sure. We agreed to keep what we had just learned confidential, at least until we knew the facts. Letting this out would cause widespread panic, it had already among the directors. What was peculiar was that the guys who might be responsible were very much part of any solution. In Malcolm's case – if we wanted to raise money fast, it was only him who had that sort of cash. So we just had to live with it.

I wanted to suspend a load of them, but I couldn't. I wanted to set about the people I felt were responsible and get them by their collective throats, but I couldn't.

They might have been the problem, but I needed them for any possible resolution. You don't throw the captain over the side when the boat is rocking. This position was one that I was to become very familiar with in the weeks and months to come. We were all reluctant bed-fellows from that moment on....

But right now, I needed to be calm. No public executions. No rocking the boat.

"Let's just get to the facts and then see where the solution lies," I said.

The next few days would be critical. The solution has to be there some where.

123

Recover or die

The suddenness of this shocking information and the complexity of it was way out of my sphere of intellectual and emotional experience. I didn't know what an appropriate reaction was. Coolness? Fear? Anger? I certainly didn't know what to do about it. I knew some form of leadership was required and that all eyes were on me, but inside I didn't feel up to the task. We decided we'd take time out to analyse and establish our exact position, but to try to make contingency plans should they be needed. The difficulty is that what we faced was uncertain. What was the worst case scenario? We didn't need to wait long. Myles was back.

"Well, I don't have final figures and getting them is going to take longer than the time I honestly believe you've got. It's my job to be straight and frank with you, so forgive me if I just get straight to it. How it happened, and what can be done can be debated later; right now this is the position as I see it.

"You'll need at least one million pounds dropped into the client account to keep the company on the right lines of solvency. This needs to be done immediately. Put another way, you're a million quid light at best guess. Worse still, the word's out in the market that something is wrong. Rumours are starting already. I'm trying to keep a lid on it without actually lying – I have my integrity to think about. I hope you guys fully understand my position?"

It flashed through my mind that I'd also need to look at the confidentiality clause in his consultancy contract, but I kept those thoughts to myself. I just tried to absorb all he had to say; knowing that to miss something might be terminal.

"People know I'm here and they've almost stopped asking about the management buyout and have started to ask what my exact role is, and what's wrong. Your company has stopped doing new business, they know something's wrong."

This was true; the market was going through a tough period and most of our guys were more interested in renewing business then chasing new stuff.

Myles continued: "If they all come for us at the same time under their agency agreements we'll be dead meat. We're behind with insurer payments, even on those that aren't disputed."

"A million pounds?" I mouthed, barely audible.

"Cash," Myles replied. "It's needed to keep your company afloat. It'll buy us time, but it may only do that. I don't honestly know where you are at the moment."

We turned to Malcolm; he was the only one around the table with that sort of cash. All my money was tied up in Woodland Grange and cars; it would take ages to liquidate and there wasn't the time. I'd always thought of my shares as my pension. I didn't do savings.

Malcolm offered neither comfort nor his immediate view as to the accuracy of this assessment. Just a faint look of bewilderment that suggested he'd been informed about this before me, and like us, couldn't quite take it in.

Malcolm always worked on the view that it was best to keep quiet and look an idiot rather than open your mouth and prove that you were. Well, we all looked like one here. What on earth had happened to his leadership as group finance director? What were James and Patrick doing in the bunker room? I wanted to scream it all out, but I couldn't. I couldn't turn on them now. I needed them on the inside.

Malcolm promised to think about it and come back on Friday with an answer. It was now Wednesday. I called Peter and Jim into a separate room. They confirmed that they, like me, knew nothing of our troubles. Peter had been going around Insurers with Paul. They'd been well-received with the notable exception of one or two. Jim looked quiet and reflective; Peter looked pale and scared.

"This is just going away from us," I said, breaking their stunned silence, and stating the bleeding obvious. "What's good about the business, the size and the volume, may turn around and kill us. We need quick and decisive action. The figures are too large; it's not going to be easy. We know the company is worth well in excess of ten million plus for the group; on a good day, maybe twenty."

"This isn't a fucking good day," Peter said, quietly - a master of understatement.

I decided to head down to London. Peter agreed to come with me, with the purpose of introducing me to a couple of agents who specialised in selling books of business. We had a book of special errors and omissions business – it was our Crown Jewels, highly profitable for an underwriter, high commissions, and very few claims. Everyone would want it – there's nearly a million pounds there, we agreed. We'd get our million and then, when we got back, we'd make changes. Bloody big ones.

We had an urgent meeting with a consultant who'd made discreet enquiries previously. We'd laughed and thanked him and said never. Now we knew how silly the word 'never' was. I resolved not to use that word again.

We arrived at an ordinary upper floor office that could have been anywhere in the middle of London. It made sense that they weren't prestigious offices; people liked to come and go anonymously. If the wrong people were seen coming in or going out, it could knock fortunes off your share price or business valuation.

It struck me that it didn't look much different to the original sex shop where we'd so enjoyed people-watching in those early days. I thought how visitors were just as furtive going in and out of this place – collar up, head down, don't meet anybody's eyes and hope you don't bump into a neighbour. Do the business and leave.

We got straight to the point: "We're in Shit Street."

The consultant listened patiently and, having listened intently for ten minutes, had some encouraging words. We wanted to talk, explain what a shock it was, which was of no interest to him.

He interrupted: "You guys think you're the only ones. You're not."

We stopped.

"You'd be surprised how many people come in here from known companies that have had some trouble or other. But your business is basically good; very good, actually. Not many can put on business like you and keep it. Sort yourselves out. Buy some time, cut your cloth and start again. It's not as if you don't know how to rebuild."

"It's a ridiculous situation to be in," I stated, glad to have unburdened myself. "Frankly, half our expenses are on salaries that we can cut, will cut, and keep cutting, until were down to that last three of us if needs be. It's not like we have a massive amount of capital equipment hanging around."

We should never go bust. We just needed to cut our cloth. We just needed to know where we were with the figures.

"If we knew that, we could go forward - we could contract and start again," I said. "But we need to buy time, that's why we're here."

"Keep going, boys," he said. "Just keep trading. I'll sell the E&O for a million, easy."

"How long will it take?" I asked anxiously. "Realistically."

"One month."

"Shit! We may not have that long!" I said in blind panic.

"Of course you have guys - fortune favours the brave. Keep trading and I'll work as fast as I can to get it away."

The whole business was worth ten to fifteen million as a going concern; we wouldn't miss one, we told each other on the way back.

"It's going to be okay, Peter," I said as I looked into his white face. "You heard the guy, we just keep going."

"Mike, don't you realise that if that guy talks to his friends, he can get a buyer for a million, but if he waits maybe six weeks, when we're bust, they could pick it up for next to nothing?"

"What can we do Peter?"

"On one side we need to tell people, to help us solve it; on the other we don't want anyone to know. It's a bastard and I don't know what to do. Ordinary rules don't apply here."

We sat in silence, with nothing more to say. Not for the last time we were completely in other people's hands. It didn't feel good.

Malcolm was there on Friday. We snatched a meeting with all group directors and Myles. Malcolm opened the meeting.

"I've looked this over, Mike; I can't just put a million pounds into it. No one knows if that will be enough, anyway. My business is a family one and I have to think of the guys "

"Great," I thought, biting my lip. So much for being able to fucking well sleep at night.

Malcolm continued, in as aggressive a way as he ever could, which was just above quietly spoken: "I wish I'd never have listened to you, James, when you said the client account was okay and it was just a load of ledger entries that needed correcting." Putting his fingers in his ears, he said: "I should have done that."

James looked upset, positively fuming, but said nothing. No one did.

Turning to me, he said: "Mike, I'm sorry about this, but if I'm putting a lot of money into this God knows when, or if, I'll get it back. I need to buy the entire business and free funds to put into the client account. I will pay you a penny for the Corporate company, with its liabilities. Once we see what's what, I'll look to see if I can cut you all in on some deal."

"Fucking great," said Jim who had, to that point, kept his views to himself. "I knew the business was for sale and I knew we'd get a buyer. Just didn't realise the price! Glad we got something for it – how will you spend your share, Mike?"

Myles looked astonished, "You lot are unbelievable. You're facing complete financial ruin and you're still making jokes. I've never met anybody like you lot."

"Gallows humour," I explained. "What would you expect? Tears?"

There was plenty of time for that, but we weren't going to show it to this man.

"Malcolm, when can the deal be done?"

He was beginning to look the entire world like an opportunist – one man's misfortune, *et cetera*.

"Next week, Mike. But I need my consultant to work on it a bit more."

"Okay, then. If that's what has to be, let's do that. We have to take you on trust, we have no choice. In the meantime, Peter and I will pursue another solution in the marketplace, but at least we have a backstop position."

"I'm saying that's what I hope to do, Mike. I've more work to do with my consultant, and then I have to go back to talk to my brother. It's our own company money that's going to look at buying it so I have to persuade him."

More bloody accountants. How many do you need to ruin a Business? Whatever the answer, don't believe it. They'll get the figures wrong and qualify it in writing.

Peter and I worked all week on getting the E&O in a financial package ready for sale.

This represented our best plan, our 'get out of jail free' card, which in this case might be a literal translation of a well-know phrase. We got it down to London in a few days, and decided to reconvene the following Monday.

The weekend dragged on. I couldn't rest at Woodland Grange. I talked about the problem with Holly and my parents. They seemed strangely remote from it. I guess they'd heard about it all before, my fits of stress-induced temper. They didn't quite see where this might head, what might actually happen

I looked into their faces. They'd other things to do, to concern themselves with. Ordinary concerns, ordinary life. I decided to leave it. What could they do anyway, other than worry? If they knew, there'd be no release from the tightening knot that persisted in my stomach and around my chest.

Monday came. Myles was waiting for us when we got back. He'd done a lot of work, and in fairness was genuinely concerned for us. He looked deadbeat, with red eyes and black circles around them. This didn't augur well. He didn't want to lose a good business that he had consulted on, either. He was a man of some arrogance and pride. He was tired. He'd gathered what accountants he could within our business; he needed more support from Malcolm as well.

"Guys, I know we're all stressed, but I have to ask you this. I need a personal cheque for this, and for the next month. Otherwise, the way things are going I might not get paid. I have my own expenses; I'm a self-employed consultant. I need to know that I'm going to be put first and get paid."

This had a terrible effect on me. It somehow became more real, that we might go bust, and people were starting to queue up to be paid, to make claims on us. And the first one was the guy who probably understood our position better than anybody, as Malcolm didn't seem to be coming forward with advice. We paid him.

"Now then. I've heard of a man who I'm told is a good corporate recovery specialist. I think it's wise for him to take a look at things. He's much more of a specialist. I'll get him in, see what he says. He has more experience in these circumstances."

Another bloody consultant.

He was there in an hour. Adam had obviously been well-informed of our troubles; in fact, everyone seemed to know more about our position than the board. A young-looking, sharp-suited guy, with too much hair and a too-broad smile, he strode into the boardroom. He gave a quick resume of his background.

"Relax. I know your emotions are going through a whirlpool at the moment but my team and I are looking at your position. We need to make decisions in the next week or so. I've been there, seen this. I'll get back to you in a few days, and I'll see you around the place."

It surprised me how he hadn't waited for an invitation.

I ruminated on how this used to be my company, but somehow people were behaving differently. It didn't seem like mine any more. Strangers were all over the place.

I got the auditors on the phone; they'd been bloody quiet. I'd wake them up, this was as much their problem as it was ours, I decided. One of the guys pointed out, though, that they'd still be in Business in a month and we wouldn't if I angered or upset them. The sad and awful truth was that these people were best placed to put it right if it could be put right.

At least, that's how it seemed then.

When the auditors came in, it seemed to me that their first priority was to put a respectable distance between themselves and any blame for our being in this position. "We have to watch this Mike. It's obvious your sales have collapsed since 9/11; there's been a downturn in income causing this trouble," said the senior partner.

"No there hadn't," I thought. I knew we hadn't had a downturn. Four weeks ago or so, we were pretty confident of making a million pounds. The auditors had presented and signed off a report and accounts showing £600K profits just a couple of months ago. If they were meaningless, why bother with them?"

Our problem was a total collapse of our accounting functions, and they had looked after us for years. Now they were distancing themselves. No point in falling out with them, I thought, we'll have enough enemies coming out of the woodwork.

I just have to try to keep everybody on side, keep the team together. There were a lot of shocked and nervous faces out there. I needed to be strong, show leadership.

But however much I tried in the office, I was a wreck and so was Peter. Jim seemed to shrug his shoulders: "I don't know, Mike. I know diddly squat about Bo Diddley."

I couldn't sleep. I walked around the estate by myself trying to get some quality thinking time, waiting for that eureka moment. It didn't come. I thought through all the characters involved in sorting the business out. Who was genuine, and who wasn't? I tried to remember that the enemies of my enemies are also my friends, and I needed all the friends I could get at the moment. But who was the enemy within the company? How had this happened?

The land was full of crisp leaves on the ground; the advanced stages of autumn. Would I be here in the spring? Where would all this end? And what would we all be like at the end of it?

Adam brought in his own team of people. More consultants. Myles had his lot; the auditors crashed in more people - it seemed to protect their position rather than the company. Malcolm walked in with another guy I didn't know.

These people were all over the place. None of them spoke to me. Little groups gathered and whispered in corridors. Each company was threatened as all the businesses were connected to the holding company that owned the shares. The bankers were the same for all.

It's easy to see this house of cards in retrospect. How I wish we'd separated the companies, each unconnected, each with their own future. This hadn't been a new idea – it had been minuted when James got involved and I think he wanted it as much as I did. But the finance people after Chris in the good old days always said it was difficult as we shared the same assets – computer leasing, management charges and the like. The auditors also talked about tax treatment not being advantageous, but they were distinct businesses trading in different markets, and I'd always seen them as separate with profits hoisted up into the non-trading holding company. I had of course taken different salaries from each of them as well. I had not thought of them as being together for many years, something that in itself was going to haunt me in the months to come.

But while promises were made, new Sage systems purchased, even a Sage consultant employed for what must have been six months, it never came about. I should have insisted on it years ago. The consequences of not doing so were clear in my face when I contemplated a future that couldn't have been imagined six weeks ago. Here they all were, little groups in corners; sometimes together; sometimes with Adam; sometimes with Adam and Myles; sometimes with Adam, Myles and Malcolm. But not with me. This was unreal. I kept thinking, hoping, that I'd wake up and it would all be a bad dream. But it wasn't.

One person's ceiling is another person's floor

A few days passed with more and more strangers walking around the place. I didn't know whether they were accountants, insolvency consultants or just concerned creditors. Either way, no one was speaking to me.

I eventually cornered Malcolm with Peter as soon as he came into the office and asked if he would have a coffee with us. I was tired, anxious and had developed an unnerving shake but tried to keep it under control.

I needed to keep calm and try to think clearly. I had a sense that what would happen in the next few days would live with me for the rest of my life, but even then it was all unreal, as if I was just a disinterested observer. All this was going on, but I seemed to be viewing it on the outside. Maybe this was what shock felt like. I didn't know. But I had a hard job trying to keep myself in the present.

Peter and I heard from the sales consultant in London who was trying to quickly raise a million pounds for us by selling our 'Crown Jewels' the book of specialist E&O business. He was having a hard time getting anyone to commit, like moths around a flame. We had a lot of interest but no commitment, simply because the longer it took, the cheaper it was.

"I think all these players who are expressing an interest know your position, Mike, so they're working on the portfolio, but they're playing a waiting game. Someone is leaking your troubles. It isn't me."

Just as Peter had predicted, they were waiting to pick it up for nothing. Vultures circulating around a dying body. Human nature at its worst; I remembered Chay's warning: "Any fool can make money, Mike - it's keeping it that's the clever bit!" How I wished I could turn the clock back. I called the sales agent.

"All's not lost, I'm hoping to get a company interested at a discounted price," he said.

"How long?" I asked.

"As soon as, Mike, I can't give you a timescale. I know your position. Keep going – remember, you must keep trading."

Malcolm's view of life was critical at this stage. I needed to know for sure what he had in mind. I'd seen him in tight circles with others. Maybe it was paranoia, but as soon as I got close to any huddled group voices would suddenly fade away and start up again when I walked away. It was hurtful even if he felt it was necessary. Maybe I was just imagining it, I didn't know.

Peter and I dragged him out the office. It had come to something when I felt more comfortable out of the office than in it. We sat and had a pizza before we were due to go straight back to the group meeting. I needed to know his thinking before that. I'd seen him in the boardroom with someone I didn't know, scanning over papers. I had seen lots of strange and strained stressed faces around.

Malcolm quickly got to the point.

"I can't do it, Mike, I've been advised against it by my consultant. To keep this business going I'd have to guarantee creditors that I'd step in to pay the difference, whatever that is. That's effectively an open chequebook. I just can't do it."

The news was devastating.

"Surely we must be close to knowing exactly what the problem is?"

"Myles doesn't know, nor do any of the accountants or accounts staff. It's at least a million, which is a big number in anybody's book, but it could be a lot more, and that's the problem."

Didn't I know it? I was close to tears. I kept thinking of a previously smiling Malcolm at that fateful dinner with James. His voice stating assuredly: "Don't worry, Mike, I can ensure you sleep at night."

And what about that bloody client *No (2)* account where we had for sure transferred over half a million because of a simple addition problem? If I were going to shout, kick over the tables, now would be the time. But I was too tired, too beaten. I had to admit to myself that I was also too scared.

We gathered for a Group Plc meeting. I'd invited a few management guys in for their information; there was a lot of fear around. Those who trusted me asked what the position was.

"Tell you what, come in and hear it in just the way I am," I said. They deserved to know what was going on. There was too much second-hand information and rumour. Adam got his small team around the table. Myles was there. It was crowded and tense.

"Well," Adam started. "Mr Myles's view on needing a million pounds is about bang on as far as I can tell. But it may need more. There's no guarantee. I think it's going to take three months to find the underlying cause of this, and of course you've been carrying this problem for at least that long already. You don't have any more time. Unless Malcolm is prepared to buy the business and put some cash into the client account immediately it's your duty, as directors, to consider alternatives."

We knew this was almost a rhetorical question, as Adam almost certainly knew of Malcolm's view.

"He isn't buying," I said.

Malcolm looked straight down. This was news for most of the others around the table who'd just been getting used to the idea that Malcolm would be our elder statesman, the father of the businesses, the new boss. Our saviour.

"Well then," said Adam. "You have to trust my experience on this, seen it many times before. As directors, you've done everything you can. You can't be criticised. But if you keep trading now, you're going to do so illegally. That's in all companies. You have to suspend trading. The accounts are in a state, but it's reasonable to believe that you're insolvent, and the test 'reasonable to believe' is all you need. You have to cease trading. That's the bad news. If there is any good news it's that I can offer you a people a pre-packed administration."

Who were "you people? I wondered. But I didn't have a chance to ask.

"The lot has to go into pre-packed administration. I suggest we get administrators in. They're appointed, if you will, as trustees of the group, and they're answerable to creditors. They effectively work for them. They'll seek to get the best and quickest deal in selling each of your businesses as a going concern. As this is the type of business where clients will flee within days, you need the absolute support of your insurers. They'll be your main creditors, but only when in administration, not before.

"So my action plan is to go to court. Get an order. We reorganise ourselves and then we go in and straight out of administration and off we go again, leaving the debts behind in the old companies. It's done in a day."

This arrangement sent frissons of excitement around the table. There were people there who immediately saw this as a get-out-of-jail card. There were those there who thought their most miserable day might have just have turned around to be their best one. It certainly did when the idea of a pre- packed administration sank in and what it meant for the minority shareholders. It already had with me.

Adam was offering minority shareholders an opportunity to buy the company on an almost guaranteed basis for next to nothing, and they could go forward and trade, leaving the mess behind. How good was that for them?

Are you part of the solution or are you the problem?

Who could and could not be part of the new buy-out team was likely to be dictated by the creditors. It was they, after all, that would have to sanction this arrangement at a subsequent meeting.

For them to do that, they needed to be given clear definitions as to who were the good guys and who were the bad; the winners and losers. They weren't going to authorise such an arrangement without having heads roll; somebody had to be made responsible for this mess. I knew instinctively that any pre-packed administration would not include me and, deep inside, It didn't feel fair that it should.

I'd presided over this mess, albeit innocently, but I was the only one who could have sacked the main operational players. Pre-packed administration effectively meant that unless you were part of the solution, you were for sure going to be labelled the problem. The more who could be labelled the problem, the more likely the administrators would satisfy their natural blood-lust. The group, and all the companies, were effectively screwed.

Each guy around the table had to get together in their respective teams and prepare an offer to the administrators; they would either accept or reject it in determination of the best interest of the insurers, who were the only likely creditors.

"Who do you recommend as administrators?" someone asked.

"CBA," Adam replied. "I've taken the liberty to gee them up on a confidential basis. We want to ensure they're appointed so they can get the pre-pack away. They work with me all the time, they're sensible guys. If the offer is okay they'll accept it. We don't want a bun fight with loads involved and I know them.

"You'll need lawyers to draw up an administration contract. I'd suggest the lawyers. Is that okay with you, Mike?"

I'd been quiet and I believe this unnerved Adam. I could hear him, but I couldn't speak.

"Okay with you, Mike?" I heard again. I nodded. I knew I'd been screwed. There was nothing I could do there and then to rescue the situation.

There were ten directors around the table. A quick calculation suggested that seven of them would be the solution. They'd have the chance of a lifetime to own their own companies at a ridiculously low price. Three would be the fall guys and face complete and immediate financial and emotional ruin.

With one discussion, that prospect had shattered the loyalty built up over the last nine and a half years. Why would they want to keep trading when it might be illegal, and just for a minority stake, when they could leave the trouble behind and own the business?

Everyone got up and left. Peter stayed and Jim, seeing we were still there, came back. "Don't ask me, guys," he said. "I just don't know any more."

"We've got to keep trading," I said.

Peter was visibly upset. "Don't be a fucking idiot, Mike. We're in Shit Street already. If we keep trading and it goes belly up we don't just lose the fucking lot, we all go to fucking jail."

I wasn't listening to that. I was thinking about the practicalities of continuing to trade. Insurers knew what was going on. Myles was fending them off with no comments while putting a note out saying *due to accounting errors the group was looking at its position.*

I thought about telling Malcolm to fuck off, showing Myles the door, slinging Adam out – but how long before there was a knock on the door from the corporate police? We were a regulated business. Some regulation. Our client account and systems should be monitored; we paid more to the auditors for that privilege, but it was useless – here we were. Jim brought me back to reality.

"I'm going back to London, mate. Let me know what developments there are."

He left. Peter and I looked at each other.

"You know, Peter, any pre-packed administration won't involve us. No matter what they say. They have to get agreement from the insurers, who they need to trade again. They're not going to give that to any company we or James are associated with."

"I know, Mike," Peter said resignedly. "I'm near the end here. I can't sleep, I can't go on. I don't want any more involvement. I can't go through this again, I just can't. I want an ordinary job where I can sleep at night."

"I know, mate," I said, placing a hand on his shoulder. "I really know."

We walked out of the office. Adam was there, waiting for us. He obviously knew the distress all this had caused. He'd done it before, many times, and wasn't beyond understanding and empathy. Whether it was part guilt or just an acknowledgement that his business was by nature a nasty one, I don't know.

"Guys, come back, sit down."

We went back into the boardroom. We had tears in our eyes – I'm still not sure whether they were due to the loss, the stress or the plain shock of the situation.

"Look, you know all these guys are out there trying to put a package together for CBA. They'll need to do presentations. I know it's hard but you know, don't you, that you can't be involved. Trust me, you will get back to where you were in three years, you'll get it all back eventually. I'll help you – I always have opportunities coming through and I'll put you top of the list. There's plenty to do in the future, you just won't see that yet. But you'll rise to the surface – trust me."

We were silent, beaten. Adam waited and continued: "But we need to work quickly. I'll get the legal document to you in the next few days, Mike, three or four at the latest so don't go missing on me. Okay?

"I know you have Debby to go back to, don't you, Peter? That's good. Just go home and collect your thoughts. Mike, you have Holly. She's a good girl from what I hear. It's important you have your family, remember that."

Adam had turned therapist;

"Let's get out of here, Pete," I said. We were both near to breaking down and we didn't want to give them that. They had everything else.

James had already gone. If people thought he was the problem and not the solution, no one had yet told him yet.

CHAPTER 10

Going home

I drove home in the Bentley, such luxury contrasting starkly with how I felt and how I saw my future. What future? This was idiotic. I was an Idiot.

Here I was, surrounded by all the trappings of success; people looked when I drove by and, as they gazed in, I thought they should be careful what they wished for. I'd gladly climb out of the car, hand over the keys and just walk away.

I drove straight home. If I hadn't, I might have kept driving, never to return. I'd let everyone down not least myself and the consequences were starting to crash in on me. Life had changed for ever.

Yet the process of dismantling everything I had and everything I was had not as yet started. I was now in a holding position, awaiting inevitable financial disaster.

The gates opened and I was met by the normal buzz of busy, happy, domestic life. Dogs ran and barked; the housekeeper was busy cooking something on the Aga; the estate manager was making white noise about the cost of getting some new fencing up around the perimeter of the estate.

And there was beautiful Holly, who always came to the door to greet me. Little things like that made me feel very special, when clearly the special one was her. I didn't meet her smile, although I appreciated it. She looked at me expectantly.

"It's all over, darling. I don't want to talk about it right now. I'm just in complete shock," I said, tears flowing from my eyes.

"Darling... Darling, come in."

She shooed everyone else away and we walked through to the drawing room. There was a big log fire burning and Christmas decorations had just gone up, making my misery even more intense. It was December 19th 2002. It should have been the happiest time, one of great expectation.

Helen poured a large glug of shiraz and sat on the floor beside me, long legs curled under her.

She would have music wherever she goes... The old nursery rhyme line came into my mind. Her intense blue eyes looked deep into my mine. I wondered what she might see in them – shock, disgrace, fear?

"Don't worry, darling. We're together. That's what matters. We have our health You have to keep your health, Mike. Tomorrow, I'll take you to the doctor. You need something to make you sleep and calm your nerves, sweetheart," she said, stroking my hair.

I was shaking involuntarily.

Jim phoned: "Are you okay, mate?"

It was lovely of him to think of me.

"You weren't looking too good today, wanted to make sure you still have your pecker up if it's at all possible. Thought at one point you were going to really kick off, and who could blame you? That would have been a bloody relief, to be honest."

"I'm okay, Jim. Had a little cry to be honest, but all right now. How about you?"

"Jesus, Mike, I don't know. I don't know how I feel. It's all happened so quickly."

"Have you heard the rumours?" I asked.

"I've heard so bloody many, Mike – which ones have you picked up on?"

"That James deliberately planned this. Brought the business down to a lower level so he could adjust the purchase price for his management buyout of Corporate. Then he couldn't control it and it all went away from him."

"Yeah, I heard that," said Jim. "But never gave it serious consideration, to be honest."

"I'm with you on that. It's too easy to blame him alone. We'll never know the truth but that's not it in my view. We had so many bloody qualified accountants and finance staff... The whole accounting system is totally fucked up. That's all I know. What do you think?"

"I think a load of people just didn't do their jobs, and that includes senior management and accountants," said Jim.

"I saw James looking like a broken man with his head in his hands when I left. He was close to tears. He doesn't have a future with Ward Evans, he'll not be part of any rescue plan. He's not well-liked by a lot of the team – none of us are, now, everyone is looking to the next guy to blame.. Strange how quickly people turn against you. Anyway, whatever they think of us, for sure they want to ditch him. He's trying to get back into the corporate buy out and plans to come to London in the next few days."

"Well if they can have him in the team then they could have the three of us," I said

"What are the chances of insurers agreeing to him being involved in anything?"

"None at all, Mike. It's not going to happen. They've drawn lines and James, like you, is on the wrong side of it. It's bleeding unfair, but there's nothing we can do, there very angry and you cant blame them."

"What about Peter, Jim?"

"He's not in a fit state to do anything, Mike. He wants no part in any new set up. He wants out of insurance all together. He's simply had enough."

"Jim, you mustn't hold yourself back. There's an outside chance those insurers would agree to you being involved going forward. Let's just say your style lends itself to thinking you weren't involved in this in any way."

"You mean they think I'm bloody daft, Mike!"

"No, just honest. And let's face it, you were in London and somewhat distant from it all. I'm worried about Peter, though – talk to him, would you?"

"He's next on my list, mate. What about you?"

"I'm screwed, Jim. No one's talking to me. No one catches my gaze. They walk past almost with a sneer on their faces. People in groups go quiet when I'm around. And because I've got all the material trappings it makes me look such a bloody idiot if not a crook.

"I have this recurring dream where I'm invited to a fancy dress party. I go into a dark room where there's lots of noise, and its just pitch black. Someone turns the light on and everyone's dressed in dinner jackets but I'm in a clown suit. Everyone's laughing at me. I don't need to analyse that too much, do I?"

"You're no clown, Mike, you just trusted people too much. It's just not bleeding fair." Jim was getting angry now.

"Forget it. I'm not taking any notice of the bastards," I said. "Let them say and think what they like. I know the truth. Call Peter, he'll appreciate it."

"Stay in touch, Mike. I'll pass on any news if I hear anything."

Jim waited a few seconds, but I had nothing else to say. Where would I get another business partner as generous-hearted and special as Jim? The loss I felt wasn't just restricted to money. In not being able to work with Jim, his humour, his take on life and his honesty, I'd lost something very special.

Off to see Jerry

Jerry was the local doctor, one of life's lugubrious, joyful characters. He was knocking on a bit, thin, with a craggy face and wide smile. He loved to be outdoors and knew more about my estate than I did.

All the woodland, the lakes and flighting ponds were familiar to him, and he regularly walked the land with my blessing.

He operated from his own house and gardens, a veritable Dr Doolittle farm with all sorts of wild and exotic animals, most of which eventually found a peaceful and useful end in his homemade sausages which he cooked with gusto on an open brick furnace he'd built himself.

His sausages were the most sought-after in the village. An entertaining party game might have been to guess just how many European legislative laws he was breaking in this one-man sausage factory, although he never charged for them.

He'd been around for dinner a few times and enjoyed telling stories. He loved a few glasses of wine and was a fantastic, approachable, personable sort of man whose party trick was to stand up at the end of dinner and sing about ten verses of a very rude and funny song that ended: "Aunty Mable's farted and blew herself inside out!"

Only he could remember the verses and hearing him sing it again and again, at the top of his voice and with gusto, was always a new joy.

I thought people could usually be separated into two groups – boilers and radiators. Those like Jerry were definitely radiators – they radiated happiness and always contributed to a party, always had a trick or two up their sleeves.

This familiarity allowed me to be completely frank with him and he was typically kind and generous with his advice, time and concern.

"You need some chemical help to get through this, Mike, some anti-anxiety pills. They aren't anti-depressants – I'll keep you off them as long as I can but I want to see you every week to monitor you. You need something that's not going to knock you out, as you'll have many legal meetings and maybe court proceedings. You'll need your wits about you, and above all you need to remain calm."

Calm? Court? What was that about? Did he know something I didn't or had rumours already hit the village? Not only was I going to be broke, but also was I really going to have proceedings hanging over my head?

Jerry continued matter-of-factly: "It might have an effect on your love life, too. That's the pay-off. Tell Holly, she'll understand. And don't drink."

Great, I thought. No sex life, going bust, can't get pissed. Possible court proceedings. Just bloody marvellous, Merry Christmas.

I got back to the house and decided I'd have to tell the staff and give them all a month's notice. No matter what happened there wouldn't be anything like the money I'd had previously. I simply couldn't afford them.

And we'd have to look at getting rid of the horses and the cattle needed shifting, as they were another big job through winter that cost a fortune.

The staff took it very well. They must have heard something was wrong. I hate how bad news travels so fast in this country. You never read good news in papers. It doesn't sell.

The staff understood I wouldn't be doing this if I didn't have to. I promised them all that if I got through this I'd have them all back without exception. They were like family to me and it was a forced goodbye.

I gave the estate manager, Lou, a great reference and he eventually moved his family to the south of France to manage a country estate owned by a member of the Sainsbury family. That wasn't a bad result for him, at least – south of France versus East Yorkshire. Nonetheless, I knew he would have preferred to stay. This whole process of dismantling my life felt like death by a thousand cuts.

Holly interrupted with a phone call from Gibraltar. The bank accounts were set up and ready to go; they just needed a date for the expected millions in transfer.

"Tell them it's been delayed, Holly. Say it will be after Christmas. I'll face it then. I can't speak to them now; I don't know what to say."

Peter called. "Hello, Mike. Look, you know I'm really down here and Debby is taking it badly. She's in a state of blind panic. I've told her we'll have to take the kids out of school, sell the house."

I realised I hadn't yet thought about the children's school. I'd have to face that one myself. I drifted away thinking about how Sue would react.

Oliver had just got back to school after as much disruption to his little life as any child should endure. But he was so far behind his classmates now, for obvious reasons. If he moved to a state school he'd at least have a chance of being somewhere in the anonymous middle. That at least was a benefit. Every cloud and all that.

"We're going to lose everything, Mike," Peter continued. "And as you know we've just moved into this bloody house. Debby's in tears all the time. I've booked a few days in Spain. I'm not going to the boat, that would be too painful; it's been moved to another, cheaper mooring, I hear. Greg heard what was going on as far away as Palma. Anyway, I've a mate out there. I can get easyJet, so it won't cost me a lot.

"I can't stand the idea of going back to the office, seeing those smug bastards with smiles on their faces, thinking they're getting our business for fucking nothing."

Peter had a point. As soon as Adam had let the cat out of the bag and effectively offered the business to those around the table for a super knock-down price in administration, we suddenly had a board of directors working for an ending that didn't involve us. Why wouldnt they?

Just when we needed to get our heads together and roll up our sleeves, we had a load of natural opportunists who looked at what they needed to do to swap their minority interests for majority ones. This was *their* chance of a lifetime; it was a natural reaction, even if it was a display of the most basic human behaviour.

On the other hand, the pre-packed administration idea by Adam was however inevitable and well meaning a corruptible one as it divided the board in each and every way, where the thoughts of pulling together were superseded by those of individual gain and natural self-interest.

Existing people around the table might have three per cent of the company, and the alternative view being spun was that we all might go to jail for continuing to trade when we had a 'reasonable view' that the company was insolvent. The choice was at least for some of them a larger percentage of a new company, leaving the debts behind and the resulting shit to be carried by guys who are not part of the solution. It was just a no-brainer for them. The only thing to stop them was loyalty, but no one exercised it. It was put to one side, old friendships forgotten. It was a shame it was feeding off the corpse of the group where, at least in my eyes, the patient wasn't technically dead yet. If it were, then at the very least they seemed to me to act like a well-organised team of grave robbers. It was the worst form of corporate cannibalism imaginable. How could this be best for the company, for the creditors and for the shareholders?

I felt like Caesar surrounded by enemies. I knew it was coming, but from which person? Who would deliver the fatal blow? I had to watch everyone and remember that the enemies of my enemies are surely my friends. Which of the directors among my extended family were on side and which weren't?

Peter left for Majorca. I hoped it would do him good and improve his health and ability to cope. I went back into the Leeds office. It had changed. There were quiet groups huddled together.

Adam got hold of me. "We've talked to the bank. They won't support any more funds going in, Mike. None of us thought they would anyway, that was just a formality. But I did feel I should ask on your behalf."

"Really?" I said. I had the impression Adam was ticking boxes, going through the motions so the prescribed objective could be achieved in a pragmatic way – to get into administration as quickly as possible and out again in record time, with the same guys apart from one or two notable exceptions and a very different shareholding.

"The last time I was at the bank, only six months ago, Malcolm, our acting group FD, was saying to Clive, our senior account manager in the city, just what control he had of everything and how we were looking forward to a good year," I said.

Adam ignored this. That wasn't going to get us anywhere as far as he was concerned. "They were supportive of the appointment of CBA, as I suggested." He seemed pleased with that; I couldn't care less.

"They're coming in today for a chat. I'm having the legals drawn up by the lawyers – that'll be on your desk in a couple of days."

"What's the first thing the administrators will do?" I asked,

"They'll listen to the presentations, try and establish the new money that's on the table, and decide if it's enough on behalf of creditors."

"How do we know if it's enough when no one can tell me what the hell is wrong in the company in the first place?" I asked in anger.

"Mike, it's not your fault. It's hard, I know. I also know you *will* rebuild from this, but right now you have to put self-interest to one side. It's your responsibility to think of all the staff you have here going up to Christmas who won't get paid if these three administration deals don't go through."

"What about the deals?" I asked, "Do they mean the employees will be protected?"

"They get TUPE pension rights, Mike, as if the contract hasn't been broken. That's as much as we can stipulate at the moment. It's better than the alternative."

"So they may be made redundant?"

"That's up to the buyer, but it's standard unbroken contact terms. One week for every year worked."

"That's not exactly secure, is it?" I said.

"It's the best out of this situation; there are no good solutions here."

"What's the deal, then?"

"I can't say, Mike. It's confidential at this time and no one has put a firm figure on the table."

"Who are those guys over there?" I pointed to a group of huddled strangers.

"They're accountants from another broker looking at the figures. We have to be sure we're getting the best for creditors."

"Well this fucking circus isn't the answer!" I exploded. "The group's worth more than £15 million!"

"On a good day, maybe, and with time on your side. You have neither. Mike, I'm sorry. This isn't easy for you, I really know it isn't, and you're coping well. I understand how you feel but I've to put that to one side and deal with practicalities."

"Fuck it. I'm not staying here watching this pack of hyenas picking at the body. I'm off to Ireland for a few days. I'm going off my head here."

"If you're going away, Mike, don't stay long, and keep in touch. Do you understand? CBA will need you to sign some documents."

"I bloody know they will, sign my life away in a cloud of confusion, treachery and deceit."

"I know why you feel like that Mike. Let me give you some advice for nothing. I'm trying to keep you out of jail. Remember that." Adam's voice hardened for the first time. Suddenly the parameters were changing. Now that was frightening.

Adam continued: "Keep trading and you're committing a criminal offence, that's the top and bottom of it. You'll not get all this back from Ford Open Prison."

It was the first time Adam had shown his teeth and it scared me. This was his specialist subject, not mine. I was beaten.

"I'm off," I said. "By the way, Peter's in Spain."

"What's he doing there?"

"Counting the money we stuffed in a load of fucking suitcases just before you turned up," I said.

At least he had the decency to smile.

Ireland

Holly had planned to see her family in Ireland a few weeks before Christmas as she had agreed to be with me at Woodland Grange. She was expected to make an appearance and it was only fair she honour the commitment.

Seeing how down I was, she suggested a three-day break would do us both good. So with a heavy heart and a *carpe diem* attitude, I boarded a flight to Shannon and then on to Tipperary. At the risk of a very obvious joke, it did seem a long, long way away from the comings and goings of the Leeds office.

I obviously wouldn't be the best company, but the family was very kind and only very gently asked questions about my current status.

Holly's sister's long-term boyfriend pulled me aside very discreetly.

"I don't want to pry, but Holly's been on the phone home. She's very worried about you, concerned about you both. Anyway, look, just between you and I here's £3,000 in cash to keep you going." He pushed an envelope my way. "Family's family; pay me back when you can – and not a word to the girls, eh?"

It was such a lovely gesture. I'm sure Holly would have never known had I taken it, but I refused.

"It's so kind of you, really, but I don't need it at the moment. I do appreciate your concern. I'll try my best to protect Holly from whatever is going to happen."

"All right," he said. "If you insist. But it's there. How much do you really need? For the company, I mean."

"A minimum of a million, apparently. Trouble is, no one can say for sure and we just don't have enough time. This catastrophe has rushed upon us."

"A bit more than this three grand then." He shook his head, recognising the numbers were too big for any acts of singular kindness.

"All the best, pal, I'm sure you'll find a way through. How do you feel in yourself?"

"Stressed to shit, bewildered, confused, let down – I don't know. A mixture."

"Listen, all you can do is try to relax, go with the flow. Eventually things will calm. Remember, everything passes. This will too. Let's join the girls."

It was a sweet thought and very kind of him. Everywhere I went in her family I saw worried, if kindly, faces looking back. There was something different about these people and I couldn't think what it was. Then it suddenly came to me – I was used to seeing them smiling and joyous. Now they were concerned and talking in hushed tones. My business had become their business.

We went back into the living room. Everyone was gathered around the fire. It was a peat fire that I'd never seen in England and smelt beautiful. I got lost in the flames, as I pondered what the future might hold.

Holly broke the silence, noticing my quiet stare: "Don't worry, Mike, there'll always be a place for you by the fireside."

I found tears flowing down my cheeks, without warning. I couldn't say anything other than mumble an apology. This was not the Christmas I expected or that Holly and her family deserved.

I'd been their great hope for Holly. I'd brought excitement and a little glamour to their lives. We'd buzzed her mum's house in a helicopter on the way to a wedding, sent a chauffeur-driven car to the house to collect her mum and sisters only a year earlier to attend a dinner at a local hotel. Yet here we all were now.

I felt ridiculous. I'd let them down. I'd given such expectations, only to dash them at the last minute, as they began to believe in me and Holly as a successful partnership.

We left the comfort of the fire and checked into a local hotel to be alone. It was a relief; if the family wasn't worried about me before, it certainly would be now.

"I know this isn't good, Mike," Holly said. "I guess you'd prefer to be back home at the moment."

I didn't know where I wanted to be. I had a feeling of awkwardness, of not belonging, that felt it might take years to lift. We made the family rounds and left the next day. I was pleased to be home.

I'd only been back a few minutes when the phone rang.

"Mike, fucking hell, where've you been? I've been trying to track you down all over the place in bloody Ireland."

"Hello Peter. How are you feeling?"

"Never mind that," he said anxiously. "I was telling our story to someone I met in Majorca. He knows our business. I've told him everything. And he's willing to make a punt for it. He'll share it with me, you and Jim once it's all sorted. He's serious, Mike. Wait, he's here, I'll put you on."

"Hello, Mike," a quiet and reassuring voice spoke. "I know we have to move quickly. I have an agent in Manchester, another corporate recovery guy. Don't worry about that, he'll work for us, not the other buggers.

"I'm going to split between you, Peter and Jim on an equal basis any profits once we buy it, sort it, and sell it within a year. We just need to get moving, and quickly. Get into the office and see those buggers get the name of the guy that's dealing with it on our side, right? Whatever you do, don't sign the admin order until we have our deal together, just let them know we're in play. They have to consider my offer. They don't need to know that you personally are going to be involved, that's between you and me. You're just going to have to go with me on trust."

He went on: "Thing is, Mike, I know with you original three back at it you can sort it and get it in good shape for the best sale. So it makes perfect sense. Now, act quickly. I'm getting legals and the like together. Get in the office and get it started."

A surge of adrenalin flowed through my body. Something I hadn't felt for ages. My mood instantly lifted.

I just had time to go and tell Holly, and then I jumped in the car and drove at speed and caught the first flight out.. I hurtled into Leeds. This was it. This was the break we'd hoped for. We still had time. We'd turn it around. My prayers had been answered.

Fighting back

I arrived at the office unannounced and certainly unexpected. People obviously thought I'd given up and just walked away.

I felt as if I'd walked into a room full of burglars who'd been caught in the act. Either I was an embarrassment or they were embarrassed by what had transpired here.

I guess most of my previous family of directors had had enough time to visualise their new beginning. A new company with a different ownership. Seeing me still on the scene might have been a bit of a blow; I didn't fit in with their vision of the future. Nobody greeted me; nobody smiled or acknowledged me other than James, who was first to appear and one of only a few people who seemed happy to speak to me.

"Holy shit, Mike, I wouldn't rush back here if I were you. You've missed nothing. It's bloody carnage, painful watching the dismantling of this lot," he said, shaking his head. I could see he'd lost weight and looked tired, drawn and enormously stressed. Whatever plans he'd privately harboured had gone south once the corporate recovery guys got involved. He was obviously not in control of anything anymore. Just like me. He unburdened himself whilst I did a quick scan around the office.

"I went to London to assist with a pitch for Corporate and was told it wouldn't go ahead with me in the team. So that's me fucked. They practically told me to piss off there and then. It broke my heart, honestly it did."

He talked without any hint of irony. "I'm just trying to help. If I don't, there have been strong hints at what might be said in the Directors' Conduct Report. It's terrible. I'd watch your back if I was you. They really are hard bastards, CBA, and that Scottish twat who's in charge of them."

"What else is happening?" I asked.

"Malcolm is all over the place - I think he's looking to buy at least Financial Services if not the Direct business. He may end up yet with the whole lot. He's not prepared to pay much, that's for sure. I mean it's fucking awful. No one's collecting the premiums, so the debts are getting larger and larger. It's such a mess, and I know who's going to take the drop when it's all added up. But whatever the problem was in the first place, it's a fucking damn sight bigger now. What a bleeding mess.

"Whatever the problem is, it'll be five times what it was because no one seems to be managing it. Nobody listens to me any more or talks to me. I'm treated like a bloody leper."

I knew how he felt.

The bank had agreed with the potential choice of CBA. All I needed to do was formally appoint them. Once I signed, that would give the guys legal control, which would be for a matter of hours only. Then they'd sell the businesses as going concerns within hours, as part of the pre-pack arrangement - straight into admin and straight out. Goodbye debts, and let's go get the bad guys and make them pay. Not a bad strategy, if somewhat unfair from where I was standing.

"Where are the guys from CBA? I haven't even talked to them yet."

"In the boardroom. Why?"

"What are they like, James?"

"Awful, like corporate policemen."

"Who's the guy in charge?"

"The Scottish guy I met called Graham Shelley. He's a complete hard man, gives nothing away. Very unemotional."

"Talk in a minute, James." I wanted to keep my powder dry on that one.

I walked in. No one stood up or even moved; no one greeted me.

140

"I'm Mike. Who's the senior partner here?"

"Hello," said a Scottish voice with all the warmth of a hangman working out how much of a drop I'd need.

He continued without any attempt at niceties, even those that might have been appropriate at this difficult time.

"We're nearly done here. The document is on your desk. Timing is critical. We didn't know when you were back. We were just talking about making contingency plans."

"Is that right?" I said, trying not to be intimidated. "I told everyone I'd always be on the end of the phone. I haven't done a runner yet."

"Look, I'll get to the point. I've a syndicate in Spain. They're serious people and want to buy the group."

One of the guys leaned back in his chair, shook his head and said, "We're selling the business in three parts."

"Okay, they'll buy them in three parts."

"Insurers won't deal with you, Mike, just like they wouldn't with James," Graham said helpfully.

"Well I don't know why the fuck not because I haven't been operational for three years, everybody around here knows that even if it doesn't suit them to say it right now! But I'm not buying it or fronting it. I just believe this is a better deal for all, including the creditors."

"You'll get a call in half an hour. Take it, please, and we'll go from there."

"I'll be outside." I looked around. Just before I left, I turned and paused for effect. "Continue using this office for now. I'm happy for it to be used today. I'll have it back in the morning."

I walked out to silence. I'd just put a spoke in their collective wheels and many other people's unbridled ambitions. I got onto the Spanish contact in Manchester – George, a very calm man, was on the other end.

"Don't worry, I've done many of these. I've got all necessary instructions."

"Okay. Well, I just met the main guy – his name is Graham Shelley."

"I think I might know him. Do you know anything about him, Mike?"

"No, other than he's Scottish and has a miserable face. And I'm clearly not his favourite person at the moment. It's clear he's made his mind up about me!"

"Probably a blessing," George said. I didn't know what he meant but moved on. It seemed there was a small but powerful club of corporate recovery specialists around the UK, all scratching each other's backs. There was a buyer, there was a seller and, as we knew, that meant a lot of fees for the middlemen.

Ten minutes later George was on the phone again. "Yes, he is miserable. And he's making it difficult for us. We need to transfer a million in cash by nine o'clock tomorrow morning for our offer to be considered seriously. We need to prove liquid funds. If not, it's not going our way at any price."

"Why? The others haven't put a million pounds down."

"That's what I said, but apparently the other players have done a lot of work on it and insurers are ready to agree so they're not taking us seriously. Don't worry, they will when I deposit the money. I'm onto it now and then they'll have to listen. They have a legal duty. By the way, who's Malcolm Curtis?"

"He was supposed to be our group financial director. Why?"

"He's buying Financial Services and he was buying your Direct arm, but he's pulled out of that one and left your boys in the lurch. They're busy looking for new backers. Anyway, we don't want Financial Services long, Mike, but we may need to buy it as part of a package. You, Jim and Peter are going to have your hands full sorting out the problems in Corporate, to get it ready for the return on my client's investment. You need to straighten it out and will be expected to sell it within a year with a split of the capital value gained. That should still be a tidy sum for all.

"So, if you know anyone who wants to buy Financial Services in isolation, I'd get onto them urgently. The more we can clear our initial outlay, the more profit for all. Can you talk to people to get that company away?"

"Sure," I confirmed, "I know just the people. Given time, that is."

"Well, we'll buy it if needs be, so long as you're confident you can get it away. That's not the issue here. It's just that when we put a million in, it would be nice if we could reasonably quickly claw some money back. Keep in touch every half hour."

"Will do," I said.

I came out of the private room.

"What's going on, Mike?" one of the accountants asked.

"I'm arranging to buy the company back when it goes into administration," I confirmed. "And I know who'll be the first to go when I'm back in power."

And having revealed their hands and shown themselves for who and what they were, I dare say I had now done the same.

The final hours

I continued to refer back every half hour until I finally got a note that the transfer had taken place and confirmation that funds would be available in cash to an amount of one million pounds for the purchase. The guys had come through with the readies. Now it was a question of what CBA wanted in terms of liabilities and finer detail. There was nothing I could do; I wasn't representing the syndicate. It was up to George.

I checked that the administration document was in my name as chairman and chief executive, awaiting my signature, and left. Everything was fine for the morning, when the formal offer would be made to CBA.

More relaxed then I'd been for a long time, I directed my attention to best offers for Financial Services. Also, I could get Peter to resurrect the E&O portfolio sale. That, with time, would raise at least a million. The Spanish consortium would be delighted. We could clear their funds with that alone; everything else would be profit.

I talked to Peter. He was resigned to whatever might happen.

"Just do your best, Mike; it's all you can do," he said.

"I'm trying, Peter. It's our last chance, we're still fighting!"

I got a call from George. "I've dropped a fax off to Graham at CBA. It confirms the money is available at nine in the morning, ready for transfer, as they have asked; once we agree final terms, it's a goer. However Ive told them that this whole issue would be best dealt with after Christmas when we can get around the table "

I was still unsure. "Is there anything else that can be done now, George?"

"No. Relax, it's just the finer detail and I'm taking instructions on that. We want to get together with you at eight in the morning - Queen's Hotel in Leeds, okay? I'll have a management team with me that I'm hoping we can use for the first three months; they'll help you with disposals, and generally steadying things down. We're all going to make money, Mike. We're looking forward to working with you."

I was looking forward to seeing a few new friendly faces for a change. Most of the new ones I'd met recently had nothing more than a sneer on them, as if I'd been caught with my hands in the till or fallen asleep at the wheel. I went straight out to a financial services company that had previously made discreet enquiries.

"It's yours for half a million," I said. We'd previously talked at around two million. They were delighted but shocked to hear what had been going on. But they'd benefit and were helping out the major shareholders, so I persuaded them that it was a case for celebration, not sorrow, given what the alternative might have been. We had well over £100,000 in renewable income in that business so four times that value seemed to be the going rate with an additional add –on for the production team. Half a million seemed a good price.

"I'm meeting the team at eight in the morning."

"Great," they said. "Let's grab a few drinks, it'll be a difficult few hours to pass."

I thought it might have been a bit too early, but I had nothing else to do. Everything was under control and adrenalin rushed through me. I just couldn't go home to sit and wait. It would be a long, long night and tomorrow was crucial. I phoned Holly and told her the potential news

"That's great, darling. I know you'll get through this. Enjoy yourself, get a taxi home and let off some steam."

"Let's have a few," I said to the financial service consultants. I called a few old school mates who came down as well. We could smile again. The drinks flowed more out of relief than celebration.

It was 7pm when I got a tap on the shoulder. It was Adam, waving the administration order in front of my face. He'd been trawling around the bars in Leeds looking for me.

"Mike. I'm glad I've found you. I need you to sign this administration order right now. Insurers are insisting this is completed tonight. They won't wait any longer."

"Piss off!" I said. "I'll look at it tomorrow when I've done my deal."

"It needs to be done tonight. If it's not, insurers won't support the pre-pack. It'll endanger everything – they'll apply to have the group wound up."

"As if another bloody night makes a difference, Adam. I've told you, fuck off!" I squared up to him. My friends did as well. I grabbed the contract. Did he really think I'd sign it pissed up? I pulled it out of his hands and threw it over the bar.

"Just fuck off. I'll see you in the morning at nine. We've got our own deal," I said.

Adam looked furious and did a second take of the guys that I was with as he disappeared into the night

"That bloody told him," the financial services guys said. "Cheek of it, trying to bully you into a corner."

"Well, he hasn't got it signed, has he?!"

But the encounter brought a sobriety to the occasion and soon after I got a taxi home. I needed to be up early in the morning. It was going to be a big day.

The last chance

I woke to a bright, sharp, winter frost. Woodland Grange always looked its best at this time of the year. I made a coffee, dressed and pulled on an old coat for a stroll around the lake.

I tried to remind myself what was at stake today. All this was in the balance and God knew what the future held. I was still confused as to why my life had been brought to this - a point where I had an equal chance of continued success or financial disaster. All decided on this day. It was too much to take in. Life shouldn't be like this. I had always liked to live life and 'feel alive' but this was too much. A simple, pivotal point. Life's ups and downs should flow with natural consequence. This wasn't like that. This was a cruel, haphazard, win or lose occasion. It was fate.

I set off for the Queens Hotel and got hold of Jim.

"Hello, mate. How you feeling?" he said.

"I'm great. Don't hold your breath but I'm hopeful of signing a deal this morning that'll kick us in for at least twenty five per cent of any disposals. It means you, Pete and I keep our jobs and share in any successful disposal. Okay, it's not what we wanted or expected, but we'll still get significant money. It's better than we could have expected a few days ago."

" It's over, Mike. " Jim said, deadpan.

I was shocked at his downbeat view, this was very unlike Jim.

"No, it isn't. Adam came to see me last night. I told him to fuck off."

" I was told it was done last night, Mike. You need to speak to Adam," Jim insisted.

"I will, but right now I'm seeing the management team that will work alongside us. Soon as I come out I'll call you. Peter's on a plane home today. It might be a good idea if you jump on a train up here."

"Just have your meeting, Mike, and we'll take it from there," a strangely subdued Jim said. "Call me when you can." He rang off.

The guys were there. I just wanted to get back to the office and tell Adam we'd done a deal for the lot for a million pounds and a commitment to look at all corporate liabilities.

They happened to be nice guys, but I'd have taken anyone as a partner. Beggars can't be choosers. Maybe I'd learned I didn't have to like someone to work with them. I'd had enough of making pretend friends out of work colleagues. Those sort of friendships die when mutuality of interest dies, I had learned that at least the hard way.

I asked if the team wanted to come to the office. They declined, saying it might be seen as provocative. We didn't want a mass walk-out. We needed the root and branch guys to look after the remaining clients. They'd have a couple of meetings with insurers while they were here; they were familiar with them as one of the team dealt in that sector.

"Just get back there and sit on CBA," I was told.

Again, George told me to relax. He could see the stress etched on my face.

"They're not going to get a matching offer at this time. Right now, time's against them for once and not us," he told me. Not bad for a quick conversation in Spain. I made a mental note to thank Peter; he'd got this deal started in his usual low-key way.

I came out of the hotel to a bright blue sky and was walking back to the office when Adam tapped me on the shoulder. How long he'd been lurking around there was anybody's guess. Was it an accident that he'd bumped into me or had he been watching?

He was smiling, as ever, but it seemed to be out of sympathy. He held out his hands to me. "We were worried about you, Mike. You have a lot of people back at that office who care for you, and they're really sorry you can't be part of their team. No one's blaming you."

"Well, they're not going to be in my new team. I've secured the million cash. It's in the bank. It's been confirmed and arranged in three days. Your lesser offer has taken four weeks to put together. I'm proud of what we've pulled off."

"It's over, Mike," Adam said, still smiling weakly. "The administration order was signed last night."

"No it fucking wasn't. I threw it away. I told you I'd deal with it this morning. It has my name on it, mate. I'm the major controlling shareholder, I checked it last night. It has to be signed by me."

"It was signed last night. We called an emergency board meeting; those who were there formed a quorum and moved that the name on the document be changed. It was sent to the lawyers turned around by them and brought back and signed.

"I'm sorry. I know how hard this must be for you. You have to understand. Time was of the essence, that's what I was trying to tell you last night. We needed to move. Insurers were getting anxious."

"You can't do that, Adam. I control the group board. I'm the majority shareholder."

"We can and we have, Mike. CBA are in court, the administration order is going through as we speak, as is the sale to the three parties."

"Who signed it? Who fucking signed it?" I said, exploding with anger.

"Declan ."

"What?" I could hardly contain myself. Declan wasn't a senior player –he was a mummy's boy! "The bastard! I'll tear him apart when I see him. Bastard!"

"Come on, Mike. No point kicking off now. Let's go to Starbucks and have a coffee. Talk things through. It's gone, Mike, you have to accept it. Everybody is impressed with your resilience, your desire to carry on, but it's over, it really is. Now you have to deal with the reality."

He went on: "When you go back into that office, hold your head high. People still look to you, Mike. How you act now will define their memory of your time with the company. You need to act with dignity.

"This is all part of the corporate game, you should know that. Guys like you are never down for long, and I'm going to help you. I'm always given a load of disposals to move on, some better than others. I'll put you top of my list. Not insurance for a few years of course, but you're a businessman – you can turn your hand to anything."

I was on autopilot. I didn't know whether to chin him or hold his hand in desperation. I was a scared, broken, shattered little boy.

I sat in Starbucks a hundred yards from what had been my office and gathered myself together.

"I'll sue the fucking lot of you, Adam. If you believe half of what you said about me, you know I'm not going to let you get away with this. You'll all fucking pay for this."

"Everything we've done has been legal, Mike, in the best interest of the creditors. I know you're angry, but let's not talk in that way. I wouldn't threaten legal action. It would be civil action, not criminal, and that means you need to fund your own court costs. I doubt if you'd want to spend what remains of your money on chasing a tiger's tail. There are a lot of big players here with deep pockets.

"These guys are professionals, they know what they're doing. They've got excellent reputations and the first job you need to do is rebuild yours. You'll not do that by mudslinging."

Tears were falling at this point.

"Look, Mike, you're not thinking clearly at this point. I see it all the time. Your concern right now should be what Graham at CBA says to the DTI about directors' conduct. That goes in as a formality. You've done everything good so far. You need to be on the right side of them. They *are* powerful people and you don't want to create problems for yourself in the future. How you feeling, Mike?"

I was conscious of people looking at a grown man with tears flowing down his cheeks while another guy had his arm round him.

Adam went on: "I need you to come in to the office. Sign two TUPE agreements that say you're not going to pursue your employment contract rights with the new companies. That's just a formality, obviously. I mean, you don't want to be seen taking more money out of the business to the detriment of creditors. They've lost enough and it will go on your directors' conduct report if you sign your rights away. It will look good for you, and that's what you need right now.

"Obviously it's up to you, but if you don't, the sale agreement states that the sale monies may be reduced by that precise amount. That means you get the money, not the creditors – trust me, you wouldn't want your name on that. It would be a red rag to a bull. Get your head down. Stay silent. Tell them the truth if they ask. There were accounting glitches and you've taken it on the chin, as chief executive and chairman. You've held your hands up.

"You'll be back in three years, Mike, good men always are. You'll be fine Are you ready to go?

"You're doing great, mate. You have character, they told me that. Head up, Mike. Let's sign the contracts and then I know you can go home. Get your thoughts together. I'll meet you in the New Year and we can talk about some of the business opportunities I have. I'll help you get funding, don't worry about that. Okay, let's go."

Into the office

I walked into the office. I could see empty champagne bottles from the previous night. I wasn't the only one who'd celebrated.

There was an attempt to hide them but they weren't discreet enough. It sickened me. I was ushered into a private room. Those who bothered to raise their heads looked as if they'd seen a ghost. They probably had. I signed the TUPE agreements. One of the junior directors brought the form in and burst into tears.

"I'm an emotional man, Mike. Thanks for doing this."

"I've no choice," I said. "There's been a lot of treachery here. You're more than aware of that. I hope you can all sleep at night. I know I couldn't if I'd have been involved in what's happened here."

I didn't see Declan, thank God, but I also knew that he hadn't acted alone. I felt as if I was in some sort of trance, signing my employment rights away without thinking too much about the consequences. I was, in effect, giving up over a hundred thousand pounds in that single action. Money that I might need in the future to keep me going, as there'd be no other source of income for quite a while.

I took the lift to the basement where I'd left my car. It had been clamped. The security men were still there.

"Sorry, Mike, orders of CBA."

I went back up in the lift and sought out Graham Shelley.

"Yes?" he said, barely lifting his head. His whole attitude towards me had hardened. The deal was done, I could just fuck off as far as he was concerned.

"My car! Get it unclamped!" I was boiling at this point.

"I need to see the registration document. One of your ex-colleagues says it's a company vehicle, in which case it stays here."

"It's not a sodding company vehicle. Wait a minute." I called Holly and told her where to find the ownership document, asking her to fax it through.

Nothing was said while we waited for it to arrive.

"Okay, get security," he said. "Unclamp the car."

He said nothing to me. I waited.

"Yes?" he asked.

"What about a bleeding apology?"

"I'm not going to apologise for carrying out my professional responsibilities in this administration," he said with a slightly heavier Scottish accent then previously.
"Well your bloody formality shouldn't prohibit decent fucking manners," I said.
"Mr Kenney," he said, "I believe you have plans to leave the country?"
"Not any more," I informed him. "Gibraltar would have been nice, but hey ho."
"Good," he said. "We'll be in touch."
I left.
Sounded like a threat to me…

Home – to what?

I'd telephoned the Manchester team and told them what had happened; they were as astonished as I was sad.
There was talk of legal consequences, but I knew in my heart the group had gone. There wasn't a new investor on earth who'd spend loads of money and time on a legal battle against this pillar of insolvency establishment. It was too much hassle and a waste of their money. Who was to say they had done wrong? They needed to act quickly and that's what they did. We were the losers,simple as that.
Acceptance overcame shock at what had occurred. It was truly over.
Holly could tell as soon as she came to the door of Woodland Grange to greet me that it hadn't turned out as I'd hoped. She poured me a large glass of red wine as I sat by the fire. I didn't want to talk; I just let my mind wander; making shapes from the flames as I tried in some way of coming to terms with the day.
When I accepted an invitation to go for a walk to clear my head, everything seemed to stare back at me with an accusation of failure. Every beautiful thing was there only to say goodbye. It was a cruel beauty. I'd surely lose this place.
I had no money coming in. My business was my savings, my pension. Sure, I had assets, but just as in the business, time wasn't on my side. In a fire sale, everything would at least be halved in value
The unique position, size and responsibilities associated with running a small estate meant that what was so special about it was also the reason why it would not sell quickly.
I wish I had a four bedroom terrace house that I could dispose of like that, I said to Holly, clicking my fingers. "Who's going to take on this lot at a moment's notice? The animals, the cats, the dogs, the horses, pheasants, cattle, sheep?" They all seemed to look at me with doleful eyes, dependant on me to ensure their feed.
The fear and uncertainty was overwhelming. I simply didn't know what to say or do. I've always been able to manage my position, had excellent credit references and an unblemished track record, but this was entirely different. This looked way beyond any hope of managing.
Lou, the estate manager, offered to help me move the animals. People came from far and wide to get their free livestock. Holly did her best through Christmas and New Year. We stayed in and sat in silence a lot of the time, only venturing out occasionally.
Fortunately we'd had the children the previous Christmas, so we didn't have to pretend to be happy for them. Having delivered a few presents that had already been bought, we returned to the temporary sanctuary of the estate.
Stress inevitably showed. Holly was reluctant to go to the matrimonial home as previously planned. She, like me, wanted to stay in alone with her thoughts.

It was unusual but I figured that she was embarrassed for me and didn't want accusing looks from Sue, who'd obviously heard the news as the direct debit of £5,000 a month stopped. She'd been a slightly sympathetic observer to my predicament, but now found it crashing in on her life. It started to dawn on the people around me that their immediate family also needed to consider adjustments. Everything was up for change.

News of the group's demise hit the papers. There I was on the front page, smiling and looking slightly ridiculous, certainly out of context as I launched the Atlantic Challenge. The headline read: 'Yorkshire company collapsed as chief executive criticised for champagne lifestyle.'

It was certainly clear that this mad world of insolvency practice seemed to attract colourful people who to my mind perhaps existed and operated at the lower end of pond life. They liked a good story, maybe for the benefit of unfortunate creditors, but it seemed that there had to be good guys and bad guys clearly defined. Somebody was leaking this character assassination to the press. It was nothing more than a pantomime.

If you weren't part of the solution then you were part of the problem. In that regard, it was obvious where everyone thought I stood.

Jim had managed to get a job with the new company set up to replace Corporate, I think because he was in London and away from the decision-making process. He'd also been involved with Financial Services and most of the attention was, not unnaturally, on Corporate. He was given a chance to start again and I wished him well. It made me smile to think of the forensic questioning he might get from CBA, only for him to shrug his shoulders and talk about 'diddly squat'.

I was pleased he'd escaped the terrible and uncertain future that surrounded Peter and me. I felt for Peter. It might have been his proximity to me that pulled him into the vision of these corporate inquisitors, or simply that he was one of the senior directors of Corporate or, he was simply a name who wasn't part of the solution.

In any event, lines appeared drawn as various comments had been leaked by someone or some company in a matter of days about the initial findings of the administrators. Peter, James and I were very firmly in their sights. I tried to be philosophical about it, but was shocked that I could make such headlines. I could hardly bear to look but forced myself to read it. Probably not a good idea but, like a nasty accident on the motorway, you have slow down for a quick glimpse as you pass. I wished I hadn't.

It talked about missing millions, how at first examination there was a suggested shortfall of £3,000,000.

I wondered how that could be. I knew nobody seemed that interested in collecting that which was owed by the clients, and I knew some insurers might bang every invoice they could onto the account in the hope of increasing the debt and getting more pennies in the pound in final settlement. But not to the tune of three million. That was just outrageous.

It was the New Year and I got on the phone to James.

"How are you?" he asked.

"In complete bewilderment, confusion and anxiety," I said.

"Nice picture in the paper though..." he replied.

It was clear that any side deals he might have thought of or hoped for hadn't come his way. He was on his arse like Peter and me, but he was still cocky with it which I admired to be honest. I wanted to ask him about the missing money.

"What the hell is this quote of £3,000,000 about? Jesus, as if we wouldn't have noticed that lot going missing!"

"Yeah, I know, Mike. It's all over the papers, isn't it?"

"It bloody is!" I said. "I'm been called Champagne fucking Charlie, and on the next line they're talking about serious investigation and three fucking million gone missing, James! It's not exactly a good connection, is it? What the fuck has gone on?"

"When a company goes into administration or receivership, they consolidate all the debts. So, for example, if we had ten years left on a £100K lease then there's a debt at the end of the day of £1 million. So that's what they're doing, consolidating all the leases *et cetera*."

"Well it's hardly fucking missing, then, is it? Anyway, won't these new companies take on the leases?"

"That depends on the offers that have been accepted by CBA. It looks likely that they didn't insist on that as part of the purchase maybe because of the time scales involved"

"So there's loads of lease agreements that the new companies don't have to have?"

"Exactly. It's a form of window dressing. Think of all the company cars on lease that will be rolled up, properties and computers. It will be millions. But it's not exactly missing, Mike, that's the point; it's just in deficit."

"How do you think people reading the news reports will think?"

"I know what they think, Mike. Have you been in your local pub recently?"

"No, I've been lying low. Surprisingly, I haven't really felt like going out."

"Well, when you do, you'll get an idea…..."

I felt physically sick. This was way beyond business failure. This was a personal attack that I had to take. I couldn't quite believe it, but here it was. The fact dawned on me that just because something was printed in the press, it had a hold on people – it was persuasive and they believed it.

Holly looked at me with a mixture of sadness and alarm. Even she began to realise what we were dealing with here. Things you don't want to believe need greater illumination because you have to stop deceiving yourself and face the truth. For her, there it was in all its glory, on the front page of the *Yorkshire Post*.

But the person portrayed there wasn't me. Where was the guy she'd been engaged to? She'd had had her hopes, dreams and future shattered. Now she was living everyday in close proximity to a man who appeared to be wasting away at his centre. She didn't recognise that man.

CHAPTER 11

Telling the family

If opinions were changing, it was because opinion-formers – like newspaper comments in the local press and specialist magazines – painted a very damning picture of my high lifestyle.

I continued to read it – I couldn't resist, even though I knew it would leave me filled with hurt, anger and outrage.

The stuff I'd expected was there, comments on yachts, cars and big houses. But here was something, a quote from someone I didn't recognise saying how Kenney always insisted on having a refrigerator at the London flat constantly stocked with quality champagne.

Thus the name 'Champagne Charlie' seemed to be the one the press ran with. Nice, I could see where this was going. First champagne lifestyle, then this refrigerator stocked up with it, all at my insistence.

The reality was quite different.

I asked that anyone who drank the one bottle – only one – that was in there, or any of the beer, cider and the alcopops Jim used as a quick heart-starter or party ice-breaker, replaced it. That seemed fair enough to me, the polite thing to do. That way, there was always a bottle there for anyone to enjoy – employees, guests, or me and my family. If you use it, replace it. It's good manners.

I began to see with my own eyes how a half-truth is manipulated in the interest of a good story and realised I'd better get used to it.

I also needed to see Mum and Dad. If the press was damning, God knew what my mother would say when she realised I'd lost all my money! Holly declined to come with me.

During the collapse of the business, another tragic situation was taking its miserable place in my world. My father suffered a serious stroke and had just managed to survive with paralysis down his right side. He could hardly speak.

I'm sure my situation, and the worry it had caused, hadn't helped. He'd always followed my career with interest and enjoyed many trips to see Leeds United as they enjoyed a honeymoon period at the top of the Premiership.

He'd just come out of hospital and we were all glad and relieved that he was home and safe. We had, as a family, seen enough of hospitals to last a lifetime.

It took enormous effort for him to make himself understood. I could only imagine his frustration, as he surely would have had a lot to say about all this in better health.

There was a look from my mum like I'd stayed out all night and been a naughty boy. Dad smiled a beautiful, lop-sided grin that said more to me than words. He'd obviously seen the paper and understood this was going to be a bit tricky.

"Bloody hell, here's Gunga Din!" Mum said, announcing my arrival to all, including my big sister who was visiting.

"He's not that anymore, Mum, he's Champagne Charlie!" said Lorraine. She started to sing:

Champagne Charlie is my name,
Champagne drinking is my game
There's no drink like fizz fizz fizz!
I get by with whizz whizz whizz!
I'm the idol of all the barmaids

Champagne Charlie is my name!

"Bloody stop it!" Mum said. "Our Michael's lost three bloody million and you think it's funny."

I remembered the fuss over the pink slippers and hardly dare wonder what she made of this.

"How the hell can you lose that lot?" Things you never thought you'd hear your own mother say. She's more familiar in what a full house in bingo might pay. I felt like a boy who'd lost his bus fare home.

"Come on Michael, where have you buried it?" my sister ribbed me.

It might have been a joke but people couldn't believe we'd be that far out. People really believed it had been grabbed and hidden somewhere. I shook my head.

"I've lost everything, Mum," I said. "And everyone is taking the piss!"

"Shit to them!" she said. "You haven't lost everything. You've still got your children and you've got your health. And you've got me and yer dad, hasn't he, Tom?"

"I've lost around ten million personally which is the true value of the shares," I continued. This was too much for her to take in. Shaking her head, she tried to make sense of these large numbers.

"How much would that have been a week in my hand Michael?"

"Forget it, Mum. It's not worth thinking about; you don't have big enough hands."

"Anyway have you seen the lovely new wedding ring I've bought your Dad?" Mum continued back to normal life. "It's lovely, isn't it Tom?"

Why he needed that after having a bloody great stroke, I had no idea.

"The other one was cutting into him, wasn't it love?" she confirmed. Dad nodded. That's all he could do at the moment. He could hardly talk.

"Great," I said. "They'll think you're my fence and I'm moving into gold bullion!"

"Who's a bloody fence?" Mum said, confused.

My sister and I laughed. "It's a good job she really doesn't understand," I said to sis, as we retired to the kitchen to make more tea. I thought a lot of tea might be drunk before this little problem was worked through.

"Best not buy any more gold for the moment, Mum," I said, returning to the lounge. "Interpol will be here soon. I've confessed everything to them. I've said Dangerous Doreen the Dollar made me do it; I gave her money, but she always asked for more. She has a habit you see, it's terrible. I asked her to stop, to get help but no; she wouldn't until I had to bury the money. It's the bingo, you see. She's a gambling addict. She always says she's a few numbers off winning and her luck's bound to change soon. She's always saying that, but she needs the money now!"

"You bloody fool," she said to the sound of laughter.

"Yes, you're going to get followed to bingo with people asking where's your Michael buried the dirty wonga. If the press turn up it's because I've told them I'm only following your orders. They're looking for Dangerous Doreen the Bingo Queen."

"Eh?" she said with a quizzical face.

"All you have to say is: 'It's a fair cop, guv, I'm bang to rights and no mistake, but I'm not turning grass on me and me own, whatever the porridge. You're wanting Champagne Charlie, are you? Well you're looking on the wrong manor, my old cock; you'll never take him sober.' Then tell them to go shit, Mum."

Fits of laughter reverberated around the house. Sis and I always shared the same sense of ridiculous humour. It was good to laugh again.

"What the bloody hell you on about?" Mum said.

"Nothing, Mum, just taking the Mickey. I'm off home while I still have it. See you and Dad later." I turned to my sister. "Keep reading."

"Ho, I am, love," she said, "This is much more interesting than that exemplary entrepreneur crap! See you later, Charlie!"
I felt better for that visit. Families, eh?

Before they hit you, they hold you still

I'd been back at Woodland Grange for just a few minutes when there was a knock on the door.
"Mr Michael Kenney?"
"Yes," I replied.
"I've this for you," the man said, thrusting a brown package into my hands.
I wasn't in a hurry to open it and placed it on a sideboard. It sat there menacingly. Whatever was inside, I knew it wasn't going to be good news.
I didn't need to wait long; within half an hour, Peter called.
"Shit, Mike, they've frozen all our personal assets. They've issued a freezing order on everything," Peter said. "The bastards! They've had everything else, now they're after our personal stuff. Have you seen it?"
"No – I have it but I've not opened it. I knew it wasn't going to be good news."
"They've implied that I was planning to leave the country and run to Spain. I mean, what are they thinking, Mike? They applied to have our passports confiscated because they think we're going to do a runner. What are they trying to lay on us?"
I cast my mind back to the administrator's words: "You're not planning to leave the country, are you?" and "We'll be in touch."
They'd surely had this in mind all along. They hadn't even got stuck into the forensic financial investigation at that time, but they'd already separated the good guys from the bad. It possibly showed a certain mind-set from the start. What did they think we were going to run from? What were they being told, and who by?
"Try not to get upset," I said. "Let's get together in the morning and work it through. The judge didn't make us surrender our passports, Peter. Take comfort in that."
"But what are they really thinking, Mike?" he repeated.
I didn't feel he needed or wanted an answer. What they were thinking seemed obvious to me and Peter was taking this very badly. I was worried for his mental health.
"And where's Malcolm in all this? What's he saying about us?" Peter, getting angry, now demanded to know. It was a good question.
"I'll try and find out and get back to you, mate. Take it steady. Things will get better, Peter; just take one day at a time. That's what I'm doing."
James was next to phone. "Peter's been on the phone and he's very upset about this order to say the least! What happened to Malcolm in all this?" I asked.
"Nothing, Mike.."
"What? Surely he had to be at least partly responsible for the financials, hadn't he? I trusted him with the accounts; he said it would be okay."
"You don't need to tell me that, Mike. You've been let down and so have I. All those bloody people in the finance department, four qualified accountants and all."
"Well how can he have escaped this shit, for God's sake?"
"Mike, he bought Financial Services along with Declan and others. He bought it for what seems to be a ridiculously low price."
"Shit. So that's their solution. What about his position as acting group financial director?"
"I've heard he's denied that entirely. He doesn't appear to remember the conversation

we had with him at Pool Court, said he'd been asked to help out and did his best for us. That's as far as it went as far as he's concerned. He was merely showing concern and doing what he could for us both. End of story. That's what he's saying to CBA."

"What?" This was unbelievable. "As if I'd allow a business to be run without a group FD, for fuck's sake! What about the contract we had with him? Doesn't that count?"

"Nope. If you remember, that was a service contract for his consultancy in the group and payment was to be made to his company, not him. Bet you weren't thinking that when he said it would be okay just to have a contract with his company rather than an employment contract with him!"

"So, no fucking contract, no fucking position, no fucking responsibility?"

"Correct, and in that case it's all back to us, mate! Happy days!" said James.

"Wouldn't have helped us anyway. He's saying he asked for more resources and you said no."

"Bloody hell, I only said there was no point throwing more money after it, that's all. How many did they need? We went from around four people to twenty seven in three years. That's not just ignoring it, or not attaching enough importance to it."

"I know, you don't have to tell me. It's like history being re-written, the prize the victors always get. It's unforgivable."

I tried to gather my thoughts and changed the subject. "Peter's cut up, James."

"So he should be, Mike. They're going for a writ against us for damages."

"Who are? How much? Why? Haven't they done enough?"

"They want heads on a plate, Mike, and ours are the biggest. If they can get Peter as well, so be it."

"How much, James? How much are they going to sue us for?"

"Around three million and counting. Christ knows what it will be once the dust settles. Fucking outrageous, it really is. Anyway... Chin up, chief! Let me know if you've hear anything. I'm off to see my lawyers, suggest you do the same."

James was as well-mannered, efficient and irrepressible as he always appeared to be. I mused about the fact that if he said it was all a terrible mistake and they had the wrong company, I'd have believed him.

Facing the future

From a financial perspective, the best Holly and everyone in my immediate family could make of this catastrophe was that at some point I could realise money by liquidating my personal assets – capital in the house and the like.

We'd previously talked about moving abroad, cashing in what we had and going to France. We'd even started to look at suitable properties in our price range once the estate was sold.

A quick back-of-a-fag-packet calculation suggested I'd clear around half a million in cash after all liabilities. My family thought it would be enough to go away, lick my wounds, take a year off, learn the lessons and start again. Wherever, whatever.

Teach me a lesson, nothing too life-shattering or serious. I now knew differently. I wasn't going to walk away from this with my life intact. Those still close to me had heard enough bad news.

I'd just been served with a freezing order, which is the equivalent of someone holding your arms in a fight. Totally tied up I couldn't do anything, but of course interest would build up on the mortgage without any income. Debts of a personal nature couldn't be paid. Then I learned that a writ for corporate negligence was on its way, which would effectively deliver the fatal blow. This noted a claim of something in the order of three million pounds. I would go straight to jail should I dispose of anything. If I wanted to spend what little money I had left from cashing endowments, I'd need to apply to the High Court, which costs in itself. Accountant after accountant, lawyer after lawyer.

I thought about where all this would end, and what would be left of me. It was too horrible to contemplate. I knew this was a time to stand tall, to show courage, be strong and wise.

But it wasn't fair. I was in the middle of a complete corporate bloodbath and had no means of fighting back. I looked at Holly and wondered whether it was even fair of me to encourage her to stay with me, and whether she'd want to anyway. She was thirty three and wanted to start a family. She'd made clear what she wanted and I'd led her to believe I could deliver. How could we go forward in this situation?

I was living on edge here. The loneliness of my position started to have a physical manifestation and overwhelm me. Holly got a job in physiotherapy, but that in itself involved a long journey to and from the hospital in Lincolnshire. I could see it taking its toll.

I'd managed to buy a car before the freezing order so she and I could get around. I'd put it in her name, perhaps for the first time contemplating what might loom in the future. If Holly noticed this, she didn't say anything.

She didn't know the exact nature of my concern. She didn't know what was contained in those legal documents. When I heard about her plans for our rebuilding our lives together it hurt so much. I wanted to scream that it was more awful than that, how we would more than likely end up with nothing, absolutely nothing. I carried around in my mind the famous picture of the silent scream by Munch. That's how I felt. But how could I say it? And what would happen if I did? I was scared of the consequences.

I was in a lonely place. And it was about to get worse.

The writ was delivered with the customary knock on the door and the serious-looking man handing over a brown paper package with an air of: "I wouldn't like to be in your shoes."

I opened it, took a deep breath and, rather like a student getting important exam results, my eyes darted around trying to make immediate sense of its content, heart beating wildly. I was looking for a figure. How much were they after?

Eventually I saw it. Six million pounds.

I threw up.

Peter leaves for Spain

Peter dragged himself to Woodland Grange looking beaten, pale and disinterested in everything. He was completely defeated.

From a massive high of contemplating life with a few million in the bank he had, like me, had a hard landing. He contemplated the total disposal of his assets and starting again after ten years of living this rollercoaster, looking at the real possibility of total financial and emotional disaster. He had planned to move his family abroad anyway, so he was determined to do that rich or poor. What was there to stay here for?

This determination had prompted much speculation among the creditors, who were almost all insurers, that the alleged missing money was squirreled away in some fancy overseas trust account.

"I'm not joking, Mike. I'm sure I'm being followed and my lines are tapped," Peter said with a worried look.

I didn't know whether this was paranoia or real. But it wouldn't have surprised me. There were a lot of people out there gunning for us.

What was very real was a phone call each of us received from a threatening-sounding man with an East End accent, dialling from abroad. I knew that because I tried to trace his line.

"You guys are in trouble. I have a mate who's owed money from you lot. You moved your boat from the mooring without telling him, and here I am."

We hadn't – it was probably the administrators – but this guy wasn't going to listen. And I didn't feel inclined to argue with him.

"I don't need the whys or wherefores, boys. Don't get into more trouble you can't handle. I want the three of you to pay a cheque to this address..."

He gave a Spanish destination, clearly and slowly.

"You make sure it's here within four days. It saves me coming over to collect it. Rest assured, I will."

The line went dead. I wished I'd had him in our accounts team – he might even have made a good group FD.

We agreed we'd better get the money across to him pronto, even if we had to borrow it from family. It was a considerable chunk of what was left of the income the courts allowed us to have for the month, though we could hardly say we needed it because a big man was threatening us.

"I've phoned Greg. This guy's a nasty bastard. There's no point in saying it should be the others who pick it up. They wouldn't listen. And it's our health. Let's just pay it, Mike. Trust me, he's the real McCoy. He'll come and collect it one way or another."

While Peter was at Woodland Grange we saw some newspaper hacks kicking around the gates. I lived miles from anywhere so they couldn't doorstep my neighbours. But they did Peter. All this was excruciatingly painful for him. He was essentially a private, quiet and dignified man, and these guys were knocking on neighbours' doors asking pestering questions, such as "What's he like? He's a bit flash, isn't he? Have you seen a lot of nice cars around here? Kids at private school, eh? Does his wife work? Where? Does she earn much?"

It was the first time I've ever thought about invasion of privacy. They have laws for this in France. I could see clearly why they should be here. The red tops feed off ordinary people, which by definition isn't newsworthy. Politicians and celebrities have signed up to be in the public eye.

We'd not committed a criminal offence, yet the papers were out to rubbish us. This was not legitimate journalism; it was harassment from workplace to school gate. Peter was physically sickened and just wanted to leave it behind, start a new life with or without money in blissful private obscurity.

The next day, sure enough, there we were in the papers again. Extravagant life style, suing for millions, leaving for Spain, a picture of my house. Not bad, I thought. I think I should phone them and ask them to use the picture on the front page of my house for the one in the property section at the back. Saying I'm accepting offers subject to the freezing order. All monies would have to be paid into court.

The piece about Peter was horrible. It said a neighbour believed a car similar to Peter's big Porsche was sold recently, secretively and quickly. They couldn't be sure if it was his, which of course it wasn't or he'd have gone to jail. It got worse, before the freezing order the helpful neighbour described how Peter had sold a lot of his possessions at a car boot sale.

"As bloody if!" Peter fumed.

This sort of gossip delving into his very personal life was almost impossible for him to bear. I felt I wanted him to leave, even though I would miss him dreadfully. His private life was being ripped apart and he couldn't face going into his local pub. He withdrew. The sooner he was out of here, the better. I'd miss my friend Pete.

Better get a lawyer

I had put it off for too long. I'd been dealing with a lot of them and it was about time I had one to represent me. I had to force myself to see one; my heart wasn't up to a fight.

The first one I chose said they'd act for me and then quickly took a back-step when they realised we were up against CBA. They apologised and mentioned conflict of interest. Good start, I thought, wondering how powerful these people were.

I eventually found one and had £400 per month that I was allowed to spend on legal preparation. Goodness knows what the other side's legal bill might be. David and Goliath, how fair is that?

It was hard for me to walk round Leeds to see my lawyer. It scared me. I felt embarrassed and ashamed. I thought everyone knew my story and was looking at me in a disapproving way. They certainly would if they were reading the papers. I got there and sat in reception feeling very self-conscious as I watched seemingly busy and efficient-looking people walk quickly by, sometimes darting an occasional glance in my direction

I didn't feel as if I belonged there. Does society still survive on degrees of separation? Us and Them. Rich or Poor. Good or Bad. And, finally, Prosecutor and Defendant. I was scaring myself silly. I tried to take my mind off things as I scalded my tongue on hot coffee thoughtfully provided by reception. I fidgeted; I couldn't reach for the papers neatly laid out at the side of me in case I was in them.

Eventually, a smart middle-aged man strode out of a side office with a secretary in tow. With a firm handshake and a few pleasantries, I was shown to the relative privacy of an interview room, and talk turned to my options.

The lawyer looked at the submissions.

"It will cost you a lot of money to fight this," he said.

"How much?" I asked innocently.

"Could be a three or four week trial in the High Court. Lots of unwelcome publicity. I've had a word with them off the record."

Here we go again, I thought. Of course you have, isn't that what always happens in these circumstances? Bloody gentlemen's club. They don't give a shit. First, it was the management buy-out guy, then the corporate recovery guy. Then it was a team of insolvency experts, then its administrators, and then it was lawyers acting on behalf of the administrators. Then its trustees in bankruptcy, no doubt.

It was a bloody big industry, corporate disaster. Who was paying for it, this band of associated people who drank in the same bars, went to the same clubs and swapped good client stories over good wine? I guessed that's what I'd end up – an amusing story in some wine bar over a liquid lunch.

The lawyer continued: "There are no good choices for you here. Don't forget the good and bad news is that this isn't a criminal investigation. Not yet, anyway, and from what you have said previously there are no skeletons in the closet so it's unlikely to go that way - at least you can take some comfort in that.

"What you are facing is the legal consequences of the initial investigation of the administrators in civil action. The bad news is that, consequently, you're unlikely to get legal aid to fight this action, Mike. You have to pay for it yourself. If it was criminal, then while that's obviously bad news in a way, the good news would be you could apply for legal aid."

"What's the cost?" I demanded.

"Somewhere between £30,000 and £50,000, and that's conservative. But you certainly don't have it in liquid assets to pay me right now, not if the financial submissions I've seen are right."

I wondered if this was standard practice. Bollocks to the bundle – the legal papers - let's see what the guy has in terms of wonga first.

"Then the administrators may apply for you to put monies into court in case you're found guilty. They'll take the view that if you are found guilty you don't have the money for their costs, which is likely to be more than £50,000, as they'll go to town on you with barristers and the like. You're fighting establishment here, Mike, and that's never good news. So you're going to need to prove liquid assets of at least around £100,000. Then there are the actual damages if you lose. It's a non-starter."

A £100,000 figure was not too far away from the amount I signed away as per my rights under the three employment contracts that I had signed copies of so the deals could go through for the benefit of the creditors. That was a good decision.

"The money you were drawing in salary from all the companies will attract a lot of adverse publicity," added the lawyer.

"But we filed £600K profits and were on line to make a million, even with my salary, and I never took dividends," I protested.

He continued: "The award that will go against you if you're found guilty, and don't forget they're going for you jointly and severally, could be as much as the six million in theory."

"What six million? How the hell did they get to that figure anyway?"

" Well it's largely irrelevant after the first few million, I wouldn't bother wasting your time on directing me to look into that. What's the point? If it's a million, it's still too much for you. Forget that part."

This was just impossible. We both knew I had no option but to plead guilty.

"Thing is, Mike, the documents suggest you were a director of all three trading companies."

"But I wasn't!" I protested, yet again, "I resigned in the most public way possible at the Rudding Park product providers' dinner. I gave a bloody speech. How many people resign like that?"

"Sure, but they say you were a director du jour."

"What does that mean?" The last time I had heard that expression, it was on a menu in the south of France.

"It means you acted like one, so you were one."

"But they're saying I didn't act as one, which is why I'm being sued, and I'm saying I wasn't at board meetings, not through negligence, but because I wasn't a bloody director. I hadn't just fallen asleep at the driving wheel; I wasn't in the bloody car!

"I've tried to get the board meeting notes to prove this, but they've gone missing. I don't have access to my old office anyway. They're quoting selected e-mails from me, where I threw a few boulders into the pond because I was getting concerned at lack of progress, but what's wrong with that? But I don't have access to my e-mails so I can't refute the evidence. Even emails dating from August to December that I know existed have gone missing or been deleted, so who's done that? Peter will confirm it, as well. Why isn't there an investigation in that?"

"Well, moving on. They say you should have known what the financial position was, as chief executive. You had a legal duty under corporate law. That title carries consequences."

"I tried to know what was going on," I said. "And because I tried they say I acted as a director, but not a good one! There were twenty seven people in the finance department. I'm no accountant, I employed them - I wouldn't have done that if I wanted to fiddle the books, I wouldn't have allowed James and Malcolm to employ four qualified accountants."

The lawyer stuck to his view that nothing I said would make any difference.

"They say in the legal document, you knew or ought to have known about the company's position when the old group financial director was signed off sick."

"We just knew he was coming out with silly, or at least different, figures that changed all the time. Even our existing external accountants couldn't understand it," I explained. "I've emails that suggest that for one reason or another, opinion was the guy was overwhelmed with the job.."

"There you are then; he appeared to be, that's obvious. You didn't know, but you should have known, and that's where they get you."

"How can THEY insist on knowing something I didn't know? The first time I knew something was seriously wrong was when Myles told me. Then I knew!"

"They're not saying you knew, they only have to prove - and remember only to civil law standard - that you ought to have known, and, to be honest, you ought to have known, Mike, even if you didn't. Because it's obvious if you didn't know then what happened to the group was a consequence that flowed naturally from that. A financial melt-down. And that clearly ought not to have happened to a company that was in its tenth year trading at the levels and volumes you were trading at."

This was going nowhere and he was MY lawyer! I wondered what the opposing team would say. I had no money to defend this action. I was even limited by the freezing order at to how much money I could spend on preparing my defence and it was clear that legal opinion was I should just roll over, take the hit, and go bankrupt.

"Look, Mike, it's obvious you're an entrepreneur. An ideas man. This is the price you pay for that. I'm a company man; I can't do what you do. So take bankruptcy and all this goes away. In eighteen months you're free to start again. Think about it, that's my advice. I could spend all the money you have left on legal fees, fuelling damaging publicity for you, but it's not going anywhere. You don't have much of a chance. The bottom line is you were the only guy as chief executive who could have changed things, but you didn't. You take responsibility for this; the buck stops with you."

"But I didn't know. I paid others to know....." My voice faded.

"Well, we've been through that one. Okay, take care and stay in touch."

I was quickly shown out. That was as much legal advice as I was going to get – a quick "You're screwed, Mike; now off you go."

I eventually got back to the estate and logged onto my email. I had a message from Peter; I knew he'd been seeing his solicitor today as well. Would his advice be any different to mine?

Mike, this is going to be hard, I know. But I've been advised by my lawyer to keep my distance from you. Not to be in contact with you after today in any way. He says it would be bad for my position. It may be construed that we are

*in collusion together, that we are acting in concert, against the interest of the
creditors. It won't help my personal case. I know it's hard, but I've got to take
their advice. So I won't see you or be in touch with you until all this shit is
over, Mike. I hope you understand. Good luck, take care of yourself.
Love Peter.*

I was heartbroken. I'd sat at the opposite desk to Peter for over nine years. We not
only worked together, we socialised with each other. He was my friend, my
confidante. We were in this together. I was devastated he'd take and act on this
advice. I felt totally isolated.
I cried, and cried. I cried in front of Holly, and I cried all night. She now knew the
truth as well. I was scared, alone and miserable. For the first time, so was she.
I started drinking too much. Bad tempered, isolated, nothing apart from notifications
of other legal proceedings against me on the smallest bills like electricity and heating.
I couldn't see the point of paying them, even if I had any spare money from my court
allowance.
Holly decided to go to Ireland for a break. I understood why. I was no joy to be
around. Even the dogs looked at me accusingly. If they could have gone, they would
have surely taken off too.

A life with daytime television

There was no one around. At least I could be as untidy as I wanted. I was advised that
if I was going down the bankruptcy route I'd need to have all my bank and credit card
statements for the past few years.
All these documents were spread out, a blanket of old receipts, a financial blueprint of
my old life over the dining table where only a few months before I'd broken bread
with friend, neighbours and works colleagues, some of whom were now refusing to
take my calls.
There is a reason why no one makes reservations in an empty restaurant, and I guess
that's how people must have seen my situation. There was no fun to be had with me.
I'd developed a habit of taking to my bed for hour upon hour. The term 'a living
nightmare' took on a new meaning. I only had peace when I went to sleep. It was
when I got up that the full horror of everything came crashing around me.
When I was awake I just sat, occasionally falling asleep on the couch, sleeping
fitfully, watching television or just staring around the room.
Bloody daytime television. Property makeover programme after property makeover
programme. They were all about ordinary couples who had just done up a terraced
house in Blackpool and made fortunes. Programmes based entirely around property
development, pure greed and increased valuations. A uniquely British disease.
But I had to remind myself that I'd been one of those people recently, all happy and
full of smiles without giving a toss for those less fortunate. How perspectives change.
I flicked across to the other side to see A Place in the Sun – another happy couple
moving to Spain for next to nothing. The programmes seemed to be saying: "What are
you doing, Mike? What's your future hold? What's your game plan now, clever boy?"
Jesus, this was driving me mad. I had to endeavour to live in the present. The problem
is, you get locked into your problems and can't find a resolution. I needed to find a
good reason to move forward. I tried to persuade myself that one would be back soon
- Holly. That was something to look forward to.

There was talk of a new start. I didn't want to stay in the north. Holly had mentioned Cornwall, I had mentioned France. I had nothing, but I looked at properties that I could previously have bought, which would and should have made me happy and set me up for life. Now I couldn't afford the air ticket. My dreams and nightmares were disturbed only by the unwelcome rattle of the letterbox in the mornings; the avalanche of final demand letters edged me closer to financial oblivion.

First to call was the taxman. Of course. He reckoned I owed the Inland Revenue around £15,000. It seemed to put the cap on things. I had always been on PAYE, no fancy stuff, no dividends, so it was easy for our tax consultants and PAYE team to organise payments, yet they'd apparently screwed that up for me too.

I didn't have access to any advice anymore but had paid around £200,000 in tax personally in the last financial year. No mention of that was made when I was being vilified in the press as Champagne Charlie. Not for me some fancy bloody tax avoidance trust.

I tried to be straightforward and honest, declaring everything, even putting details in that I didn't need to do. Someone on behalf of the Revenue turned up to take a look around and document some of the assets. I told them they were all subject to a freezing order and even they couldn't touch them. That was a nice moment. Such small victories mean a lot when you're in this situation.

He went away scratching his head; it was such an unusual legal order in these circumstances. It really brought it home to me and made me realise that the administrators had got us treated like terrorists or drug dealers.

Sufficient evidence must have been presented to a High Court judge, subject to further detailed information, that all our personal assets were more than likely illegal, perhaps ill-gotten gains which needed to be impounded and protected immediately from disposal before I fled the country.

Better not let anyone catch me watching A Place in the Sun,' I thought.

I read the original court papers and it was clear the judge had considered taking our passports away. This frightened me more than the results of the legal action, as it was an important indicator of the thinking of CBA. They were determined to go for the jugular.

Days dragged along. The diet of daytime television, along with double doses of anti-anxiety pills swilled down with red wine put me into a twilight world. And that's what I wanted, reality at the furthest point away that I could manage. I knew what was going on but I didn't give a shit. If they wanted me, here I was. Do your worst.

I ventured into the local pub and with some good-natured piss taking, I had them on about being chased by the *News of the World*.

"Whatever they say, for God's sake, don't mention the Russian prostitutes," I pleaded. To my astonishment, they believed it. What was happening? Had everyone gone mad?

"What? Bloody hell, what's that about?" they'd ask, wide-eyed.

"Ho, you'll read about it, I guess!" I teased. "But I didn't know until it was too late that one was actually a bloke! You have to believe me on that one."

It was amazing how this caused frisson of excitement. They'd already read some pretty astonishing things about me. Right now, an ordinary life like theirs was something I wanted and admired, but I still felt the need to break their stares with some extravagant quip or other. I asked for credit at the pub until I had chance to dig some money up, which was met by them inspecting the £10 I put over the bar.

It was all taken and given in good humour, but inside I was sinking lower and lower. I couldn't look at anyone doing work, digging holes, cleaning windows, and serving in the pub without wondering how much the jobs paid and whether I could do it.

Missing Holly

What could I do now? What was I for? Everything and everyone seemed to have been assigned a purpose. But not me; mine had been taken away.

I should have listened to my father, who always said that a trade would be good as no one could take a learned skill away from me. Why did I have ideas above my station? What made me think that people like me would be greeted and accepted in the closed ranks of establishment? They'd certainly taken away my opportunity away to work in the insurance industry.

I was the bad guy; no one would give me a job or an agency to transact business in the future. Yet out of seventeen directors in the group, fourteen were part of the solution and were still trading with the same insurers that formed the creditors' panel authorising CBA to go for my blood. It hardy seemed fair.

Nothing much had changed for them, other than the majority of them had increased their wealth significantly by increasing their shareholdings in the new ventures. These were the very same people who ran my businesses and were well-paid for it.

They were the ones with operational control, that still had it. All had been on high salaries to perform for and on behalf of the company and its shareholders. Yet here they were making money for the same insurers and for themselves now. Happy days!

None of this made sense to me, no matter how I looked at it. The administrators advised the creditors' panel that they had initiated an accountancy investigation that might take a year to complete. A year? To find what? Hell, it appeared to take them two weeks to separate the good guys from the bad, and now it would take them a year to substantiate that decision, backed by a hell of a lot of creditors' money.

This made my heart sink further. What were they looking for? I knew there were enormous fees to be paid for this action. My assessment for that was around a million pounds for a year's work, including costs. We were instructed to attend a meeting at the company's auditor's office. It was compulsory, a legal responsibility to complete director's statements; otherwise you'd never have got us all in the same room again. Did I tell anyone I wasn't a director? No matter. I thought because I was *du jour* I'd better go. Jim told them all to fuck off, whatever the consequence, nor did he send any statements in. He said diddly squat because he knew diddly squat.

The auditors wanted not unnaturally to protect their own interest and insisted on recording the meeting of directors' discussions relating to the agreement of financial information that needed to go into a final Directors' Statement of Financial Affairs. The information had to be agreed by all, to the best of knowledge and belief. Other than Peter, James and I, the guys were still in the industry with access to all insurer statements. Significantly, Peter, James and I played no part in the calculation because we weren't in the office anymore. We had no access to records. But the others did. They appeared to obtained the figures easily. We'd obviously stopped trading, which meant clarity of previous transactions wasn't mixed up with new ones. They then asked insurers what we owed them. They checked this out against a 'does it look right?' analysis. They took off what the clients owed us. Simple.

This was similar to what Malcolm said he would do by stopping all transactions in account *No (1)*, and initiating his client account *No (2)* projects for all new transactions. That account got polluted again with adjustments on previous transactions. Much to my annoyance, that and the small matter of the computer glitch that meant that one minus one made two. The financials relating to the shortfall in client account monies, according to the guys who brought this information to the meeting with the external auditors, was assessed at no more than £800,000 deficit. This figure was recorded and agreed to go into the director's submission of financial affairs. Given we screwed up and lost £500,000 on account *No (2)* in the six months it operated due to an IT error that Myles had identified earlier, the sad, awful truth was it looked like we hardly had a problem at all, at least not one that we couldn't have coped with.

When we had the meeting with Malcolm at Pool Court that night, our problem would appear to have been no more than £300K on transactions going through our account of over £20 million. Even that should not have happened.

But given the volume and the changes that had taken place within the finance department, it was easily manageable if we'd known where we were. It was so frustrating; I had a rage in me I could not express. We had a group of businesses worth over £15 million go down for this. And I had been made to feel broken, isolated, publicly humiliated and was very likely about to be made bankrupt.

Peter, James and I wanted all the previous Corporate directors to issue a press statement recognising the figures given in the directors' statements. They refused. They wanted nothing to do with the three of us. We three offered our sincere apology publicly to all creditors. We all knew this wasn't going to placate them, but it was in any event well meaning. The rest didn't want to be guilty by association .it would appear. I knew that my pain and discomfort was not in any way over. I made the point that if we'd had the information earlier, the companies wouldn't have fallen like a pack of cards. It was a tragedy of Greek proportions.

One year later, and a massive amount of money spent on fees, CBA never agreed or established categorically what the final deficit was. From what I understand they said it was impossible to tell. All this could have been fixed, if we had that information and the main board had stuck together and worked the problem through.

I also had to look at myself.

What aspect of my leadership at the moment of crisis was found lacking? The whole circumstance had been beyond any sphere of experience that I could possibly draw upon. I had lost a fortune; worse still, I'd lost my will to carry on and fight. I was devastated, and they had forensic accountants poring over the figures looking for anything that they might construct as fraud. They would need something to hang this lot on, if only for the sake of the creditors. Credibility amongst the big players was something they desperately needed.

This gave me another concern. It's like driving past a police car when you know you're okay but still feel intimidated. That's how this felt, only a hundred times worse and it was a constant 'drive past'. In normal life, investigations of this type should only give concern to the criminally-minded. But this was beyond that, and it deeply unnerved me. What might they find? What might I have done? Maybe the fact that I put a lunch for £80 down as a client lunch was fraud? What about the company car I gave my sister to drive?

No one lives their life, corporate or personal, in a way that can stand a forensic analysis of this nature without feeling nervous. But I was sure I had never, ever signed a cheque in the last five years of trading let alone a client account cheque. I'd never knowingly done anything dodgy. I tried to reassure myself with that. I was my father's son and I was straight. Let them prove otherwise.

But I still had sleepless nights, tossing and turning. I started to take sleeping pills as well. I was getting quite a collection together overall. I wondered where all this was going and when it would end; what would become of me at the end of this journey.

I missed Holly terribly. I was needy, clingy, vulnerable, and insecure. So much had changed so quickly. I was upset with her, didn't feel she understood what I was going through. How could she? She didn't feel the shame that I felt, and when I tried to look to the future, I didn't see one.

Perhaps it was because Holly had seen me at my most vulnerable that it made me angry. I was running on empty, I had nothing left in me to give, financial or emotional.

She eventually called to say she'd returned from Ireland and was heading for London to stay with friends for a few days. She wasn't exactly rushing back to see me, that was obvious. And who could blame her? I was a car crash.

She turned up a few days later; my relief was palpable. She persuaded me to go for a walk around the estate. I realised I hadn't done that for some time; it was too painful. I think we both felt that we were saying goodbye to it.

I'd been told to make an inventory of all my goods, possessions, and personal clothes, in preparation for the possibility of going down the bankruptcy route. I'd decided that if that was my reality I was going to jump and not be pushed. I wouldn't allow anyone to have the pleasure of putting me into bankruptcy. It would, at least, be voluntary. Having arranged my clothes, I decided to do so for Holly, all colour-coded and on neat hangers. In doing so, I stumbled upon a book by an Irish Author. I read the foreword.

It was an emotional rollercoaster where a lady fell in love with a man. She deeply loved him, but for reasons not obvious in the foreword, she had to leave him. No matter how hard it was, they had to part. The book was called *He Has To Go*. The writing was on the wall; a title could not be more prescriptive.

I wept and howled in total panic. I had to confront her but was scared of what might happen as a result. I didn't know what I'd do without her. I looked at her and she was the best and only thing that the whole establishment machine couldn't take away from me. Yet she was thinking of leaving. Was it yet to be decided, or had she made up her mind to leave this sinking ship when she was in London, or perhaps over a family discussion in Ireland? I knew their first concern must be for her.

I showered and changed. I got myself together and put on a helpless smile. I opened the car door for her when she returned from work. I'd made dinner and was trying to keep things together. I lit a fire for the first time in ages.

I took a deep breath, "Holly, darling, I wasn't prying but I came across this book. It's really disturbing for me."

She looked surprised and slightly taken aback.

"Don't be silly, Mike;" she said. "It came free with a magazine. I just picked it up. It looked good. I haven't read it yet, you can see that. I didn't buy it. It was free. You have it if you want; I'm not bothered about reading it."

I didn't want to confront her anymore. Maybe she'd changed her mind and, having seen me again, had decided to stay.

"I just wondered, honey...You know I love you, don't you, Holly?"

"Yes, sweet," she replied. "I know you do," she added silently, almost to herself.

We said nothing more about it. She retired early to bed.

I took a pill and waited until I felt drowsy. I didn't want to confront the truth. I'd had had enough of all that. I just wanted to sleep and never wake up again. I couldn't contemplate more loss. As I lay there downstairs on the sofa, I stared with bleary eyes at the receipt I'd found inside the book cover.

My head pounded, I didn't want to confront what was there right in front of me, her credit card receipt that proved she'd bought it at Shannon airport.

If in previous weeks she'd discovered something new about me, it was certainly true that I'd also discovered something new about her.

CHAPTER 12

Gone

When I awoke the next day, Holly had already quietly left for work and let me sleep. I'd tried to get up for breakfast with her previously but sometimes felt so awful I just stayed in bed.

It was a Friday, and this time I'd try my best to ensure we both had a great weekend. The children were due on Saturday to stay the evening. A bit of life around the place might be just what we needed.

It was lovely to see the house wake from its quiet, depressing slumber. The sound of children and dogs cheered the place up; for a moment life seemed almost normal. But as always, the time eventually came to say goodbye.

Sue had agreed to come across rather than meeting halfway, which had become the norm. Two cars stopping in a car park, a swapping of prisoners like a hand-over during the Cold War, grabbing of clothes and possessions and off without a word of goodbye.

This time she trudged around the house, looking for school clothes that the children might need during the week. It raised the tension in the house, albeit innocently. Holly didn't like anyone else on her patch; I could understand why.

Sue must have been at least as concerned as Holly regarding my perilous financial state, even more so with my three children to feed. It created a sort of Mexican stand-off that I hadn't experienced before. The children left, waving goodbye, oblivious to the sudden change in mood. So did our dinner guests, who were a little more sensitive to it. I could see Holly was in a bad mood and the burning issue of the book I'd found didn't help. Something had to give.

"I don't know about you but I'm going to have another glass of wine," I said, breaking the silence

"Why not?" she said. "We're going nowhere, doing nothing!"

We swapped looks that indicated an electrical charge in the air.

The wine was drunk quickly and quietly and then she fixed me with a stare. How would this kick off? What would be the spark that set off the explosion?

"I can't understand you Mike. You talk about leaving this country to go to France. If I had children, I wouldn't want to abandon them."

"I'm not bloody abandoning them." I was more than ready for her; this argument was a long time coming. I'd seen the clouds gather and now here was the storm.

"You don't know how it feels; thinking people are pointing at you, laughing at you, talking about you behind your back and reading shit in the bloody papers.

"You want me to go to Cornwall, for God's sake – that would be six hours away. With easyJet I'd be only hours away in France and it would be cheaper to travel."

"I don't want you to go Cornwall, at least not yet," she said. "I was thinking of going for a while to take a look around and see how things are while you get sorted here. Then we can take it from there."

So that was her plan; moving to Cornwall and it didn't involve me, after all.

"Well piss off and go then," I said, wounded.

"Do you want me? Do you really bloody want me to? Because it's not exactly great up here babysitting you all the time."

She'd called my bluff and she knew I wouldn't back down. To hell with the consequences.

"Yes, fuck off!" I said. She knew I would, of course. She didn't need telling a third time. She went upstairs; it was obvious she was packing.

I told myself not to go upstairs. I didn't want a big scene. She'd calm down in a minute and she'd have to come down and walk past me to get out of the door. I'd talk to her then, deal with the book and the receipt, pull things around. It's was just stress. That and too much drink on both sides.

I waited. The packing had clearly stopped so where was she? The house was quiet. I eventually made my way cautiously upstairs to our bedroom. Most of her clothes had gone. I came downstairs and looked out of the window; a car had gone. She'd left through the conservatory door so she didn't need to pass me. She'd really gone. What an idiot – what had I done?

The aftermath

I drank the remaining wine, welcoming the soft muffled blanket of oblivion. I had a future without hope and nights without dreams. If Holly was my anchor, I was surely adrift now.

I woke on the kitchen floor lying like an up-turned beetle, feeling stupid and helpless. The dishes and remains of our lunch party were still on the table. The dogs noticed me stir and heaved themselves from their basket, padding across to lick my face. I don't know whose breath was worse, theirs or mine.

The lights in the house blazed and my head thumped in time with my heartbeat. The dogs jumped up and became giddy, trying to call me into action. The back door was open but they'd stayed in, perhaps from loyalty as I lay there in a useless heap.

It all came crashing back in cruel flash backs. Holly had gone and I'd told her to go. I was a bloody, bloody fool. Why sabotage the last hope of happiness I had? What would happen to me now?

I poured myself a glass of milk and took two aspirin, two sleeping pills and one anti-anxiety tablet. I'd be drowsy in minutes, so I opened some dog food and called the animals in. It was comforting to be with them; they at least had stayed.

I locked the doors and turned off the lights. My watch told me it was around 3pm. It must be Monday, I thought, as I went upstairs. Why do I feel like this at this time of day? What's happened to my biological clock? I wonder what the guys are doing now. Have they met their targets? How did the Monday sales meeting go? Strange how these thoughts crowded in, out of habit. The dogs looked up with tired, accusing eyes; it wasn't a normal day for them, either.

I curled up in the foetal position on the bed and pulled the sheets over me. I wanted to sleep and never wake up. I was more than alone; I was in an empty void mostly of my own making. The quietness scared me; I felt vulnerable. I searched in the bed and there it was – the white silk blouse Holly kept under the pillow to sleep in. I could still smell her perfume. I placed it under my cheek and cried with a fever-like sickness.

I tried to think good, positive thoughts. Maybe she'd return in the evening, and tell me to forget the fight, that she was still with me. She'd understand. We were both just letting off steam, like in the films.

Maybe all my friends would turn up, just like in *It's a Wonderful Life*. Where was my guardian angel? He should be with me by now. James Stewart was accused of taking the missing millions in the film but truth holds and lies are beaten in a fair world; one of justice, and the simple belief that if you do the right thing, everything will turn out okay in the end. I slept a black, comatose, dreamless sleep.

I woke with a start and looked at my watch. Tuesday evening! What the hell had happened to me? The previous few days' events flooded back like unwelcome guests. I resisted the temptation to take more pills and went downstairs – the dishes were still there, along with half-eaten food and the general mess of the previous day.

I heard a tune in my mind that I couldn't get rid of, with the lyrics "lipstick on glass that you don't want to clean". I saw the glass Holly has sipped wine from; it was the only remaining trace of her.

I understood the sentiments of the song - *What a Good Year for the Roses* by Elvis Costello. It played on a constant loop in my head. I took a deep breath and cleared the table as the dogs padded around, happy to see me.

There was a letter on floor by the front door. The envelope just read 'MIKE' so it was obviously hand-delivered. From Holly? Had she come back and been unable to get through the gates? She had a key, though. I put the letter to one side; I'd clean myself and this place from top to bottom and then read the letter as a reward.

I had to get myself together, be worthy of her love. I worked hard, lit a fire, stroked the dogs and threw away all the alcohol. I made a cup of tea before going into the drawing room, carefully opening the letter with nervous excitement.

It wasn't from Holly but Jerry, my doctor and family friend.

Mike...

Holly phoned me yesterday. She's worried about you. I've heard about all the shit coming down on you. If you need a shoulder at the moment, then please use mine.

I'm working all day tomorrow at the surgery. Make an appointment. If you don't come then I will have to come for you. Keep your chin up, and don't drink with those anti-anxiety pills.

Jerry

It was lovely of him to care. I was glad I'd got rid of the alcohol before reading the letter. I was so disappointed it wasn't from her, but at least she'd got in touch with someone and was concerned about me. Surely that was a good sign?

I took two sleeping tablets and went back to bed, to fall into a black sleep once more. I'd phone Holly first thing in the morning. I'd apologise and beg her forgiveness, say whatever was needed to have her back for good. We'd get through this as a team.

I couldn't survive this alone. I hadn't been alone when I'd had money. I had so-called friends coming out of my backside. Everyone wants a lift in your limo, but when it breaks down you want someone alongside you who's prepared to catch the bus.

They were a bit thin on the ground, but surely Holly was one of them? Holly, who I loved beyond words. She'd be back, and she would stick by me. We promised each other, thick or thin.

I woke early on Wednesday morning, took a deep breath and called her. She'd surely had enough time to calm down now? Her phone was off. This panicked me but, trying to stay calm, I thought that she'd been in touch with Jerry so might phone him again. I'd go and see what he knew.

As soon as I walked through the door of the surgery, I got to see him. He took a good look at me. "You been drinking?"

"Not in the last twenty four hours, Jerry, but mines a pint if you're asking..."

He didn't laugh.

"I threw it all away, Jerry – the alcohol and my life."

"Good about the alcohol, you can't afford emotionally to drink right now, Mike. There's too much going on in your life, you have to quit it for a while. Depression and drink don't mix."

"I'm not depressed, Jerry, I'm just bloody pissed off! But I'll do anything; I have to get Holly back. I can't handle this on my own, I really can't."

"Mike, bugger that! From what I've heard, I don't think she's thinking in those terms right now. Just do it for you and everything else will fall into its natural order. Look, I'll refer you to a guy called Terry. He's a top psychiatrist and an even better man; he'll help you talk things through. Get your head straight.

He went on: "We all need help from time to time and he's available this afternoon. It's up to you, Mike, but I strongly advise you to go straight away. I'll phone him to say you're on your way, so you'd better turn up. You're a good, strong guy – you can get through this, with the right help and determination from you."

"Now, medication. I'm changing your pills to anti-depressants. They're a bit stronger than the others; they won't kick in for a few weeks so stick with it. Don't drink!"

And I was out of the door with an address, before I could change my mind. At least I had something to do to occupy my mind for a few hours. This was hard love. No indulgence there but good, honest, straight talking.

"One last thing," I said. "If Holly calls you, put in a good word for me, would you?"

Jerry looked at me sympathetically and shook his head. "The best I can do is to tell her that you at least turned up here. That's a start, eh?"

I drove to Hull, thoughts swirling in my brain. Jerry had got this guy to drop everything to see me and give me some emergency counselling. They must think I needed it. But I'd always considered it as psychobabble shit. I just wanted Holly back, and they were sending me in the wrong direction. I also realised that if I didn't go and Holly found out, she'd never come back. I'd better do what they said for now.

Terry came bouncing into the room. The place was a drop-off centre for all sorts of ailments – drug addicts, alcoholics, failed corporate hooligans like me. We shared one thing in common – we were screwed up or had screwed up. Terry settled me down, made some tea, talked in a gentle voice and got me to say what was on my mind.

I was in floods of tears as I finished telling him my life story. It was the first time I'd cried when the other party wasn't moved to console me.

Far from it; he told me to let the pain come out and go. That said, I was the sort of person who cried when their snowman melted. He encouraged me to get to the core of who I was, what I was, what was truly bothering me and what I could do about it. Simple questions really, just bloody difficult to answer. It was obvious I was severely depressed and the trigger point was obvious. I mean, if your house burns down you don't need to go back to childhood, do you?

"Ten bloody million, Terry. Ten!"

"I bet it's nothing to do with money, Mike, but it *is* about loss."

"Okay, Terry. Get it back for me and I'll tell you what else I've lost other than money."

Against this confrontational exchange, Terry set out to bring me back from the edge, to make me feel normal again. He worked on cognitive behavioural therapy following Gestalt theories, whatever they were. To me they we're just words. Getting me to prattle on about anything and everything, with seemingly little structure, in reality was very disciplined. It challenged wrong-thinking, with the patient adjusts behaviour through moments of clarity according to that new reality and way of thinking.

Well, mine was that I was in a shit place, going bust, with no mates, no girlfriend, no prospects and no future.

"Analyse that," I said. And he did, for two days a week for around twenty weeks. I don't know how he had patience; even I was pissed off with hearing me go on and on. "You know, Mike, most ordinary people have very little control of anything in life. To such an extent that if they realised it would probably cause great trauma in their lives. You couldn't control what happened to you - Oliver getting ill, business going to the wall, Holly leaving. It's outside your control. But you're privileged to be confronted with this reality; many people go through life not having that experience." "Yeah, I know that, Terry. They're called lucky bleeders!"

He waited a moment and then continued: "It means you'll start to live with a new understanding. An easier acceptance and wisdom of what you can and can't change." "You mean cooperate with the inevitable?"

"Yes, exactly."

"That's another line for do nothing, roll over and die, Terry."

"Is that how you see it, Mike?"

"Look Terry, fuck the new wisdom. I'd rather have my old life back."

"Of course you would right now, but this is an opportunity for growth. There's every chance that in the future you'll look back at this moment as a very important and constructive phase of your life that, once completed, you might not wish to have changed even if you had the power to do so. By considering your past you may decide that the changes you make for the future are a power for the good, and what you had surrounded yourself with previously was simply false."

"Hey, are you having a pop at our published accounts now too?"

"Did your colleagues and 'friends' hang around because they liked you or because they were on your payroll?"

Now that was a bloody hard and personal question. A chocolate-covered hand grenade lobbed straight at my ego. Iron fist in velvet glove, he wasn't giving in easy and dared to ask a few hard questions. I recognised it was one of the first I'd been asked in many years. No one ever asked me hard questions. Why was that? Was that a moment of clarity?

"Ouch! That hurt, mate! Okay, you win, Terry. I don't care."

"It's not winning or losing, Mike, it's about getting to the truth and adjusting our thinking and then behaviour where we think it's appropriate. That's what we need to explore."

The first session ended too quickly. Doctor Jerry had got me in with Terry on an emergency; if I wanted him to continue, I'd have to go private. I wasn't being referred due to any drug or alcohol problems, though God knows I could have easily met that requirement.

I might have met my match here. If I wrote to the administrators saying I needed this, maybe Terry and I could come to an arrangement and I'd be in therapy for as long as possible; at least they wouldn't get the money. I didn't mention this reason to Terry, but I did get permission to see him twice a week for as long as appropriate. We never did exploit that; I truly needed Terry's advice, even if I didn't recognise it at the time. My priority was to get Holly back. She'd taken a car that I'd put in her name as a precaution against it being taken off me should I go bankrupt. Surely she'd drive back soon? I tried to call but the phone was still dead. She hadn't just turned her phone off; she'd bloody well changed her number. I tried to call her mother, who I'd been close to. She put the phone down as soon as she realised it was me.

Now that was fucking great, I thought, as tears fell again. That woman used to work for the Samaritans in Tipperary. Get it? Fucking Irish Samaritan putting the phone down on me! Even I could see the funny side of that.

I poured my heart out to Mum and Dad. Mum was furious.

"She always was a bloody gold-digger, son. I told you, didn't I, Tom?"

Mum was on a roll now. She shouted, turning to my father who was listening intently but couldn't talk very well.

"None of you would listen! I knew she was a wrong one, there for the bloody money. She'll have her claws into another fool by now, mark my words!"

"You never told me, Mum," I said.

"Well, I was told by your father to mind my own bloody business and not interfere!"

Dad smiled apologetically. He hadn't said much. He couldn't after his stroke.

"The trouble with you, Michael Bloody Kenney, is that you think and act like you're still bloody chief executive. That's your bloody problem. You go your own way and listen to no one. You take no notice of me and you never bloody have. Letting everyone take advantage of you. You're just a bloody fool," Mum rounded on me.

Dad suddenly got out a sentence: "Well he is, Doreen...He is chief executive."

"Of bloody what, exactly?" Mum retorted, razor-sharp and with a laser tongue that ended that discussion. It was a winning blow, she had a point. She didn't mean to hurt, she was just blind with anger towards Holly and her family. She could see what was left behind and it wasn't pretty, but she didn't have them in her range. She was frustrated because she claimed to have seen this all along.

Dad wasn't finished. Everyone told Mum to quieten down as he wanted to say something. He slowly whispered something to me, in a deliberate and concentrated way. I was in tears again. I leaned over and he held me with his good hand.

"Holly, Michael, Holly..."

"Yes, Dad, what is it?"

"Cast her to the wind, son, cast her to the wind."

Talking to Terry

The house felt like a museum. A quiet empty shell reminding me of better days, a previous life – all now firmly in the past.

Wherever I went in the house I sensed images, sounds and smells of what had been. I was truly by myself and felt scared at being completely alone. I couldn't escape my own company, thoughts and emotions. Everywhere I went, there I was.

Sue had become less willing to bring the children to see me. They'd suffered disruption and some trauma as they were pulled out of school and put into state education.

I believe Sue became embarrassed about me and her loss of economic status with her public school friends, who probably stared and gossiped about what read in the papers. I'm sure she felt my disgrace.

She was angry with me for what 'd brought to the door. She'd received £5,000 per month, a Range Rover and convertible BMW to assist her lifestyle; this had stopped. She'd thought she was set up for life, too.

In reading the papers she had, like many people, read between the lines. Implications of dishonest behaviour and speculation with regard to the missing monies had an effect on her. She'd heard me talk about being off-shore in Gibraltar and travelling the world and drew her conclusions quickly – she thought I still had money squirreled away. She wanted me to understand what this financial devastation was having on her, her life, and importantly my children. She implied she knew what I was up to and demanded access to foreign accounts that didn't exist.

I couldn't make her believe the truth. Sometimes people don't because they simply prefer a different answer.

"You can't have ten million and lose it all," she figured. There must be some money somewhere that the authorities didn't know about. I must have known something was wrong in the business, she and her friends reckoned.

Well, whatever they thought, I wasn't expecting this. I hadn't planned it. If we'd known where we were accurately, we could easily have solved the problem. As I've said a thousand times, I wasn't aware of any financial problems.

When the money stopped, she needed somebody to blame. She couldn't blame the financial team, as she didn't know them. So she blamed me. The children stopped visiting, but there again it wasn't a happy place for them to be, and they probably didn't want to come. Who could blame them?

The one occasion they did stay they woke early, having had a conversation between themselves the night before. Oliver was concerned that the quad bike his granddad had bought him when he first got out of hospital would be left behind.

I told him I wouldn't be able to move it as it wouldn't fit in the old estate Shogun that was left for me. So early in the morning there it was, with Oliver and my other two children standing proudly as the quad bike balanced three-quarters of the way in the car with flags hanging out of the back for safety and ropes tied everywhere. It was a proud, happy moment for them. They weren't going to allow anyone to take what they legitimately thought was their stuff.

We set off on the back roads travelling at ten miles per hour, hazard lights on, loaded with all their gear, the electric blue quad bike taking pride of place along with two dogs that weren't going to be left either. It was a veritable caravan of children's possessions on the move.

I prayed we wouldn't be stopped by the police. I felt so proud of Oliver and the children for not taking no for an answer and quietly arranging things. I wished I could have the same never-say-die attitude, but I didn't. I also knew in my heart that when the children took control and moved their possessions out, they'd never return. They had said their goodbye, in their own way.

I felt suicidal for the first time. If this is how I felt when I was masked with anti-depressants, God knows what my true feelings were like. The only thing to look forward to was my sessions with Terry; at least we could have some verbal sparring.

"Hello, Mike. How are you?"

"I'm okay, Terry, as you can see. Just bloody marvellous. How are you?"

"I'm fine, Mike."

"How's your day been, Terry?"

"Okay, Mike. Tell me about your day."

"What's interesting about mine, Terry? It's the same as ever. Why might you be interested?"

"It's my job to be interested, Mike."

"Is it, or is it just to listen, regardless of interest? Can't you just do your job without being interested? After all, you can't be interested in every client, can you? That wouldn't be interesting, that would be all the same, and all the same isn't interesting."

"Mike, why do you try to use your intellect to avoid my questions?"

"Do I, Terry? I hadn't recognised that. Can you give me an example?"

"There you go again, Mike. If I'm not careful I spend the whole session talking about myself, and you don't speak at all."

"How long have you been feeling like this, Terry?"

No one was laughing, so I continued on another vein.

"I hear counsellors have to be in therapy themselves, Terry, is that true?"

"Yes, Mike. We all have to clean ourselves from personal issues so we don't bring them into consulting with the patient."

"Am I a client or patient, Terry?"

"Whatever, Mike. Shall we move on?"

"Sure, just that client is a transaction, and a patient means I'm a loony. What do you want to talk about?"

"There you go again, Mike."

"Nearly caught you there, Terry, you must admit!"

"Mike, do you think you have bought friendship and might have tried to buy Holly as well? Might you have considered and treated her as just as another asset?"

"Bastard! Got me right back there. Bit of a low blow. Well, you're married aren't you? How do you know your partner isn't the same? How does anyone know the answer to that question? At least the poor have one advantage, don't they? Because they know they're loved for themselves? You're not poor, Terry, so how do you know?"

"Because we share things in a way that's much deeper than money. I don't know what your relationship with Holly was like, but I can see the debris of what remains. Mike, we each have to meet our own needs. If my partner left me I would be very upset but my life would go on. Do you think you're currently meeting your own needs, Mike?"

"I don't know because I'm not well, am I? Let's hope you never have to test that theory, Terry."

"Mike would it be true to say that you operated from a platform of arrogance?"

"Bollocks! What's the point of paying you all this money to come out with crap like that? If you're going to talk that shit I'll get myself another psychologist!" I shouted, and immediately realised that I'd proved his point.

We both saw the joke. I apologised when I had calmed down.

"Look, Terry, can you just tell me how it is?"

"That's the point, Mike. You have to tell me. In doing some constructive challenging, we can test the thinking and adjust it. You might then decide to adjust your behaviour, and hopefully increase your awareness of emotional intelligence."

"I didn't know emotions had intelligence," I said.

"There you are then, you've learned something. You can adjust your emotions, Mike, but not your feelings."

"Well, that's no good because my feelings are full of shit right now. Adjust that emotion, Terry," I said and left. I'd had enough for one day.

The letter

I was devastated Holly had gone to such lengths to be rid of me. She'd been the undoubted love of my life, and with her I had something of a future.

Without her, I couldn't contemplate one at all. Maybe that was what Terry was on about with regard to meeting my own needs.

She had changed her mobile number and her mum wouldn't speak to me. I felt completely abandoned. I needed to talk to her, if I couldn't see her. I needed her to know that together everything would be ok and we'd be even better for this experience. That getting through this would make us indestructible. But I couldn't do all that at a distance.

The only time I didn't banter with Terry was when I talked about my feelings for Holly, and when that happened the mood changed and I could hardly raise my voice above a whisper.

Rather than curse the darkness, I wanted so hard to do something positive – like light a candle. I did that, metaphorically and physically. Every evening as darkness fell, in the window of the kitchen where we spent most of our happy times, I'd light a scented candle. I hoped in some spiritual way that Holly would see the light and come home.

"You know, Mike, from the little I know of her, although you told her to fuck off, she had already gone from you. There's no point blaming yourself for angry words – she'd have left anyway," said Terry.

"It's likely she'd made her decision and was waiting for the time to go. You gave her permission to slam the door on your life. Look how she's gone and not left any means for you to contact her. Even if you were in a position to try to persuade her to come back, you would only be beginning another ending. Maybe you have to face up to the fact that, for reasons that might never be clearly explained to you, she doesn't want to come back. It's a sad fact of life that the one that loves the least has all the power."

I was traumatised by with this clarity, this realisation. Terry could see that.

"Terry, I'm engaged to be married. She still has the engagement ring. She'd have written by now to call it off if she was planning to leave me completely. She's giving me time, that's all. She wants me to prove I'll be okay, that I can stand on my own two feet and get through this. Then she'll come back.

"You wait and see. She hasn't said no. If she has gone from my life, then I want to say goodbye to her, I want to tell her how much I love her and always will. She needs to know that I'm sorry how all this has ended, that I know her dreams have been destroyed in all this chaos. I want her to know I understand that. It's not her fault. She's giving me time. That's all, Terry, that's what she's doing, giving me time."

Terry listened patiently. He could see my agony. He might well have seen my deception, too. But at the time, I believed those words. Not to have done would have been unbearable.

"Mike," Terry talked in the gentlest way. "Sometimes people have to face a future without ever saying goodbye to their loved one. People die after arguments. They have a row, hard and bitter words are spoken, they jump into cars and crash. One has to face the fact the other is dead. It happens more than you probably realise.

"Life is like that, and so sometimes are endings. Sometimes we don't get neat and tidy. Imagine how distressing that must be. You know Holly is alive and well somewhere in the world. If you know that and you truly love her, you must be content that she's happy. She doesn't have to be your possession, Mike; if you love her, you really do have to let her go, wish her well and acknowledge her right to do what she wants, however cruel that may seem.

"Let her go, Mike. You have to at least contemplate the process of moving on. You will, in time, if you give yourself a chance. If you don't, you'll stick in this purgatory. You'll carry this pain for ever. You know, in the Buddhist religion the highest are taught that pain is like a golden ball in your hands. They are taught to drop that ball. You have to do that, Mike. Then you can begin to see a future without her, but you won't say hello to anyone again in your life without first saying goodbye to her."

I was beside myself with grief. The emotional pain was real; it didn't have a physical manifestation, but was stronger than anything I'd felt before. How could I recognise my soul in this darkness?

"The pain comes in waves, Terry," I said, with silent tears streaming down. "It submerges you in a way that strips you bare. There's no pride and no hiding. Then the intensity leaves a dull, constant ache, a longing for the comfort only a loved one can give. Then the wave hits you again, and what's left is completely submerged in grief."

Terry listened quietly.

"It's awful that Holly hasn't and won't allow you the opportunity to say goodbye, Mike, it really is. She ought to have given you that. She owed it to you."

He looked at me, waiting for me to regain composure.

"To give you proper closure on that part of your life you both shared. A part that was so very obviously important to you...."

"*Is* important to me, Terry, not was," I said.

Terry continued: "Sometimes we recommend that you can gain some comfort in writing a letter of goodbye. Tell her all the things you want to say in that letter. You post it with the person's name on it, but no address. The Post Office keeps it for three months and then eventually destroys it. That might help you. It helps many who are bereaved and your loss is like bereavement, Mike."

"Letters?" A light switched on in my brain. Letters.

"Letters? There haven't been any for her, Terry. Don't you see? She usually gets some mail. But there hasn't been any for ages, not since she left. She's registered a change of address. Don't you get it? I don't know where she's gone, but if I write to her and address it to Woodland Grange it will be re-directed to wherever she is! Fucking genius, Terry, just genius!"

I skipped about. The mood had suddenly lifted. I didn't feel so helpless; I could do something positive and light that candle.

Terry let out a gasp of exasperation. "Oh don't, for God's sake, leave it! I was hoping you wouldn't figure that out, Mike. We were making real progress in getting you to let go. Don't do it. You have a responsibility not to do this rather than one to do it! Don't put an address on it. Face it, Mike she doesn't want to be contacted by you and you have to respect that. If she did, she would let you know herself where she was."

"Stuff that, Terry. She doesn't know what I'm going to say yet! Let yourself out, Terry, I'm going to be busy. I'm off to write a letter."

Poor Terry. Despite his best efforts, he was getting used to seeing himself out.

The telephone call

I sat at the writing desk in the drawing room; it was full of beautiful stationery bought at Smythsons of Bond Street. The letterheads and personal embossed address with the blue-lined envelopes had been personally chosen by her in better days. It would be familiar to her.

I wrote and re-wrote the letter, but when it came down to it the message was simple. I loved her, missed her, was sorry to bring all this to her door. But together we could get through it. We would be stronger and wiser as a consequence.

That was the bones of it, however it was written. Although it didn't feel as if I'd said enough, I had to stop drafting and re- drafting it and send it, courtesy of Woodland Grange Estate, and hope it didn't end up on my doormat.

I enclosed recent photographs of the dogs looking doleful and hoped beyond hope for a reply. As the days ticked by slowly, the good news was that the letter didn't appear so must have been re-directed. The bad news was there was no reply.

Every day I waited for the postman. He must have thought I was mad, as I willingly took all the final demands in search of a handwritten letter that would say everything was okay, she was coming home and we'd start a new future together.

The only thing that caught my interest was an offer from Provident Financial. They said they were very happy to give me a loan. Me? I thought. Yes, there it was. A loan for up to £500 at an average APR of 177%!

"Bloody hell," I thought. "The poor bastards that borrow at that level of interest because they've got no alternative."

Those with no money at all were being ripped off, and it disgusted me. Surely there should be a limit to the APR?

A new world was opening up to me, and not a very pleasant one. In a matter of months I'd moved from a select group of people who were invited members of Black Amex Charter to another who, if they wanted credit again, would be paying 177% for the privilege.

I thought I was going mad with frustrated anticipation. I've always imagined I was in control of most things in my life but here I was, waiting to be evicted from the house, all but a few friends gone. I was a broken, shattered, lonely man.

Eventually I decided that if Allah wouldn't come to the mountain, the mountain must go to Allah. I'd contact a London-based off-record private investigation company that I knew I would get pretty much anything I paid for. I obviously didn't have a lot of money but reckoned this expense would be worthwhile. They could get any telephone number at any time, regardless of confidentiality. A frightening prospect, but useful.

I rang a mobile number and was redirected to a phone somewhere in Europe. I could tell by the ringtone that it wasn't in the UK. A guy with a heavy East End accent asked a few questions; he didn't ask why I needed it.

He told me the price, which I paid, and said it would be invoiced as artwork.

They got back to me within twenty hour hours with a phone number. I couldn't quite believe it and didn't know how I felt about it. I stared at the digits. It was like looking at the winning lottery ticket, but I didn't know if I felt that lucky.

I carried the number around with me all day, sometimes taking it out of my pocket looking at it. I copied it onto another piece of paper in case I lost the original, carefully folding it up and putting it back in my pocket. I felt strangely close to her, knowing I could get through to her if I really needed to. I almost didn't phone as I didn't want to break that spell. It was comforting.

I could hardly bring myself dial the number when I eventually decided to do the deed. I so wanted to pick the right moment, to say the right words, to hear her voice again. I waited until a safe time, 4pm. I hadn't been drinking.

I thought I'd have a heart attack just hearing the ringing tone. It was real. They'd got the right number. She'd pick up and I'd speak to her at last. My heart beat fast.

"Hello?" It was her. That beautiful Irish accent I missed so very much.

"Holly, darling, it's Mike. I wanted to say....."

"How did you get my number?" she demanded, her voice hardening. "Don't you dare phone me again." She slammed the phone down.

I was shocked and called back immediately. A friend answered. "Look, she doesn't want to speak to you, okay? She's in floods of tears here. Leave her alone."

The phone went dead.

That was my big call, my opportunity for reconciliation. I sat in tears, wondering just what action I had instigated to be so forcefully abandoned and rejected. I was desperate and desolate. Inconsolable.

My despair was interrupted by the phone ringing and I nearly jumped out of my skin. Could it be her? Had she had second thoughts and decided to talk to me after all? I plucked up courage to answer. Don't screw this up. Whatever she says, just agree with her and ask for a meet. Don't get upset, don't get angry, just have the objective of meeting her. From there you can work things out.

I said hello in a faltering voice.

"Mr Kenney?" A male voice asked. "Mr Michael Kenney?"

"Yes?" I said.

"This is Essex Police. We've had a complaint of harassment from a Miss Holly Oakley."

"What?" I said, bursting into tears again. "I can't believe it! What? She's said what?"

"Mr Kenney, you're not to phone this lady again. If you do, we'll arrest you for harassment."

"But I've only phoned her once. I just wanted to talk to her, discuss things. I've still got some of her stuff here and she's got my car."

The policeman interrupted. He didn't seem to want to know the details.

"I'm going to interview her. Once I've done that, I'll get back to you. In the meantime I'm officially warning you, don't call that number again. I need to note on file that you're giving me your assurance. If I don't get it, I have to put a call into York and they'll come and arrest you immediately."

"But I've only phoned her once. It wasn't late at night. I want reconciliation not this..."

"Mr Kenney, the new harassment laws are constructed firmly in the favour of the individual who feels harassed. For them, it's a question of whether they, the victim, feel as if they have been harassed. She, in my view, is genuinely upset by your call and the prospect of any more. Now you're in possession of that fact, if you keep calling her, then you are indeed harassing her and you will be arrested."

The policeman could hear my distress. "I know you have a lot of personal problems at the moment and you don't want any more, Mr Kenney. Just don't contact her."

The phone went dead. I was shocked, totally finished. I knew at that point with a certainty that was overwhelming. I just wanted to end it all. I wanted to die.

Have you gone, it's really true?
No love exists between us two...
No views to even battle with
No heart to break, or smile to give

No hope of promises yet to come
Or calming walks in Easter sun
No beating heart at fireside
No hurtful tears or silly pride

No future cosy, no warming bath
No jokes to tell, no cause to laugh
No softening pillows on linen bed
And loving words...all left unsaid.

To see you again? I do not know
But as mountains rise and rivers flow
In noisy bars beyond the din

Whilst you breathe out, I'm breathing in.

Will I again, try catch your eye?
And clouds that patch my perfect sky
Are soon all gone, and you know why
Because you won't see my heavens cry...x

"I'm so sorry, Holly," I said to myself quietly, like a prayer most sincerely given. "I'm so truly sorry for everything."

CHAPTER 13

Saying goodbye

I stayed in bed. Didn't eat, hardly drank and didn't get up. Just put my head under the now stale and sour-smelling blanket and waited for something. I tried not to think about the future. Just keep waiting until Terry arrived. I'd come to realise that I had slowly but surely began to rely on this only point of contact with the real world. The rest was just crazy.

Eventually Terry came. He was shocked by my appearance and insisted on hearing my story in detail, making tea for us both. He had long since been comfortable padding around the house, checking on the dogs to make sure I was feeding them. He always said it was good to have something else around that needed looking after. Given the sort of heaving walk each dog had begun to adopt, and their flagging tails, I wasn't so sure they'd have agreed with him.

"Well, it's hard, but let's face it – you've got your answer," Terry said when I finished the blow-by-blow account. Shaking his head, he concluded: "Like it or not, it was a goodbye of sorts, Mike, let's be honest about that. It left nothing to chance or interpretation. You now know where you stand."

"Yes – she's prepared to throw me in jail for saying how much I love and miss her. For asking after her... We're engaged! We lived together! What does she expect? How can she suddenly change and be like that?"

"I don't think it was that sudden, Mike. I think she already had it in mind to leave you. If you're asking me what I personally believe, I think that everything happens for a reason. That's not part of any psychological wisdom, that's down to my personal beliefs. There's a reason and a unique timing to everything in life.

"It's preordained and, while parting is difficult and traumatic, it has to be right for you right now. You just don't know it or accept it yet. It's been done in the cruellest way, just leaving with no contact. It's hard for you to understand at the moment, but for that matter what gives us the right to insist on knowing? It's a bit arrogant, wouldn't you say? And we don't want to go down that road again!"

"Operating from a platform of arrogance? We who belong to this world, Terry, not yours," I said, in a failing attempt at humour.

He ignored it. I'd noticed that about him before. If you annoyed him or were cynical, he'd put it aside and continue undaunted. I wished I could do that.

"Precisely, Mike. Whatever makes us believe we should know everything that happens to us in this world in the first place? Why should everything make sense to us? That's just illogical to me, it's unrealistic. I acknowledge there are things that don't make sense and, when I do, it makes it easier for me to accept them. If you concede that life, and I mean ordinary life, is difficult, it certainly seems to stop being *so* difficult, if you see what I mean. Am I making sense?"

"No, but you've just told me not to expect to understand everything!"

Terry laughed. "You still have that quick wit there, that's for sure. No one's going to take that from you," he said, plainly trying to cheer me up a little.

"Isn't that one of the twelve steps along the route to recovery in AA, Terry? The higher power and all that?"

"I guess you could term it like that. You should give thanks for the times gone by, Mike, and remember that you will gain real wisdom from this experience. You're growing, you really are. You can't fail to grow given what you're going through."

"Why would Holly do this to me? Right now, with everything else going on? Why?" I insisted.

"She's living a human existence, Mike, not a perfect one. You promised her the earth. Implicitly, that was your social contract with her and, while you deserve much better than how she's handled things, you knew in your heart that she needed all those things she regarded as security. For her to feel safe, she needed security and safety. She sees that in money and power, Mike, two things you don't have at the moment.

"But that's not love, Mike. I'm sorry my friend, but it isn't. We often label things wrongly, that's half our problem. It's about meeting our own needs again, and she doesn't appear to be doing that. She looks for others with money and power."

Terry left me to dwell on his words. He'd already given way beyond the call of duty and possibly thought that my moment of clarity had now arrived. It had certainly been delivered by him. I could see things for what they were, he thought, and maybe next time we could start moving forward.

I knew what I was going to do. It was the only thing left. For me it was a case of tying up loose ends.

I awoke early the next day and went for a walk around the estate. I was looking for somewhere quiet, somewhere private, peaceful and undisturbed. It had been in my mind for some time. The idea was first a mere thought that was dismissed in a moment, but as opportunities and options closed down it felt more realistic and had become a real possibility, the only solution.

I needed somewhere beautiful. Looking over a flight pond where I could see the birds resting before making their long journey to sunnier climes, somewhere where I too could start my journey to God knew where.

This was where the children used to climb, each having their favourite tree. I needed somewhere Holly and I had picnics, where the memories were happy, clean and un-polluted. The place I stood in. It felt right. This is where I would finally cease my torment and the pain would stop once and for all.

I tried to write goodbye letters to the children but had no words. I sat at the writing desk with tears falling onto the paper, but no words would come. If it were anything it would have been to ask for forgiveness and an understanding for what I was about to do. It might be a selfish act but a necessary one, I reasoned.

They'd understand. I wasn't seeing them regularly anyway and they'd be better off without watching their dad continue to diminish as a person in front of their eyes. Let me at least have the chance to remain someone they could look up to and be proud of, even if I couldn't be with them anymore.

There was a practical reason, too. The added advantage of a life policy in force that would pay a small amount that was just about to fall behind on premiums, but was still currently in force. I'd carefully checked the details. It wouldn't be for long and there was no chance of it being reinstated. It would be lost forever.

"Everything has a time," I thought. "Everything happens for a reason."

Terry had confirmed that. This was my reason, it was clear to me. What I was contemplating suddenly had a time limit. I had to go, whether I was ready or not. How smart would I be if I did this after the policy expired? I couldn't screw this up as well. It was now or never.

I showered and changed into good, smart, casual clothes. I wanted to be tidy. I felt almost happy, relieved, like a great weight had been lifted from my shoulders. Nothing actually mattered any more. No one could get to me; let them say what they wanted. It was a solution that would solve everything for me.

It was a strange feeling, like when you found the answer to any difficult problem. I felt in control and I liked it, it was familiar to me.

I looked at myself in the mirror – smart, smiling, actually happy. I was my old self. I'd dictate what happened, not some other authority.

I knew Terry would call the police when I didn't answer the door on the Monday. They'd arrange a small search team. No one would find me accidentally, no one would stumble over me – unless it was the bloody poachers, in which case fuck them! Serves them right.

I was happy with the decision. I trusted my instincts. If you feel good about a choice, it has to be the right one.

I got the rope from the garage. I had given this a lot of thought. I knew how to tie it, and where to place it at the right hand side of my neck, not in front and not behind. That would give a clean, sharp break. It's amazing what you can find on the internet nowadays. I knew the height, which I'd calculated from my weight. Weight was important in this and I had lost a lot.

Too small a drop and I would choke to death. Too high and it would decapitate me, a bit messy and not good for the searchers. Oh, and don't forget to go to the toilet first. I didn't want any accidents in that department ruining my nice clothes. Just enough of a drop. Quick sudden and very, very final.

I had everything with me. I turned the lights out for the last time, stared around the kitchen, warming myself in the dark next to the Aga. This was a place of such happy times. Photographs hung on the walls, seemingly saying goodbye.

I looked at the phone and decided to call Terry out of respect for what he had tried to do for me. He would have been the last to see and I didn't want him to be blamed or feel he'd let me down. I didn't want him to live with that.

It wasn't him, it was others. On the contrary, he'd done his best and more for me then anyone. I wanted to say thank you. He'd given me his home number, not something he usually did but we'd grown to become friends.

I would call; there was nothing he could do anyway, he was miles away in Hull.

"Any time Mike. I mean it. Any time," he'd said.

Well, this was the time. Sunday night always felt like suicide hour between six and seven, ironically the God spot on television. I'd try to nip into paradise while His attention was there. I didn't want fuss or bother, no cry for attention. That had already been done many times. I was looking forward to ending the constant pain, the torment and turmoil, to never feeling ashamed again.

I made the call.

"Hello Mike, what's wrong? Are you okay?"

"I'm fine. Look, I'll get to the point. I won't be seeing you Monday or any other time. I've decided that whatever the future holds going forward, it's not for me. Don't blame yourself, I'm just saying goodbye. No fuss or bother, you know me by now. I won't change my mind. I just wanted to say thank you, Terry, you're a good bloke, really you are."

"What you saying, Mike?"

"I'm saying I've had enough, Terry. Not your fault, put me down to one that got away, but I'm ending it all right here, right now. I don't want you to try talking me out of it, my mind's made up. I'm old enough to realise what I'm doing, I just wanted to say goodbye.

"We've had some good chats, you're a good bloke. In different circumstances I would have enjoyed them. We could have been mates, I mean proper mates, and I could have straightened out some of the bullshit you talk! You've tried hard to get me back to being almost human. But I can't go forward, I really can't. And you know what? I'm absolutely certain now that I don't want to. So I'm leaving you all."

Terry listened intently, careful not to interrupt. There was no more joshing.

"Mike, I won't try talk you out of it. But I want to make sure you're thinking straight. It's an irreversible process so let's just test whether you're correct in your thinking. At least give yourself that.

"You're making good progress. You can't see it, but I can. You've always said you trusted me on that. Well, I'm telling you you're making progress. You have to believe me on that one. I would never lie to you."

I believed him but that wasn't the point. I'd had enough.

"Terry, I just want the pain to end. I feel like I'm going mad. It hurts me if I look at the past and it hurts me if I look to the future. And I sure as shit can't live in the present. There's nowhere for me, Terry. Nowhere, and now there's no one either."

"Your future is going to be fine, Mike. Different to what you had before but fine, maybe even better."

"It's the pain, Terry. I can't stand it any more."

"So that's why you're thinking of suicide, Mike, because of the emotional pain? You can take it, Mike. You're courageous. You're feeling exactly what you should be at this stage. I don't underestimate what you've been through, but it will pass."

"I can't. That's the truth. I can't."

Terry went quiet for a few seconds and then changed tack. "What do you think that will do to your children? I see the victims, the ones left behind, every day. Like it or not, you'll blight their lives forever."

"They're better off without me. They can have the insurance policy."

"Christ, Mike! Do you honestly think anything good would come from the money that's left behind? This is about your wrong thinking, Mike. Money was in the way of an honest relationship with Holly, and look how much pain that caused. Now you're putting money between you and your children. They want you around, not your money. They'll never forgive you, just as much as they'll never get over you."

Warming to his theme, Terry was increasingly passionate and spoke with great urgency. "Do you think Holly would be the same if her father hadn't thrown himself in the river? Do you think she would have treated you in the same way? Would she still have slammed the door to her past and yours in such a way? When does she stop running, Mike, and which other poor unfortunate sod gets hurt as a result, just like you're hurting now? Don't you see that *her* father's's suicide caused her to run? She left Ireland at seventeen, just as soon as she could. And as soon as something goes wrong, she'll be off again, running to goodness knows where. Do you think she's happy doing that? Burying her past like it's shameful?

"Will you have your children run for the rest of their lives as well? Will they ever be truly happy again, will they ever stop running when this act of extreme violence is so clearly on them and not you? You'll be dead a long time, Mike. You're out of it, but what about those who love you who are left behind? They have to live with your decision for the rest of their lives."

I could feel the emotion and pain rising up in me and crystallising into tears.

"Your mother and father will never get over it, Mike. It will kill them before their time; you're as good as killing them as well as yourself."

I wanted to be strong, matter-of-fact, I didn't want him to change my mind. I was determined. I wanted to be happy; I didn't want fear or regret. I wanted my last moments to be happy ones.

"Terry, I just want this pain to stop."

"I know, Mike," Terry said quietly, calming himself. He'd made his point only too well. "And it will once you work through it. It's justifiable and there's nothing wrong with how you feel; it's perfectly normal and so are you. You're courageous; you're talking it through, and most don't. They just take pills and walk around in a zombie-like state, dealing with the symptoms and never the causes.

"In talking it through, you have to face things that are difficult for you, and you have. The issues have to be worked through, there's no quick or easy way, but I've told you and you know I'm honest, and I'll tell you again – you're making good progress. Don't give up now."

"I don't think I can go on, Terry. I really don't see that as an option any more."

"Mike, we both know that if your mind's made up I'm miles away and there's nothing I can do. If I call the police, you'd be gone before they found you. But consider this," Terry said in a deliberate tone. "What makes you think it stops?"

That got me. I didn't understand. "What do you mean?"

"The emotional pain that you can't stand. What makes you think that if you take your own life that doesn't go on through eternity? I wouldn't risk it. You're doing it because you think it stops. I'm saying, logically, you really don't know. I wouldn't chance it. Think about it. It's a big call, how you're going to feel for eternity.

"Are you listening to me, Mike? You're not an idiot. You can see the odds are against this idea. The damage you cause to your children, your family, and the pain might not stop. It may be with you for ever. Let's talk in the morning, okay? Mike, promise me man to man you'll be there in the morning. I'm there first thing. Have an early night and get to bed where you're safe. This will pass, if you just let it. Don't drink. I know you won't sleep, but go to bed. Are you going to call your parents?"

"No, Terry, I'm fine," I said, regaining composure. "I'm sorry, I really am."

"I know you are, but you're going to come through it. I have your promise, Mike. I'm putting my trust in you. You keep my trust, Mike."

Terry rang off. How could he spend so much emotion on someone who was just a client? I'd intruded into his family and certainly ruined his Sunday, his only night off. He must be thinking about me now, worried about this idiot.

I felt ashamed. I went outside and got the rope and some petrol from the garage. I went upstairs, and looked under my pillow and there it was. The pure white, silk Dolce & Gabbana blouse of Holly's that I'd found. It had been missed or she'd have taken it; it was one of her favourites. It still had her perfume on it; I could smell her. I hadn't wanted to wash it; I'd wanted to feel close to her. As I held it to my face I could imagine her there with me. It was evocative and comforting. I'd been crying into it. It had become my equivalent of a child's comfort blanket.

I sat outside and poured petrol onto a small fire I'd hastily put together. The blue flames quickly turned yellow as the damp wood heated up, spitting like a devil that had reluctantly given my soul another chance at living.

Eventually the fire burned clean and warm. I said a prayer and, with a sobbing goodbye, tossed the blouse onto it. It flared like the passion I'd felt in the relationship and, in the same way, burned away to nothing.

This was my unaddressed letter in the postbox. This is where it would end. I said my final goodbye to her that night, in the darkness of that lonely, desperate place. Just me, crouched in front of the fire, staring into the flames of my past until they turned to ashes, just like my hopes for reconciliation.

Eventually the wind would take the ashes. My father had struggled to say it but he had, his pained eyes concentrating on the words: "Let her go, Michael. Cast her to the wind."

Clarity

Terry arrived promptly the next morning. With something of a shamed face, I opened the door and settled down to the bollocking I felt was inevitable. It never came.

"Now I can really say I'm glad to see you!" Terry smiled. I think he meant it. "Get the tea on, then, and then you can tell me how you're feeling."

His patience and optimism knew no bounds.

"Surviving. I'm here, feeling slightly ridiculous now as well as everything else, but you'll say that's how I'm supposed to feel, eh? I'm staying so I might as well make the best of it. I have to face what needs to be done. I'm sorry about the drama I caused, and on your day off as well...Not a good Sunday night for either of us."

"That's clarity. It's better, Mike. You'll have more of them. Everything else that surrounds you at this moment is only temporary. Things will get better. But before they get better, they will get different. It's a process."

"Terry, I have to ask you. Do you think I should be sectioned for my own safety?"

"No, Mike, you're completely aware of what you're doing. By asking whether you should be sectioned you're really asking whether someone else should take responsibility for you. If you were sectioned, you'd only delay what you know you have to do, which is take responsibility for yourself, and meet your own needs. With help you'll work it through; just try and concentrate on not letting your feelings overwhelm your thoughts."

It was a turning point.

I decided to at least take control of that which was available and decided to get out of Woodland Grange before they threw me out. I was introduced by a friend to yet another accountant, Adam, who listened patiently. I didn't want to talk to any accountant again, ever, but my friend insisted and at least it gave me another opportunity to off-load.

"I really don't think this should have happened to you, Mike, but it's too late to fight back now. The best you can hope for is a good trustee in bankruptcy who won't rub your nose in it or make it personal."

It seemed sensible enough advice. He introduced me to a gentle, kind guy who didn't judge me at all.

"Let's be totally honest with each other, Mike, and agree what you can and can't take with you. So long as you're straight with me, I'll be straight with you and as flexible as I'm allowed."

I didn't ask for a lot, but there again I didn't want a lot. I had nowhere to put my stuff anyway. Where would it go when I didn't know myself where I was going?

I walked to the magistrate's court with him. With scary efficiency and an immediate but brief appearance in front of a judge, who looked at my details for a few minutes and said: "You seem to be in a little trouble here, Mr Kenney," I joined the members of a small, exclusive club that declared themselves bankrupt. It was painless and quick. I guess the consequences of such an action are rarely felt on the day and affect you over a period of time.

The trustee tried to cheer me up by giving me the statistics about how most multi-millionaires go bankrupt at some time in their life, how it wasn't such a stigma nowadays. If I was in America my credit rating would have actually increased and investors would be happier to invest in me in the future because I was more unlikely to go through this painful process again.

It was one possible consequence of being an entrepreneur and I'd accepted that risk years ago when I set up the business. I just found it shameful.

I'd never owed anybody anything. But at least my personal creditors would only be the institutions that had initiated these ridiculous claims against me. It was an inevitable decision given my circumstance and what I was up against. At least I registered it as voluntary bankruptcy. Minor victories become important in the struggle for sanity whilst chaos inhabits your everyday life.

Sue could still get half of the matrimonial home and half my pension, that was agreed with the trustee. It amounted to over £200K in total, so while it wasn't the million or so she'd planned, many wives leave a marriage with a lot less.

It wasn't the absolute disaster for her that it was for me, and quite rightly so. None of this was her fault. But I couldn't help wondering why she hadn't divorced me years earlier when we first split. Maybe she expected a big payday, and the longer she left it, the bigger it would become.

It was only when I'd become engaged that we started to discuss divorce, even though she'd been living with her boyfriend a lot longer than I had been with Holly. How things and circumstances change in such time. Her family stopped talking to me completely.

I got a few suits and shirts, a settee, a television. It was enough. I didn't deserve or want anything else. There were a few people who, on knowing my position, casually mentioned that the white gold Cartier watch I had should be 'lost'. It was worth about £17,000. No one could have proved it wasn't lost. But I decided that with honesty, rather like pregnancy, you can't be partial. You either are or you aren't.

I still felt that those who were investigating the company's affairs would see that I was honest. They would, at the very least, give me that credit even if they concluded I was also stupid and too trusting, and I would survive this onslaught with at least my honesty and dignity intact, if not my money or friends.

I thought I could at least travel light now. I heard (through the administrator) that Peter also went bankrupt. He came back from Spain and was a little worse for wear when he rolled up at the High Court in London, smiling like a lunatic. He apparently laughed in the face of this. It saddened me that he'd gone a little wild and crazy, but hadn't we all? I still feel the same way. We were coping in our own individual ways, but we were both hurting badly.

James did a deal with CBA and negotiated a settlement. I had to like James, he always could negotiate himself in and out of a corner. I always thought he was strangely talented. I couldn't help but admire him even now.

I went to stay in a flat which my Mum and Dad paid advance rent for. It was a kind thing to do as it came out of their savings; they personally had no income in retirement. I was very grateful to them as I trudged up the stairs to this tiny, third floor place. At least I had a roof over my head. What would have happened to me without their support? What happens to others in these circumstances? The thought of how quickly someone's life can unravel scared me. It sent a shiver down my spine.

Days stretched into weeks, sitting there doing precisely nothing. Only Johnny would speak to me, no other directors came near. Weeks turned into months. I tried to keep my mind active and think about business opportunities I could capitalise on once I came out of bankruptcy.

There was no point in doing anything at all until I came out of that which had been agreed for a period of twelve months. I found myself in a sort of twilight world, where everyone seemed to be doing something but me. I had never felt so disassociated from real life, as people around me continued their normal, busy lives and I stayed still.

Apparently, the ex-directors were busy making their own arrangements to take each of their new companies forward. Gossiping about the future, answering questions from CBA, getting their lawyers to protect their positions and answering the questions asked by the DTI in a uniform manner, meeting together and enjoying Friday night drinks. I wonder if they ever saw ghosts in the windows.

I obviously wasn't invited and neither were Peter or James, not that we would have turned up. Some old-time employees asked after me through the directors, but were told not to talk to me and not mention my name again - at least until investigations were completed and their own positions safeguarded.

Johnny, the best of them in occasionally keeping in touch, talked about how he negotiated with the administrators to take the sofa that sat in reception for his new company. He didn't understand this furniture originally came from my matrimonial home, purchased by my parents and donated to the company when we first started the business above the supermarket all those years ago.

For him it was just a game, spoils of war almost. For me, each piece of furniture had a history. It seemed too cruel and too insensitive.

My sister came round and talked to me at length, helping me to keep going as I saw the physical as well as the financial dismantling of the business. How stupid had I been to think that work colleagues could replace family? And how many people in business with their minds focused on it still make that mistake today?

Terry eventually and carefully let me go to take my first tender steps into the big wide world. He'd weaned me off anti-depressants and counselling. I could have done with more, but I'd had around 42 hours of discussions and had to leave the estate, so it was a natural end.

"You can get too much," he said. "Look at Dudley Moore."

"Yes," I said. "And look at you!"

He gave a generous smile. This man had helped me through an awful period and while he had made it clear there were still situations to overcome, I was ready for the world again. I was hugely grateful.

"Things will get different before they get better, Mike," he warned. "But they won't get any worse than what you've already been through, and you've coped with that."

"I don't know where all this will end," I said. "I'm scared they might find something, anything, even though I've been honest all along. I didn't know there was a problem and they're trying to really go for me; the creditors are after my blood. They're asking the others all these questions about me. What happens if I'm sent to prison? It sounds crazy but I'm scared, really scared."

Terry, still smiling, walked to the door and opened it. He turned with a final flourish and announced: "Prison? Ho, don't worry about that, Mike. Prisons are easy, at least the sort they would eventually send you to. I was sentenced to seven years in there!"

"Bloody what? Jesus, what's that all about? Let me get this straight, I've been taking wisdom and advice all this time from an ex-con?"

"There's none better, Mike. Been there, done that, bought the T-shirt."

"Holy shit!" I said, shaking my head.

"See," said Terry confidently, as he opened his car door. "We can all turn our lives around if we want to; it's never too late. Don't worry about my story, Mike, I'll tell you about it one day. You take care of yourself, meet your own needs and be open to real love when it happens. Keep your chin up!"

We embraced, and he was gone. Some man, was Terry. He had surely saved my life and, having looked after it for a while, had given it back to me as a gift. It was now up to me to do something with it.

I knew that, after the bankruptcy, I had around six months to a year before the DTI findings were announced.

In that window of opportunity I needed to set up, run and hand over a business to someone else to manage.

All this had to be done from nothing. I'd better get a move on. I mustn't waste this gift, a gift Terry had personally given me.

CHAPTER 14

The DTI report

Christmas came and I braced myself for the enforced cheer. It was a time I dreaded, as most people with emotional baggage tends to. Even reasonable moments where you feel quite normal stand in stark contrast to happier days.

I tried to remember that it was only a few days, Christmas Day and Boxing Day, and then everything could be put away and I could return to the miserable existence I'd come to regard as my normal reality.

It nearly overwhelmed me when I saw the look in my daughter's eyes. It had been made clear over many years that this was a time when she had to be a very good girl, as the angels would tell Santa Claus and only good girls got presents. She was on her best behaviour and, thanks to my extended family, all the children got Christmas presents. But Lucy's concern was for me, not herself.

She'd noticed that I didn't have many presents and, while I wasn't ungrateful and personally couldn't have cared less, no amount of thanks could disguise the fact that this year there were meagre pickings all round.

This rather reinforced a view that she had heard about Daddy, that he was a bad man. I must be very naughty if Santa hadn't brought much. She cuddled me, offering to share her presents, and tried to explain how things could get better if I made an effort and that I'd be forgiven if I was a good Daddy. She'd been naughty once but she had now behaved herself and I was told to look at all the presents she had as a result.

What beautiful, child-like logic. If Daddy could try a little harder, be a bit better, then maybe next year he might get more presents.

The DTI eventually received the Directors' Conduct report from the administrators. There was no suggestion of criminality, as had been rumoured both in the press and among some of my old colleagues, who always knew that it was both impossible and ridiculous.

No hidden money nor self-gain from this financial disaster. No apparent weight was attached to the simple truth that it seemed obvious to all that if I'd known we had a problem, we'd have cut our cloth, reduced salaries and made redundancies.

Much instead was made of my large salary, but it was described as one rather than three from the separate companies, each under separate employment contracts. I had still been employed within these companies but not as a director. I'd resigned from the actual boards and worked more in a consultancy capacity. As far as I was concerned, each was a private company with no external shareholders, so in that regard I believed we could organise ourselves as we wished.

The arrangements were all transparent with full details of earnings listed in the report and accounts under the full disclosure arrangements we always insisted on.

No reference was made to the fact that neither I, nor any other director, had ever taken a dividend from any of the companies regardless of profits made and banked in the previous nine years.

If I had, rather than a salary, they wouldn't have been able to say I'd been paid an excessive amount. It would have been better for personal tax and cash flow too, as I later understood. More great advice given retrospectively.

When Oliver became ill, I'd explained to my fellow directors that if I could earn the same money by leaving my capital in the business as by cashing it in and living off the interest, there was no immediate need to sell. That seemed an honest and straightforward way to behave and a simple test that everyone could understand. The company had always worked on the basis of being open, transparent and financially honest. Why should we not? We were proud of what we had achieved. We knew that anybody interested in making an offer for the business would simply add back the salaries of the principal directors and get a profit multiple based on that greater amount.

We always used to talk about transparent finances available to all. Everyone had access to them. I drew salary from the three companies and it was the total of these that they objected to, despite nine years of unbroken profit.

They didn't give any credit as they promised for me signing away my contractual rights, which amounted to £160K, in order that their disposals could go through for the benefit of the creditors. The creditors thought I was one of the bad guys.

All the directors' submissions to the DTI were sent to me as part of them prosecuting the case. It was difficult to read the other directors' statements, as clearly they were written at a time of great pressure and fear for their own safety. It's most unnerving being cross-examined in correspondence by someone representing the Secretary of State. It obviously hadn't occurred to a few people that these would, in turn, be passed on to the defendants. Or if they did, maybe they simply didn't care anymore.

Some of the statements contained information that, to say the least differed to my recollection of unfolding events and some were just bloody personal. One wrote that the answer to the question of our "lavish entertaining" had to be firmly placed at my door. It included by way of explanation that must have been a reference to his trips to the boat in Majorca and general social activity that it was an obligation rather than an enjoyable event.

The fact that he, along with others, frequented what was later described on credit cards slips as 'a boutique clothes shop' at a venue in Palma called The Mustang Ranch was not something that could be regarded by any stretch of the imagination as an obligation.

My personal experience of the place suggested it had little to do with clothes, indeed the lack of them would be more the appropriate point. I understand that one of the guys once bought twice from the 'boutique' in one evening he was so taken with the merchandise. Now to me, that didn't suggest any obligation. In fact, it was definitely beyond the call of any duty that even I would have tried to impose.

It was also suggested that I didn't have many friends and, as such, used to insist that people accompanied me on social as well as business events and they in turn felt obliged to be there. To have excluded the person I have in mind would have brought about a world record sulk that would have offended those unfortunate enough to see it. He had a face that could effortlessly maintain a twenty-four hour strop, a point Mum cleverly noticed this when she'd said: "There's more to him than his face suggests."

The allegation about my lack of friends was the most hurtful and cruel. I believe it untrue and I had, without exception, a high regard for the people around me, a real friendship forged from a common purpose. That friendship might have been initiated as a consequence of working within the business, but it wasn't just because of that. The kindest person who has taken an interest in my career and personal well-being left the company a year before it crashed. But, as things turned out, here I was, alone and abandoned by my so-called friends. The person who wrote that for the DTI may have been closer to the truth than he could ever have realised, as he was obviously talking about himself. I clearly didn't have as many friends as I'd thought, as evidenced by their behaviour when the business went down.

I was sorry that the administrators had never bottomed the problem from the point of view of discovering what the original financial issue was.

This wasn't a result for the creditors or the administrators, and gave them little comfort. They'd seen this investigation grind on for over a year.

Eventually, Corporate and Group went into liquidation; the others remained in administration. How could Group Plc go into liquidation when it never traded? It was the only company I was a director of and that was simply a holding company for the shares. No one bothered to tell me. Maybe it was because a couple of months before all this happened I was asked by the Financial Services directors to sign a 'subordinated loan' arrangement from Group Plc to Financial Services as "a mere formality to do with the FSA and about our liquidity under those rules, and no actual money is involved".

I never did find out, but I was a fool for not getting correct advice. The directors walked away with their company intact with the pre-packed administration. What were the implications of that loan agreement?

No evidence of criminality, no foul play was established by the administrators. However, negligence was something that could be reflected in the Directors' Conduct report. Someone, somewhere had been negligent. But who, and in what capacity? The DTI, not surprisingly, decided that out of seventeen directors three, and only three, were culpable – Peter, James and I.

Being made a scapegoat for the failure is such a timeless and unimaginative concept. I couldn't believe the DTI would swallow a view that seemed harsh in singling out just three people from the seventeen who were so obviously making decisions about the ongoing operation of the business.

Those very people who ran the businesses at the time continue to do so now, quite a few under their own personal ownership. How could they reasonably say they weren't responsible then? If I, as alleged, took my eye off the ball, was it not simply because I'd passed that responsibility onto others - and paid them well to look after things? The entire Ward Evans Group's demise was responsible for the creation of over half a dozen new businesses that continue to flourish today. I've been told that they even trade with the same creditors.

If the three of us were not part of the immediate solution then we became the problem, and the DTI wanted – needed – to slap someone. Heads needed to roll. In all of these dealings, from beginning to end, neither CBA nor the DTI interviewed me face to face. Not once.

It's another hard-learned fact that they can do this to someone's life behind faceless bureaucracy. So much for Enterprise Britain.

They said I'd been negligent in my running of the business. I presume they mean all businesses. Well, if they thought I was running the business then they might have had a point as I was hardly there! But I wasn't running the group. The directors were, and their collective salaries amounted to well over a million pounds.

I'd passed on operational control and resigned in the most public of ways at the Product Providers' Dinner – attended by lots of executives (if not exactly the same people) who eventually became the creditors. I'd even sent the DTI an original copy of my resignation speech, introducing the new Corporate board.

In a perverse way they were agreeing with me, saying I wasn't running it when I should have been. I was saying I'd delegated that authority in the most visible and public of ways.

Was this the same government department that in the same year had spent millions on looking to change its name to be more modern and user-friendly in corporate Britain, only to say "forget it" and remain as the DTI – wasting tax-payers' money?

They advised that the Secretary of State for the Department of Trade and Industry was going to apply to have me banned for six years as a director. Nice to take an interest, I thought.

I asked for legal aid. It was refused. It's not a criminal charge.

I made enquiries into what would it cost to defend. I begged a favour from the previous lawyers.

In the usual clipped, legal language accompanied by an air of disinterest, I was informed: "Well, it will be around £50K, lots of publicity. You'd be taking on a government department and that should never be encouraged. I'm happy to take the money off you, if you insist. Do you have it?"

"No," I said. "I've just come out of bankruptcy." I'd just been discharged.

"Really? That's a shame."

"Why?"

"Well, you have no money to defend this action from the DTI and it's going to cost a fortune. If anyone, including your parents, were to support you the DTI has a right to go for them personally as well if they win. That means if anyone feels outraged by this action, even if they wanted to, they couldn't financially support you."

"So I can't legally defend myself, even if I could borrow from family?"

"No – they risk financial ruin themselves if they do. It was a legal principal established in the Hamilton's Al Fayed case some years before."

How come all these major players now impacted on my life? If people really knew how civil law operated, they'd know it's a simple principle of deepest pocket wins in all but the most rare of cases.

I had no one to help anyway. Mum and Dad didn't have that sort of money, certainly not to throw on legal fees. What sort of victory would it be anyway? It wasn't going to get my companies back. I had no choice but to just agree it.

"Well, Mike, that's probably for the best. All well and good but..."

"But what?" I asked in complete exhaustion.

"If you accept this, they go and get it agreed by the court, and their costs are awarded against you."

"What? What?"

"The case will not be contested, as you've agreed you don't have the money and that's your decision. But that means the costs in investigating you and banning you will be awarded against you. That's pretty much an automatic procedure."

"But they've had lawyers onto this for nearly a year... The DTI can afford it... I've had no one represent me because I can't afford it... clearly I can't. We've just agreed all that!"

" I'm sorry, but their costs, I reckon, will cost twenty to thirty thousand pounds."

"Screw them! I can't pay it! I have no money. Whether it's buried in an off- shore account or anywhere. What happens now?"

"Well, looks like they may bankrupt you again, Mike – worst case situation."

"What? Again?" I said, blinking back tears.

"I can't face all that again. It's just not fair." As I said those words, I remembered a few years earlier Lewis saying exactly the same words to my wife when talking about Oliver's diagnosis.

"This isn't a discussion about fairness, Mike. In this case they're holding you responsible, end of story."

"What would it mean?" I said, trying to regain my composure.

"If you go bankrupt again that would be an automatic five years, as anyone who goes bankrupt more than once is showing a worrying trend."

If it hadn't been for Terry's wise words, I would have again thought very seriously about ending the struggle there and then. I was right about not wanting to face my future, but I had no choice.

Learn the lessons

I had to try to remember some of the lessons I'd learned from Terry. It was survival. Deal with one thing at a time, keep my chin up. I had to write to the DTI throwing myself on their mercy. There was nothing more that could be done. Cooperate with the inevitable, relax in the chaos. Be clear as to what I could change and accept those things that I couldn't.

I would have to agree to a DTI ban and try getting them down to something less than six years. The absolute minimum would be three; maybe I'd settle for four. Mum and Dad offered on my behalf to give them £3,000 as a contribution to final settlement of their legal bills. They agreed eventually; having made enquiries, they reluctantly accepted that I really didn't have any money. I had nothing left to sell, either. Maybe they, like me, couldn't quite believe that you could lose ten million and not have anything to show for it. As I repeated on so many occasions, if I'd known in time that we had a problem, I'd have dealt with it.

That people in the industry felt I'd swindle money rather than deal with a problem just didn't stack up. This was a subject Terry and I came back to time and time again.

"People want someone to blame, Mike. They've seen the flash cars, the lifestyle. You were high profile so you got the blame. If you accept that, you'll learn to live with it. Even if their conclusions aren't true, it will make it easier for you to deal with."

Eventually the DTI agreed that Mum and Dad could pay for their legal bills but not for my defence. And they banned me for four years.

In itself, whilst the DTI has all sorts of frightening powers, I was told that the minimum ban is two years and the maximum is fifteen, so in that regard it wasn't bad. I did, however, briefly become target practise for the press again. They'd waited patiently for the DTI announcement and let me have a few volleys. Only to be expected, really. It could have been worse.

I so wanted to go public and tell my side of the story but was advised against it by a friend, Christine, who operated in the weird and wonderful world of crisis management PR.

"You'll stir it all up and never get what you want, Mike. They'll edit it and they're hardly going to be supportive, are they? What did you want to say exactly that they might think worthy of printing? How will it sell papers?"

"Well it's a long story, and almost unbelievable," I said. "I wouldn't know where to start..."

"Precisely," Christine said. "They won't give you column space, they just want a sound bite that keeps the reader interested and bad news sells more than good, as I'm sure you're aware."

I thought about this for a moment, and the only thing I could think of that embraced these two principles was: "If you think the creditors' committee is pissed off, you should hear what my mother has to say about my losing ten million!"

Christine laughed.

"Well, what can I do, then?" I asked.

"In this business, when dealing with journalists, there's an old Chinese proverb that's usefully employed – that when you're on the end of a public thrashing, just say 'I wish you an interesting life'. Just do that, Mike, it says everything. Wish them an interesting life."

Eventually the press became less nasty and started calling us "those loveable rogues". It could have been worse, I suppose, and in some respects, it suggested some sort of grudging warmth. We weren't the complete bastard crooks they initially thought, or perhaps just thought of me.

Before my director's ban came into force I needed to kick-start a business, get it going, and give it to someone else to run so that it could continue when I wasn't able to direct it. Funnily enough, it's precisely what I did with the Ward Evans Group.

I needed something that interested me. That made me get up in the morning, put a suit on and go somewhere. I wanted to be missed by someone, to be expected somewhere. I'd begun to understand how totally disassociated you can feel from society when the everyday business of going to work or home again suddenly stops. Where do people in my position go? Everywhere I went, people were walking purposely, going somewhere, doing something. Talking on mobile phones, making arrangements, having meetings. Doing business or lunch.

I understood how envious one could become of an ordinary life. Having a home to go back to, friends to share stories with, work to grumble about, a girlfriend to love and occasionally fall out with. Disassociated is a desperate place to inhabit.

It was no sudden revelation, but this disengagement crept up on me through that old process of gradual disclosure. It saps your energy and optimism, destroys your self-worth and diminishes your joy for life. Nothing is fun. Your humour, personality and intellect evaporate in the monotony of doing nothing. Because you're not in society but merely observing it going on around you, you're left with a feeling of distance and unreality. No feeling of belonging, and we all need that.

I really understood how criminality starts in the ever-expanding club of the disengaged and dispossessed. Where people don't feel as if they have any ownership of the future or contribution to make. It destroys your self-confidence and you feel that you dare not do anything any more. All decisions are big decisions. Paralysis by analysis.

You distrust your instincts. You no longer have a 'gut feeling'. You question what was good about yourself in the first place. You re-examine what were previously strongly-held views and become separated from what used to be second nature. Your moral compass is distorted. If people speak to you they tend to bully or, worse still, pity you. They talk down to you, smile as if they knew all along what I didn't. The flash cars were the obvious indicator of the disaster that would befall me. I'd grown too big for my humble boots.

Well-meaning people tell you to get on with it, snap out of it. They smile and pat you on the shoulder like some well-meaning Dutch uncle and say you'll get it all back. You did it before and you can do it again, as if energy, time and resource are infinitely available and the industry would welcome you with open arms – which, given the bad publicity, they certainly wouldn't. They pay no attention to the timing, hard work, and enthusiasm and sheer dedication – not to mention luck – that got you there in the first place.

Ho – and I received an amusing notification to say I was being considered as an entry in the business edition of *Who's Who,* and could I check the details and fill in a few blanks. Well, at least I got a laugh out of that. I thought better of it; I'd had enough publicity for my liking and binned it.

I tried to bring to mind Terry's words of advice: "Keep it real, Mike. Things will get different before they get better. People will be different with you, but remember you are the same person. Don't measure your value in pound notes. If you do get involved with another venture, if it succeeds, all well and good. But if it doesn't, it's because the business proposition is wrong. Not you. Don't define yourself by what you do."

I started to understand better. I had to get on with something, anything. My mind was awash with creative ideas but they all cost money, like Mr Micawber in *David Copperfield*. I tried to keep an optimistic view that something would "turn up".

My parents saw me thrashing around. They said they'd put £20,000 up, part of an inheritance following the sale of their council house, into anything I chose. This was a vote of confidence and one that only a close family would make, given my track record.

I knew I couldn't waste it, as once it had gone there would be no further possibility of either my earning it or having more given. The dilemma was whether I put the money away for rent in the future or into trying to put a team together who could and would eventually run a business. Could I trust them; importantly, could they trust me, given what had been described as my 'colourful' business background?

New beginnings

I'd been made aware of the short comings of accountancy services generally…to say the least and I was aware of a man named Colin that drank in the same local pub and had seen all the comings and goings associated with the demise of my companies.

I'd briefly talked to him about how I believed that I could have done a better job of the accounts than the previous lot. This developed into a general moan about the Industry overall. With a little bit of "relaxed thinking" Colin broached the subject of my working for a newly-formed company that he might assist in setting up, which would include an element of shared ownership for me. What took the wind out of my sails was that fact he wanted it to be an accountancy company. It would be more than ironic if I set up that type of business, but the prospect intrigued me and held a special fascination. I would be doing general sales and marketing and hopefully, it would be up to me to try to transfer whatever skill sets previously learned and apply them to this sleepy traditional profession.

The deal quickly fell through when the amount of shareholding couldn't be formalised. This in itself was a blow; what I thought was a man running a business turned out to be a husband-and-wife team where the dominant person appeared to be the wife.

The shareholding had been agreed in principle at a meeting held in a hotel, minuted for the sake of clarity. There were five people around the table plus the main man. Everything was fine, I had potential investors introduced by Andrew another accountant, who had unlike the rest taken pity on me, and I had his know-how. The idea that I was sure must have started as a joke, took on a life of its own. That evening on the way home, I got a call.

"Mike," said Colin "I've got a problem. My wife's gone ape-shit over the shareholding. She won't agree it."

"I didn't know I was in business with your wife," I said.

"Well you're not really, but I can't go forward on existing shareholding, you know how it is..."

I was quietly relieved. I didn't want to be in business with her and exposed to all the domestic considerations that go with a couple, let alone the internal debates that would be inevitable within their household. I'm sure they expected me to just say bollocks and walk away, but I had grown used to the idea and there was certainly an element of "If you cant beat them join them" The Genie was out of the lamp and nobody was going to try put it back.

Research suggested that the market place was fragmented with thousands of one or two man bands organised in the most traditional of ways where the average age of the owner was around sixty five years or even older. It seemed a large number of these people were simply waiting for their retirement. The cost of service delivery seemed expensive and must have been in these traditionally run establishments where marketing was unheard of and the only way to compensate for increased expenses was to divide it by the number of available clients. These people had no real appetite to do things differently and most looked to me like they were happy to serve out their time, or get lucky and find a buyer for their business.

The idea of being charged by the hour and not really knowing how many hours the work might take reduced the client to be nothing other than a passive but very interested observer in how much all this was going to cost. A job done slowly was a more rewarding one financially for the accountant. Surely we could do better than all that?

There were lower entry bookkeeping packages on the market for small businesses that meant a lot more clients were able to provide their data electronically rather than in the proverbial carrier bag with all the associated scribbled notes that had historically taken accountants ages to decipher. Yet fees seemed to be going up regardless of how the information was provided. The fee charged seemed to have no real correlation to the amount of work done. All this seemed wrong and open for a new way and a new approach. Hadn't I seen all this before some ten years earlier within another Industry?

While I was researching this possibility I needed to seek some form of benefit. My family had insisted I should as I was entitled to it, having paid what must be near half a million pounds in personal tax over the last few years. Apparently, if I was engaged in this research activity, it could be for no more than a couple of hours per day as I had to be available for work. I needed to claim whatever benefits the system would allow, not a great deal but useful.

The thought of going into the Job Centre was, to say the least, something I wasn't looking forward to. I braced myself to claim Social Security and Job Seekers' Allowance. I felt sad and humbled by the realisation that this was what it had come to. I also had to recognise that I was no different from others and that I shouldn't feel it beneath me. It was a lesson in humility, and one that was well-needed - if not at that precise time. I found most of the staff polite and respectful.

They seemed genuinely interested in what had happened to me and what I was now trying to achieve.

"Great idea," they would say. "Let me know when it's up and running."

Someone even gave me a copy of their CV, should I be looking to employ in the future. I explained to the person at the Job Centre: "It's a simple concept, really. We have an idea and, if it works, a new company will be set up. It in turn will give me a job. So I have to work for nothing as much as I can to assist in getting the project off the ground. I then won't be able to run it once the DTI ban comes into force, so I have to find others that will. So that I give operational control completely to others."

All of which was true.

"Well, Mr Kenney, what is it exactly that you're doing within these few hours?" The lady behind the desk asked politely.

"Research," I said confidently. "It's a potential commoditised service delivery system that is transparent and transactional in a fragmented market place...

I said it again. I tried to explain what I had in mind. It was just an idea, but I wanted to tell as many people as possible so I could get feedback. Turning over my details, she said in an incredulous way, "It says here you claim to have paid over £250K in tax last year. Should that be £25K?"

"No. I guess it was around that, but it won't be this time around. Now my parents give me £50 a week, which I'm grateful for."

She shook her head. "Are you sure you're in the right place?" she said, closing my file.

"Actually no, but it's where I am and I just have to get on with it, don't I?" I said, trying to make light of it.

"What do you mean? Who put you here? What happened?" she said, handing me a reference number to confirm the interview had taken place.

When I remembered my story, I shook my head. I paused before speaking, considering the innocent question and the enormity of it.

"I'm not honestly sure. Maybe it had something to do with me, maybe it was others, and maybe it was all of us. I really don't know. I've never honestly figured it out. I just know that this is where I've ended up. Like it or lump it, this is where I am and I've just got to get on with it."

She shook her head again as she stamped my file.

"Thanks a lot," I said, "You made it better than I thought it would be."

"We're not monsters," she said. "And with what you've paid in, they should be giving you a taxi home. Take care."

I sought out Andrew, the accountant I'd been introduced to. He at least had been kind to me previously, even if it was just about listening. He felt genuinely aggrieved over what had happened. He had been interested in my views as an accountant and my general grumbling about the Industry. He had also brought along a few interested potential investors.

"You know Mike, you may just have something with regard to this accountancy lark....I've never looked at my business like that before, Its really scalable isn't it. I mean its painting by numbers if you get the sales sorted. Just like your previous ventures."

"I'm sure we can sell these services off a menu that a client picks and chooses from. We guarantee that the fee quoted is the only fee chargeable they can have as many telephone calls or meeting as they like. I mean most clients won't want to spend hours upon hours talking to their accountant. They would much prefer to be out doing business so what's the problem with that? We can spread the payments so the client has a cash flow advantage as well, what could be simpler? "

"Well Mike I've given this a lot of thought and I'm up for it if you are Mike, I can also get funding that shouldn't be a problem," Andy said, realising the potential whilst doing the simple arithmetic...

It was achievable. It had lots going for it. The Industry was ready for change, just like it had been within the Insurance Industry all those years ago. We would be selling to exactly the same people, young owner managers of businesses who just want their accounts doing fast, efficiently and on time. Nothing hard about that. Maybe in the years to come we could incorporate the placing of their Insurance portfolio alongside the accountancy services and throw it in as an added benefit! That would set the corporate broking market alight again. "Compete against that!!" I thought..... Three or four years and I could be back on a boat in the Med...

Andy quickly put the company together and I went full-time, doing initial research into how best access the market. .

I looked at an office that was going for nothing. A friend had empty space at the top of her retail fashion shop. I climbed the stairs; it was small and empty. It had a window facing out onto the main street below.

Fumbling for the light, I instinctively looked out of the window, as I'd done so many years ago. Memories swirled into my head, sending shivers down my spine. I'd hardly dared remember, couldn't help myself.

I'd been in this place, feeling this way, all those years ago when we took the first steps towards building Ward Evans. How I wished Peter and Jim were there too. I longed to hear their voices and share their enthusiasm, and fancied I could see their faces in the reflected light on the windows.

But you can't re-wind the film.

I tried to see Holly's face reflected in the window too. She must be there, somewhere in the back of my mind. Where was she now?

Try as I might, I could never bring the detail of her face to mind. I didn't dare look at the photographs of her; they were hidden away, maybe for another day, another year. Perhaps that would make it all too real. I just wanted to remember her smile and her soft Irish, lilting accent and beautiful blonde, curly hair. The frisson of excitement she created in me when she walked in the room. Too good to be true. And she was, ultimately.

I never got the chance of a goodbye, save that night in front of the fire and the flames of the past that burnt away my hopes for reconciliation. The ashes that were cast to the wind. Maybe I'd blamed her for all the loss I was feeling, however unfairly, but it was now obvious I'd never see her again to work through what was right and what was wrong. I figured she might be a married now, perhaps even with the child she wanted so much.

She made no attempt to call, or, to my knowledge, enquire about how things were going. Whether I lived or died. It saddened me to think she was still running and would never confront the past.

I was horrified I'd even contemplated something that would, in all probability, have set off the same sort of reaction in my children as her father had done to her.

What if things had been different? If the business had been sold and I was still sitting on millions? Would she have been the right girl for me and still at my side, or would the ending have been the same?

It was a hard question. Terry tried in his own honest way to make light of it: "One way or another, she'd have found a way of separating you from your money, if that's what she was interested in."

I tried to stop myself thinking about it. What good could come from wondering what would have happened if the past had been different? The answer came to me in that quiet, empty office that would become the centre of my new hopes and ambition.

It could have been very different indeed. How it used to be when Oliver was in hospital, everyone worried sick about how things might turn out. The probability equation of his mortality and his parents' chance of experiencing a happy day again. I'd solemnly prayed for some sort of divine intervention, to change the course of possible events and had been lucky enough to get what I prayed for. I should always remember to be grateful and equally glad to have paid the price. Gratitude forms the basis of all religions and spiritual awareness, but the act of gratitude has to be practised every day. I should try always to be grateful. The past could have been very different indeed.

I could see Oliver in my mind's eye, smiling, playing with his sisters. A strong, handsome boy and, God love him, healthy! That was something good to remember, to hold on to. Something to give thanks for and a reason to be there in the future.

To see him and his sisters grow. Tears stung my eyes as I gazed out of the window. Andy came upstairs, stirring me from musing over what Terry would have called my biggest moment of clarity, ever.

"It's small and cold but we can all make something of this, Mike. It will get us started. The other potential shareholders seem to be interested. They will help run it for us; they think it's a great idea."

"Yes," I said, with a new sense of life's experience. A new season, and what seemed like a wondrous sense of renewal. "Let's go."

We turned the lights out and walked blinking into the bright bustle of a busy town.

"Beer, Andy?"

"Sure; where do you fancy?"

"Let's go to the nearest wine bar and make a few friends. Bet you've never heard of a green fucker, have you? It's a great drink. I'll tell you the story about that one day; it's a real drink of friendship."

A new dream, a new adventure born.

END

Printed in Great Britain
by Amazon

16431712R00115